History of

POPULAR MUSIC

EVERYDAY HANDBOOKS

History of
POPULAR MUSIC

by DAVID EWEN

BARNES & NOBLE, INC. • NEW YORK

PUBLISHERS • BOOKSELLERS • SINCE 1873

Preface

American popular music has many faces.

American popular music is the religious hymns and national ballads which were sung when our country was born. It is the ragtime and the blues of the Negro from which jazz was evolved. It is New Orleans jazz and it is progressive jazz. It is the commercial tune of Tin Pan Alley. It is the music of the theater from the minstrel show to the musical play, and that of the Hollywood screen. It is the symphonic jazz of Carnegie Hall.

This book is an effort to provide coherence and integration to these different and varied facets of our musical expression.

The principal composers of our popular music since William Billings in the eighteenth century are, of course, discussed. But biographical information in all cases has been reduced to a minimum, including only those facts essential for the placement of these men in the proper perspective of their times and settings. The author has placed emphasis not only on the music itself, but also upon the sources from which this music sprang, upon the influences that have been brought to bear on our changing musical culture, and upon the cultural and social conditions in which this music has developed. It is for this reason that the pages that follow are often sprinkled with information about the evolution of the musical theater and the talking screen, the development of radio, phonograph, and television, and the history of organizations like The American Society of Composers, Authors and Publishers and Broadcast Music, Incorporated.

It is hardly necessary to belabor any longer the point that our popular music has finally arrived at significance and distinction. It has captured the imagination and stirred the enthusiasm of an entire world. It has been said, with justification, that in Gershwin's opera *Porgy and Bess*, in the musical plays of Rodgers and Hammerstein, in the jazz of Louis Armstrong and Dizzy Gillespie, in the songs of Gershwin, Porter, Rodgers, Kern, and Berlin, a native art has been created which is perhaps America's greatest single contribution to the cultural heritage of the Western world.

To trace the history of that art, as well as to evaluate it, has been the intention of this author.

Contents

1—Backgrounds and Beginnings

America's first popular songs were the psalms and hymns that flourished in New England before the Revolution. These religious tunes, which represented both a means of worship and a social pastime for the home and for town meetings, were the first pieces of music imported from the Old World to the New and the first to gain wide circulation. True, French Huguenots had introduced French psalmody to the Carolinas for a brief period as early as 1572, and, during a stay of several weeks on the California coast in June, 1579, Sir Francis Drake's men practiced English psalmody. However, these were merely episodes, and it is only with the landing of the pilgrim fathers at Plymouth Rock in 1620 that a continuous tradition was established. The immigrants brought with them Henry Ainsworth's *Book of Psalmes,* one of which is "The Old Hundredth," to this day sung as the doxology to the words "Praise God from whom all blessings flow."

Shortly thereafter, in 1628, the Puritans settling in the Massachusetts Bay Colony introduced there the Psalter in the version of Sternhold and Hopkins. Soon, however, dissatisfaction with the English translations of the Psalter led to the first publication in the English-speaking colonies of the New World: *The Whole Booke of Psalmes faithfully translated into English Metre,* more popularly known as the *Bay Psalm Book,* issued in Cambridge, Massachusetts, in 1640. (In 1947, a copy of the first edition of the *Bay Psalm Book* in New York brought $151,000, up to then the highest price ever paid for a book.) That first edition presented only the words; not until the ninth edition, in 1698, were thirteen tunes added.

The melodies of psalms and hymns popular in New England were sung from memory, having been handed down orally from

1

one generation to the next. The melodies were generally in a slow tempo, flexible in pitch and time values, and freely embellished with numerous flourishes and grace notes. The singing of these tunes in congregations and in meeting halls was primitive and discordant, since each singer followed his own concept of rhythm, pitch, and tempo. In 1700, the Reverend Walter Roxbury described communal singing as a "mere disorderly noise, left to the mercy of every unskilful throat to chop and alter." Another critic, never identified, scratched the following provocative lines on a pew in Salem Church:

> Could poor King David, but for once
> To Salem Church repair,
> And hear the Psalms thus warbled out
> Good Lord how he would swear!

A singing method known as "deaconing" did not help to improve the quality of song performance either. In "deaconing" the tune would be "set" by the deacon, who tapped a brass candlestick or curtain rod with his knuckles. The congregation would then repeat the tune after him line by line.

There soon appeared in New England several musical reformers seeking to establish order out of chaos by introducing some sadly needed discipline in psalm singing. These reformers objected not merely to "deaconing" but also to the "common way of singing," the latter being a singing performance from memory without any specific guidance as to tempo or pitch. After the turn of the eighteenth century, several of these reformers tried initiating "singing by note" through the publication of new psalm books that included the music as well as the words. Thus they hoped to introduce a more orderly procedure in the singing of the psalms. In or about 1714, the Reverend John Tufts of Newburyport published *A Very Plain and Easy Introduction to . . . the Singing of Psalm Tunes,* a collection that included thirty-seven three-part melodies, possibly copied from John Playford. In 1721, the Reverend Thomas Walter of Roxbury issued *The Grounds and Rules of Musick Explained,* a volume which Benjamin Franklin's older brother helped to print. In 1764, Josiah Flagg published in Boston his own collection, *Best Psalm Tunes,* engraved by Paul Revere.

A strong prejudice prevailed in New England against "singing by note," for the Puritans and Pilgrims regarded this method as sacrilegious. Despite a concerted opposition to the new melodies and methods, "singing by note" slowly replaced the older and more primitive procedure. Out of this reform came the man generally considered to be America's first professional popular composer, William Billings (1746-1800), a native of Boston without any formal musical training. Nature had handicapped him severely from birth by giving him only one eye, a withered arm, and legs of uneven length. For this reason, as a boy Billings did not mingle with others but spent his leisure time in the solitary pursuit of music. He virtually memorized Tans'ur's *Musical Grammar,* and while working in the tannery in which he was an apprentice he would scrawl psalm tunes on the walls and hides. He soon abandoned the tannery for music, devoting himself industriously to the writing of psalms and "fuguing tunes." His first collection of original melodies, *The New England Psalm Singer,* was published in 1770. His subsequent publications were: *The Singing Master's Assistant* (better known as "Billings' Best") (c. 1776), *Music in Miniature* (1779), *The Psalm Singer's Amusement* (1781), *The Suffolk Harmony* (1786), and *The Continental Harmony* (1794). By the end of the century there was hardly a psalm book published in New England that did not include at least one of his compositions.

But recognition did not come easily. His physical deformities and his personal slovenliness made him a perpetual butt for ridicule, and the unorthodox kind of music he was writing was no less subject to laughter and attack. Like the reformers who had preceded him, Billings was an avowed enemy of "deaconing" and the "common way of singing." Indeed, he founded in Stoughton, Massachusetts, the first singing class in the colonies just so that the people might learn to sing by note. But Billings was a rebel not only against tradition but even against some of the current reforms. He did not like the trim, well-ordered, stately kind of psalm music the reformers were presenting. What Billings sought was a music more robust than these genteel tunes, a music more befitting a hardy people and a rugged way of life. As he explained in the preface to his first collection, he did not feel constrained to follow the rules of composition. His

writing was filled with all kinds of crudities in harmony and counterpoint—consecutive fifths, unorthodox progressions, and dissonances. Billings was striving to introduce freshness and vigor
into the religious music of his time; a later generation might say
that he was "jazzing up" the old hymns. His psalms, as he explained, were "more than twenty times as powerful as the old
slow tunes, each part striving for mastery and victory." He
preferred a brisk tempo, a varied and energetic rhythm, and a
virile if at times discordant harmony. His basses moved at a
vigorous pace to maintain the momentum. For these practices he
was long subjected to severe criticism and at times derision. One
day, several of his fellow musicians hung two cats by their tails
on the signpost outside his house. The point they were trying to
make was that the squealing of the abused cats sounded like
Billings' music. Billings' reply to his critics was a composition
entitled *Jargon*, filled with even more alarming and reckless dis-
cords than he had used before.

Billings' music may often have been unschooled and crude;
yet it succeeded in creating a homespun musical product that
could not have originated anywhere but in the New World. Thus
Billings deserves consideration as the first composer of *American*
music. Since some of this music eventually enjoyed wide distribution throughout the colonies and since during the Revolution
Billings became a leading composer of war songs, he must also
be designated as America's first composer of *popular* music.

Outside New England, in the rest of the colonies, other kinds
of popular music were favored. The Cavaliers in Virginia were
preserving a rich literature of formal English ballads. In time
this music would be the soil from which would sprout a wonderful
literature of folk music, that of the Appalachian and Cumberland
Mountains (songs like "Barbara Allen," "Chevy Chase," "The
Two Sisters," and "Sourwood Mountain"). In still other colonies
the songs and dance music of England proved popular—"Drink
to Me Only with Thine Eyes," "The Fair Emigrant," "Green-
sleeves," Henry Carey's "Sally in Our Alley," Thomas Arne's
"Rule, Britannia," and William Boyce's "Heart of Oak." English
popular tunes and ditties were often imported into the colonies
within the framework of the ballad opera, a stage production as
much favored in the colonies as in England. The very first stage

performance to take place in the colonies was such a ballad opera—*Flora,* presented in a courtroom in Charleston, South Carolina, on February 8, 1735. In New York in 1750, John Gay's famous *The Beggar's Opera* was performed, probably for the first time in the colonies, while in or about 1765 came still another English ballad opera, Thomas Arne's *Artaxerxes.* The general practice in the colonies was to provide these English tunes with new lyrics describing everyday events and episodes of immediate appeal and interest to the colonists.

Performance in a ballad opera was one way in which popular tunes filtered through the colonies. Another was by means of singing actors, most of them English, who traveled about with their English repertory. A third method of song circulation was the publication of broadsides, sold in the streets by peddlers and newshawks for a penny a copy.

"Yankee Doodle" was one of the songs most widely circulated throughout the colonies. The precise source of its melody has never been uncovered. Some believe that it originated in England as an instrumental piece, while others trace it back to Scotland, Ireland, Holland, or Germany. In England, various sets of lyrics were adapted to the melody, the most popular being the nursery rhymes "Lucy Locket" and "Kitty Fisher."

There is reason to believe that the melody of "Yankee Doodle" made its appearance in the colonies for the first time during the French and Indian War. In or about 1755, Richard Shuckburg, a British army physician, was so amused at the ragged and disheveled appearance of General Braddock's colonial soldiers that he decided to perpetrate a joke on them. He improvised a set of nonsense lyrics to a tune he had heard in England and palmed it off on the colonial soldiers as the latest English army song. Dr. Shuckburg's nonsense song, "Yankee Doodle," made a strong impression on the British troops in the colonies. During the next two decades the British often used it to taunt the colonists, sometimes by singing it loudly outside church during colonial religious services.

In the very first days of the Revolution, the colonials took over "Yankee Doodle" from the British. When the latter marched to Lexington in 1775, it was to the tune of "Yankee Doodle," but it was the Americans who rendered it lustily as a song of victory when Cornwallis surrendered at Yorktown.

The significance of "Yankee Doodle" as a war song of the colonists points up the role played by popular music during the Revolution. Joel Barlow wrote in 1775: "One good song is worth a dozen addresses or proclamations." Important events leading up to the final conflagration were described and commented upon in numerous songs, quickly distributed on broadsides. These lyrics became a significant influence in creating an emotional climate favorable to the eruption of war. The melodies used for these hastily improvised verses were those familiar to colonists everywhere. Since the tunes sung most often at the time were of English origin, a curious paradox developed in which the colonists spoke their defiance of their mother country with English-born melodies.

"The Liberty Song," which is generally considered to be America's first important political song, was a setting of words by John Dickinson to William Boyce's famous melody, "Heart of Oak." Inspired by the refusal of the Massachusetts Legislature to rescind the Circular Letter of February 11, 1768, imposing duties and taxes on the colonies, "The Liberty Song" was first published in 1768, but no copy seems to have survived. The following year it appeared with Boyce's music in Bickerstaff's *Boston Almanac* and soon thereafter became the official song of the Sons of Liberty.

> Come, join hand in hand, brave Americans all,
> And rouse your bold hearts at fair Liberty's call;
> No tyrannous acts shall suppress your just claim,
> Or stain with dishonour America's name.
>
> In Freedom we're born, and in Freedom we'll live,
> > Our purses are ready
> > Steady, friends, steady
> Not as slaves but as Freemen our money we'll give.

The great success of "The Liberty Song" led the Tory opposition to write parodies with which to taunt the radicals and hotheads:

> Come shake your dull noodles, ye pumpkins and bawl,
> And own that you're mad at fair Liberty's call;
> No scandalous conduct can add to your shame,
> Condemned to dishonour, inherit the fame.

In folly, you're born, and in folly you'll live.
  To madness still ready
  And stupidly steady,
Not as men but as monkeys the token you give.

And still another parody went:

Ye simple Bostonians, I'll have you beware
Of your Liberty Tree, I would have you take care,
For if that we chance to return to this town,
Your houses and stores will come tumbling down.

The Stamp Act of 1765, the dictatorial Writs of Assistance, the Townshend Act of 1767, the Boston Massacre, the excessive duty on tea, and the harsh retaliatory measures of Parliament in 1774—any and every issue that served to arouse and unite the colonists against the Crown—were sung about with lyrics hastily concocted and just as hastily distributed. "Fish and Tea" was one of the songs that proved to be especially effective; "Castle Island" was another. These and similar lyrics were always fashioned to popular English tunes. Two songs denouncing the tea tax were set to the melodies of an old English hymn and of "Hozier's Ghost" respectively.

Once the Revolution had begun, the practice of expropriating English melodies for freshly conceived martial lyrics became standard procedure. "God Save the King" became "God Save the Thirteen States." "What a Court Hath England" was adapted to the melody of "Derry Down." In the same way, familiar English melodies were used for "Liberty's Call," "The Burning of Charleston," and "Americans to Arms" in 1775; for "The War Song" and "Independence" in 1776; for "Saratoga Song" and "Burgoyne's Proclamation" in 1777; and for "The Rebels" in 1778. One of the most fiery of Revolutionary War Songs was "Free America," the lyrics by Joseph Warren, who died at Bunker Hill, and the music that of "The British Grenadiers."

Songs, still to English melodies, described the Battle of Trenton, the siege of Savannah, and the defeat of Burgoyne. Songs hymned the praises of Washington and Lafayette, told of the exploits of John Paul Jones and "Mad Anthony" Wayne, and denounced the treachery of Benedict Arnold. Soldiers marched to battle to the rhythm and melodies of fife songs, all of them of English origin. "My Dog and Gun," "Rural Felicity," "On the Road to Boston," and "The Girl I Left behind Me" were particular favorites. As we already have had occasion to remark, it is altogether possible that the most famous of all the Revolutionary War fife songs, "Yankee Doodle," was also English in origin.

"Yankee Doodle" became popular during the Revolution not only in its own right but also by virtue of many parodies. One of the most famous was "The Battle of the Kegs," words by Francis Hopkinson, statesman, signer of the Declaration of Independence, and one of America's first composers of art songs. "The Battle of the Kegs" was inspired by David Bushnell's experiment of filling kegs with powder and floating them down the river for the purpose of destroying the British ships anchored off Philadelphia. When the British saw the kegs floating toward them, they began firing wildly. This episode proved so amusing to Hopkinson that he put to paper a set of satirical lyrics, using "Yankee Doodle" for his melody:

> Gallants, attend, and hear a friend
>   Trill forth harmonious ditty;
> Strange things I'll tell which late befell
>   In Philadelphia city.
>
> 'Twas early day, as poets say
>   Just when the sun was rising
> A soldier stood on log of wood
>   And saw a sight surprising.
>
> As, in amaze, he stood to gaze;
>   The truth can't be denied, sir,
> He spied a score of kegs—or more,
>   Come floating down the tide, sir.
>
> * * *
>
> The kegs, 'tis said, tho' strongly made
>   Of rebel staves and hoops, sir,
> Could not oppose the powerful foes
>   The conquering British troops, sir.
>
> From morn to night these men of might
>   Displayed amazing courage.
> And when the sun was fairly down
>   Returned to sup their porridge.

A few songs were entirely of American origin, and these are America's first native popular songs. One was "The American Hero," published in 1775. The words were by Nathaniel Niles; the music came from "Bunker Hill," a song by Andrew Law, an American. This stately melody, modeled after the English ballad, was no rousing war song, but a song tinged with melancholy, reflecting the somber spirit of the colonists when they realized that they were engaged in a life-and-death struggle.

Another exclusively American war song was "Chester," by New England's prolific composer of psalms and fuguing tunes, William Billings. Billings was a passionate advocate of the Revolution and a friend of Samuel Adams and Paul Revere. When the Revolution broke out, Billings set himself the task of writing songs to arouse the fighting spirit of his neighbors. He distributed his *New England Psalm Singer* and *Singing Master's Assistant* in army camps, providing his hymn melodies with new war lyrics. "Many of the New England soldiers who . . . were encamped in southern states," said a writer in *The Musical Reporter*, "had his popular tunes by heart and frequently amused themselves by singing them in camp, to the delight of all those who heard them." Billings' "By the Waters of Babylon" became "A Lamentation over Boston." Others of his psalms and hymns he transformed into such stirring war tunes as "Retrospect," "Independence," "Columbia,"—and, most important of all, "Chester," first published in 1778:

> Let tyrants shake their iron rod,
> And slav'ry clank her galling chains.
> We fear them not; we trust in God,
> New England's God forever reigns.

The stately melody, even rhythm, unchanging meter, and formal cadences of Billings' old psalm seem to us not particularly appropriate for a war message with ringing accents. Nevertheless, the strains of "Chester" reverberated throughout the colonies and proved to be such influential propaganda that it has been described as "the 'Marseillaise' of the American Revolution." It is America's first great war song.

Just as the songs of the colonists had been mainly religious and the songs of the Revolution martial, so the songs of the new

America were primarily political. Lyrics were created to comment upon the varied problems and achievements of the infant nation, and, as had been the practice heretofore, English melodies were borrowed to provide music for these verses.

Immediately after the Revolution the American people sang a "New Federal Song" and, to the strains of "Rule, Britannia," "Rise, Columbia." To the well-known tune, "To Anacreon in Heaven," Americans wrote lyrics named "Freedom Triumphant" and "Song for the Fourth of July." Songs appeared hymning the praises of America's first political heroes. Songs about George Washington were legion, marking his achievements, and his birthday, inauguration, and death. Among the most popular were "Washington," "God Save Washington," "God Save Great Washington," "A Toast to Washington" and "Elegy on the Death of General Washington."

Similarly, song lyrics were written for presidential candidates. In 1798 Robert Treat Paine wrote the words of "Adams and Liberty" to the music of "To Anacreon in Heaven." In 1800, "Jefferson and Liberty," to the melody of a traditional Irish reel, hailed Jefferson as a champion of liberty and expressed opposition to the Alien and Sedition Acts. In 1828, Andrew Jackson's campaign was promoted by "The Hunters of Kentucky," with lyrics by Samuel Woodworth to the melody of "Miss Bailey's Ghost."

With each successive political campaign, songs assumed an increasingly prominent role. Presidential campaigns provided a welcome form of entertainment in an era before the popularity of the theater and the concert stage. At barbecues, mass meetings, and torch light parades, songs were as influential as speeches in swinging the sentiments of audiences toward a candidate. In 1824, there was heard "The Aristocracy of Henry Clay"; in 1840, "Tippecanoe and Tyler Too" and "What Has Caused This Great Commotion?" for Harrison; in 1844, "The True-Hearted States-man" for Polk; in 1860, "Lincoln and Liberty" to the popular melody of "Old Rosin, the Beau." These are only a few random examples of campaign songs that helped to carry candidates into office. Some candidates even had an entire volume of songs devoted to them, such as *The Clay Minstrel* and *The Polk Songster.*

Numerous songsters, containing new lyrics for thrice-familiar melodies, were published and distributed immediately after the birth of the nation. These volumes were vest-pocket in size, contained about a hundred pages, and were hawked in the streets. The first such songster was *The American Musical Miscellany*, published in 1798. The emphasis then placed by songs on politics is proved by the fact that, as already mentioned, many of these songsters were often devoted to a single presidential candidate or exclusively to political subjects, as was the case with *The Nightingale of Liberty* and *The American Naval and Patriotic Songster*.

Next to politics, in the early years of the republic, current events interested song writers most. Michael Fortune wrote the words and music of "The Acquisition of Louisiana." Virtually every phase of the War of 1812 was discussed in song. Some of the more popular of these war songs were W. Strickland's "Decatur's Victory," Samuel Woodworth's "Erie and Champlain," John Bray's "Hull's Victory," Joseph Hutton's "Perry's Victory," James Hewitt's "Lawrence the Brave," and—most significant of all—"The Star-Spangled Banner," about which much more will be said shortly.

Economic depressions were sung about in "Hard Times" and in "Know Ye the Land" (1837); prosperity, in "Peace" (1815) from the *Everyday Song Book*. The opening of the Erie Canal in 1825 inspired the writing of "The Meeting of the Waters," and another song still fresh in our folk-song literature, "The Erie Canal." The completion of the Baltimore and Ohio Railroad in 1828 led a humble Baltimore musician, C. Meineke, to write "The Rail Road" and "The Rail Road March." Lafayette's return to the United States in 1824 stimulated the same Meineke to pen "La Fayette's Welcome" and W. Strickland to write the words of "Come Honor the Brave" to the melody of "My Heart's in the Highlands."

The practice of setting the news of the day and the political thinking of the times to lyrics and music led to the birth of our earliest national ballads. The first important one to survive to the present day is "Hail, Columbia," in which both lyrics and melody are of American creation. Its melody was the "President's March," believed to have been written by Philip Phile, a Philadelphia violinist who died in that city in 1793. Phile had written his march to honor Washington, and it was first published as an instrumental number in 1793 or 1794.

"Hail, Columbia" appeared in 1798, in a trying period when it seemed that young America might be helplessly drawn into war with France. In that year, Gilbert Fox, a Philadelphia singer, asked Joseph Hopkinson (son of Francis) to write some patriotic verses which Fox might perform at one of his concerts. Since Hopkinson felt that the performance of patriotic lyrics might arouse American people to a renewed awareness of their "honor and rights," he set about this task eagerly. For his melody he chose the vigorous "President's March." Fox's concert was attended by President Adams and his cabinet. After Fox had sung "Hail, Columbia" several times—accompanied by a chorus and brass band—the ovation was tumultuous. Only a few days after this concert, both music and lyrics of "Hail, Columbia" were published in Philadelphia under the title of "The Favorite New Federal Song." "Hail, Columbia," as the song came to be known, was soon heard throughout the country, and it was a particular favorite with government officials. For a quarter of a century it was performed on every American ship at the lowering of the colors; for another quarter of a century it was a patriotic anthem as frequently performed and sung as "The Star-Spangled Banner." Charles Coffin wrote in *Four Years of Fighting*: "Everywhere the music of the streets, vocal as well as instrumental, was 'Hail, Columbia'. . . . Even before that, in December 1860, Major Anderson . . . raised the American flag . . . of the still unfinished Fort Sumter. As he drew the star-spangled banner . . . the band broke out with the national air, 'Hail, Columbia,' loud and exultant cheers, repeated again and again, were given by officers, soldiers, and workmen."

But "Hail, Columbia" was the exception to an unwritten rule that seemed to dictate that our national ballads be made up of American lyrics and foreign melodies. The melody of "The Star-Spangled Banner," for example, was that of "To Anacreon in Heaven," an English song which may have been written about 1775 by John Stafford Smith for the London Anacreontic Society, a group of esthetes and art lovers. "To Anacreon in Heaven" became so popular in America that it was freely appropriated for many lyrics, including "Adams and Liberty," "Freedom Triumphant," "Song of the Fourth of July," and "Jefferson's Election."

The words of "The Star-Spangled Banner" were written in 1814 by a young Baltimore lawyer, Francis Scott Key. (He had previously used the melody of "To Anacreon in Heaven" for still another of his poems, "The Warrior's Return," honoring Stephen Decatur.) During the War of 1812, Key headed a commission sent out to the British fleet anchored off Fort McHenry in Baltimore. Its mission was to effect the release of an American physician, Dr. William Beanes, captured and held prisoner by the British. Key and his party appeared on the British vessel just before the British launched an attack on Fort McHenry. During the night of September 13-14, 1814, Francis Scott Key watched the battle. When, at dawn, he saw the American flag still flying atop the fort, he spontaneously expressed his joy with a set of verses scribbled on an envelope.

One day after the battle, Key and his party returned to Baltimore. That day, Key's verses were issued in a broadside under the title "The Defense of Fort McHenry"; that evening, Ferdinand Durang introduced the song in a Baltimore tavern. Soon after that, Key's verses were published in two Baltimore newspapers, and, under the new and permanent title of "The Star-Spangled Banner," they were issued by Carr's Music Store. Further indication of the immediate popularity of this anthem was the fact that it was included in several songsters, one of which was actually called The Star-Spangled Banner. Though regarded for many years as our national anthem, even by the Army and the Navy, "The Star-Spangled Banner" did not officially achieve that status until March 3, 1931, by an Act of Congress.

"America," second in importance only to "The Star-Spangled Banner" has, to be sure, the melody of Great Britain's anthem, "God Save the King." The new words were written by Samuel Francis Smith, a clergyman. In 1831, Smith had been encouraged by Lowell Mason, distinguished American music educator, to write a new American anthem. Mason provided Smith with several song books from which he was to pick out his melody. "One leisurely afternoon," Smith recalled many years later, "I was looking over the books, and fell in love with the tune of 'God Save the King,' and at once took up my pen and wrote the piece in question. It was struck out at a sitting, without the slightest idea that it would ever attain the popularity it has since enjoyed. . . . The first time it was sung publicly was at a children's celebration of American independence at the Park Street Church, Boston, on July 4, 1831."

Whether the melody of "Columbia, the Gem of the Ocean" is of English or American origin is a question long hotly debated but never satisfactorily resolved. Some claim that the tune came from "Britannia, the Pride of the Ocean," written by Stephen J. Meany and Thomas E. Williams in 1842. After "Columbia, the Gem of the Ocean" had been successfully introduced at the Chinese Museum in Philadelphia in 1843 by the actor-singer, David T. Shaw, Thomas A. Beckett insisted he was author of both its lyrics and music, having been commissioned by Shaw to write them. Beckett's claim notwithstanding, "Columbia, the Gem of the Ocean" was first published in Philadelphia in 1843, crediting David T. Shaw as its sole author. Beckett hotly disputed Shaw's right to be considered the song's creator, and when a second Philadelphia publisher issued the song, the title page bore the legend that this was "A Popular Song . . . Adapted & Arranged by T. A. Beckett." If this publication was issued with Beckett's consent, the conclusion is justifiable that Beckett was now ready to concede that, though the lyrics were his, the melody had been borrowed. This already confused situation is even further complicated by the fact that when "Columbia, the Gem of the Ocean" was first issued in New York in 1861—under a changed title, "The Red, White and Blue"—it was described as a "National Song . . . Arranged by Thos. D. Sullivan." No mention was made of either Shaw or Beckett.

2—The Sentimental Ballad

"The enthusiasm of a happy people," it was said in the preface to *The Harrison and Log Cabin Song Book* (1840), "always did and always will break forth in song."

Song played a prominent role in the social life of the American people in the era immediately following the Revolutionary War. Since other sources of entertainment were not readily available, the singing of popular tunes provided a welcome form of diversion. Families—often supplemented by friends and neighbors—grouped around the parlor organ for an evening's or Sunday afternoon's pleasure. The singing of songs was also basic to the clubs where men gathered by themselves for dinners, quilting bees, and ceremonies of all kinds.

The American people liked to sing and they liked to hear others sing. Singers and actors arrived regularly from England to tour America in concerts of popular ballads. One was Joseph Philip Knight who on his brief tour in 1839 wrote and introduced his most famous ballad, "Rocked in the Cradle of the Deep"—still a favorite of many a basso profundo. Another such performer was Henry Russell, about whom more will be said later.

Traveling singing families were particularly welcome, not only when they performed the day's popular songs, but also when they performed songs of their own writing. The most celebrated of these groups was the Singing Hutchinson Family. The Hutchinson Family initiated a half century of performances in 1842, when four of its younger members traveled around New England, entertaining villagers and farmers with such ballads as "The Cot Where I Was Born," "The Alpine Hunter's Song," "The Irish Emigrant's Lament," and "The Maniac."

While, as we saw in the previous chapter, political songs and songs about current events dominated the literature of the popular music of the day, other kinds were also favored. Tunes of street vendors were widely heard throughout the eighteenth century: "Oyster, Sir," "Buy a Broom," or "Come Buy My Woodenware," to mention only three characteristic examples. Street cries continued to be popular as late as 1840, for at that time the *New York Mirror* editorially condemned milkmen and glaziers for insisting on making music "enough every day of the week to set the citizen's teeth on edge." Some of the most haunting of the street-vendor cries came from the South, especially from Charleston, South Carolina. The Negro vendors there sold their "hoppen' john peas," crabs, shrimps, and other victuals to the strains of improvised melodies. In his twentieth century Negro folk opera set in Charleston, *Porgy and Bess,* George Gershwin imitated these street cries with remarkable accuracy.

The people inevitably picked up these street-vendor cries and tunes and assimilated them into their own popular-song repertory. This repertory embraced other types of songs as well. There were songs about the fashions of the day, songs about life in the city and on the farm, songs about fires and other public disasters, songs about sin and about the evils of drink, songs about the pitfalls awaiting the young and the innocent. Love—its torments as well as its joys—was, of course, not neglected. "Daisy Bell" (not to be confused with the late nineteenth-century ballad of the same name) and "Oh, No, I'll Never Mention Him" spoke of the sad plight of girls left stranded by their lovers. "Your Lot Is Braver Than Mine" described the unhappy love of two people from different social strata.

Since genteel ladies in the family parlor represented a sizable segment of the singing public, sentimental ballads flourished. One of the earliest appeared during the Revolutionary War. It was called "The Banks of the Dee," with lyrics by John Tait to the melody of "Langolee," and told of the tearful farewell of a Scotchman and his lass, as he made ready to join the British troops in the American colonies.

John Hill Hewitt (1801-1890) was one of our earliest native composers of popular sentimental ballads. He was the son of James Hewitt, the eminent violinist, publisher, and composer of what is often credited as being the first American opera, *Tammany* (1794). The son attended West Point, from which he was graduated in 1822. He then settled temporarily in the South as a journalist and music teacher. In 1827 he returned North; for most of his life after that he lived in Baltimore, devoting himself to newspaper work, editing journals, and writing sentimental ballads. On one occasion he submitted one of his poems under a pseudonym in a contest sponsored by the journal he himself edited, and the committee in charge of the award selected it for first prize over a contribution by Edgar Allan Poe.

Hewitt is the composer of "The Minstrel's Return from the War," which may well be considered our first popular song hit. He wrote it during his stay in the Southland, in or about 1825. It was published by his brother James in 1827—but with such little hope of success that a copyright was never taken out. Nevertheless, as Hewitt later recalled, the song "was eagerly taken up by the public . . . and was sung all over the world. My brother, not securing the rights, told me that he missed making at least $10,000." Among Hewitt's later ballads were "Take Me Home," "The Knight of the Raven Black Plume," and a war song popular throughout the South during the Civil War, "All Quiet along the Potomac Tonight."

The sentimental ballads of this period were often painfully realistic in their depiction of catastrophes, just as they often exploited other unusual subjects. In "The Vulture of the Alps" the agonized emotions of a mother at seeing her infant snatched by a ravenous vulture are described with almost indecent vividness and gusto. There were tear-provoking ballads about snowstorms, drownings, and other disasters. "The Snow Storm" gives an all too graphic account of a mother wandering with her child over a snowy mountain peak in search of her husband who has already frozen to death.

Much more wholesome in its subject matter and much more direct in its emotional appeal is "Home Sweet Home," probably the most famous sentimental ballad published in America during the quarter century preceding the Civil War. The melody came from England. It was the work of Sir Henry Bishop, who first published it as a Sicilian air in an anthology of folk tunes issued in England. But the lyrics were written by an American, John Howard Payne, who early in his manhood went to live in England to pursue a career as actor and playwright. Later in life he became the American consul in Tunis, where he died in 1852. While in London, Payne wrote the libretto for an opera, *Clari*, which Bishop set to music; it was produced in London in 1823. It was here that "Home Sweet Home" first appeared, Bishop having borrowed his own Sicilian air from his folk-song anthology. "Home Sweet Home" became an instantaneous success and was heard throughout the world. In the very year in which it emerged in *Clari* it was published in Philadelphia.

The most successful composer of American sentimental ballads before the Civil War was Henry Russell (1812-1900), whose blood-curdling description of various stages of insanity in "The Maniac" was from the very first a staple in the repertory of the Hutchinson Family. Russell was born in England, received his musical training in Italy, and from 1833 to 1841 toured the United States as a concert singer. For a while, during that period, he was the organist of the First Presbyterian Church in Rochester, New York. It was in that city that he inaugurated his career as a composer of sentimental ballads. It is said that his immediate stimulus was an oration by Henry Clay. "Why," Russell argued, "should it not be possible for me to make music the vehicle of grand thoughts and noble sentiments, to speak to the world through the power of poetry and song?" As his own response to that query he wrote "Wind of the Winter's Night," setting to music a poem by Charles Mackay.

Russell wrote over eight hundred songs, the most famous being those he himself performed throughout the United States to his own piano accompaniment: "The Gambler's Wife," "The Ship on Fire," "The Maniac," "Oh, Weep Not," "The Old Arm Chair" (probably the first example in American popular music of a "mammy song"), "The Old Family Clock," "The Old Spinning Wheel," "The Old Sexton," "A Life on the Ocean Wave," and his greatest hit of all, "Woodman, Spare That Tree." In the closing years of his stay in America, Russell wrote numerous ballads of topical interest, in which he pleaded for the abolition of slavery, for temperance, for the remedy of abuses suffered in insane asylums, and for other social reforms.

"He was an expert," wrote John Hill Hewitt, "at wheedling audiences out of applause and adding to the effect of his songs by a brilliant pianoforte accompaniment. With much self-laudation he used to describe the wonderful influence of his descriptive songs over audiences. On one occasion he related an incident connected with 'Woodman, Spare That Tree.' He had finished the last verse . . . The audience was spellbound for a moment, then poured out a volume of applause that shook the building to its foundations. In the midst of this tremendous evidence of their boundless gratification, a snowy-headed gentleman, with great anxiety depicted in his venerable features, arose and demanded silence. He asked with tremulous voice: 'Mr Russell, in the name of Heaven, tell me, was the tree spared?'. 'It was, sir,' replied the vocalist. 'Thank God! Thank God! I can breathe again,' and he sat down perfectly overcome by his emotions."

Since Russell sold his songs outright for a pittance, usually for only a few dollars per number, he did not capitalize on their tremendous success, which spelled fortunes for many publishers. "Had it not been that I sang the songs myself," he complained, "the payment for their composition would have meant simple starvation."

Russell returned to England in 1841, went into retirement in 1865, and died in London in 1900. Two of his sons distinguished themselves in music. Henry Russell, Jr., became a famous impresario, and Landon Ronald, an eminent symphony conductor.

The influence of Henry Russell on American songwriting persisted long after he had returned to Europe. It was reflected in many of the ballads that appeared in the years directly preceding the Civil War—Ernest Leslie's "Rock Me to Sleep, Mother"; John Rogers Thomas' " 'Tis But a Little Faded Flower"; Benjamin Russell Hanby's "Darling Nelly Gray"; Charles Blamphin's "When the Corn Is Waving, Annie Dear"; H. S. Thompson's extremely popular "Lilly Dale," in which a lover weeps over the death of his sweetheart; and also in Thompson's "Ida Lee" and "Annie Lisle," the last of which has survived as the melody for the Cornell University song, "Far above Cayuga's Waters."

3—Pearls of Minstrelsy

Before the Civil War, concerts by singing families like the Hutchinsons were one form of public entertainment for which popular songs were written and which helped to popularize them. Another was the minstrel show.

The minstrel show was, to be sure, not the first species of the musical theater in America. As we have already noted, that distinction belonged to the ballad opera. After that came broad travesties and caricatures of famous plays and performers known as "burlesques": John Poole's travesty on *Hamlet* in 1828, for example, or William Mitchell's musical take-off on the Viennese dancer, Fanny Elssler, in *La Mosquita,* in 1838.

But unlike the ballad opera and the burlesque, which were foreign importations, the minstrel show was thoroughly indigenous. It was the first American stage presentation with entirely American components.

The minstrel show became popular first in the North. By finding amusement in blackface performers, listening to sentimental songs about the Southland, and watching Negro dances, the North found in the minstrel show a safety valve for the release of passions aroused by the issue of slavery.

When the first minstrel shows appeared, the Negro had been no stranger to the American stage. There are records of stage caricatures of Negroes in song and dance as far back as 1769. Thirty years later Gottlieb Graupner was a successful blackface performer in Boston.

Nor had Negro songs been unknown before they achieved such prominence in the minstrel show. "Poor Black Boy" and "The Gay Negro Boy" were widely sung before 1800. Soon after 1800 other Negro songs attained wide circulation. The "Bonja Song," which had originated as an instrumental piece published anonymously in 1818 but to which lyrics were added by R. C. Dallas, is believed to be the number with which the banjo, as an accompanying instrument for Negro songs, first became popular. "The Coal Black Rose" and "My Long-Tail Blue," both of them published in or about 1827, were made famous by George Washington Dixon, one of the first successful blackface performers. Dixon, and another entertainer in blackface, Bob Farrell, are each credited with having popularized "Zip Coon," first published in Baltimore in 1834 with more or less nonsensical lyrics. Each claimed to have written the song, but in all probability the melody was borrowed from an Irish folk tune. Under the title of "Turkey in the Straw" and as an instrumental composition, "Zip Coon" is today a classic of American folk music.

The embryo from which the minstrel show emerged was a popular song and dance routine called "Jump Jim Crow," devised by Thomas ("Daddy") Rice and introduced by him in Baltimore in 1828. One day, Rice, a stage favorite of the time, happened to notice an old, deformed Negro, stumbling along and moving his body with absurd contortions. As he moved, the Negro chanted to himself "Jump Jim Crow," a foolish little ditty with gibberish verses. This episode made such an impression on Rice that he decided to recreate the old Negro on the stage. With borrowed tattered clothes, Rice improvised an act in which he danced with a halting, stumbling gait and sang gibberish verses beginning with the following lines:

> Wheel about, an' turn about
> An' do jis so;
> E'bry time I wheel about
> I jump Jim Crow.

His act was a sensation. Throughout the country, blackface performers began doing "Jump Jim Crow" acts of their own in frank emulation of "Daddy" Rice. Thus impersonations of the Negro on the stage in song and dance, comparatively infrequent up till then, became the vogue. The term "Jim Crow" has since then been assimilated into the American language to designate segregation.

It was not long before the Negro became the inspiration not merely for a single routine but for a complete stage production. This development, through which the minstrel show came into being, was the result of an economic depression in 1842 to which theatrical productions of all kinds fell victim. Numerous black-faces were thrown out of work. With bookings few and far between, some of these performers were compelled to join forces in a single act.

One of the first such acts was created by Dan Emmett, today remembered chiefly because he wrote a song called "Dixie." Emmett, however, is no less significant as a founding father of the minstrel show.

As a boy Daniel Decatur Emmett (1815-1904) served as a piper in an army band, as drummer boy in a circus, and finally as a performer in "Daddy" Rice's troupe. Rice's "Jump Jim Crow" act had such an impact on Emmett that he started writing Negro songs of his own, which he himself introduced as a member of the Rice company. Thrown out of work during the depression of 1842, Emmett decided to join several other minstrels like himself to form a new act. They called themselves the Virginia Minstrels and made their debut in New York in 1843. They dressed in blue swallowtail coats, striped calico shirts, and white pantaloons (from that time on a traditional costume of minstrel shows). They introduced "walk-arounds," exchanged puns and light banter, performed sentimental Negro songs, and did the cakewalk, a dance that originated with the Southern Negro. Their success was immediate. Other blackface minstrels teamed up into troupes of their own, and all of them emulated both the dress and the routines of the Virginia Minstrels.

Dan Emmett wrote for the Virginia Minstrels the songs with which he has since won recognition as the first successful composer of music for minstrel shows and as one of the leading popular composers of his time. Several of his best songs became major attractions of minstrel troupes throughout the whole country: "The Blue Tail Fly" (more familiar to us today under the title of "Jim Crack Corn"), "The Boatman's Dance," "Jordan Is a Hard Road to Travel," and "Old Dan Tucker." The last of these was inspired by a ne'er-do-well who was always getting into difficulties. A year after Dan Emmett introduced it in his minstrel show, it was used by New York farmers for a parody in which they expressed their resentment at the feudal conditions then existing. "Old Dan Tucker" is to this day a favorite of square dancers.

Like all the other songs he wrote, Emmett's most famous one, "Dixie," was originally meant for a minstrel show. He intended it as a walk-around for a performance by Bryant's Minstrels at Mechanics' Hall in New York, completed it one Sunday in 1859, and gave it the title of "Dixie's Land." "At first," he recalled many years later, "when I went at the song I couldn't get anything. But a line, 'I wish I was in Dixie,' kept repeating itself in my mind, and I finally took it for my start. The rest wasn't long in coming. And that's the whole story of how 'Dixie' was written." Emmett introduced his song with the Bryant Minstrels on April 4, 1859. "It made a hit at once," he continues, "and before the end of the week everybody in New York was whistling it." More than that, minstrel shows everywhere borrowed the melody for their own walk-arounds, and a burlesque play in New Orleans used it as a march for Zouaves. Publication of the lyrics in a broadside and subsequently of the entire song, proved beneficial to all concerned—except to the author himself who had originally sold out all his rights for $25.00. The subsequent history of "Dixie" will be reserved for our discussion of Civil War songs.

In 1878, Emmett retired to Mount Vernon, Ohio, where he lived quietly, raising chickens. Occasionally after that he made an appearance with traveling minstrel companies, proudly featured as the composer of "Dixie." "Every time he appeared before the footlights to sing 'Dixie,'" recalled Al G. Field, with whose minstrels Emmett made an appearance in his eightieth year, "the audiences went wild." Emmett died in Mount Vernon when he was eighty-nine.

If some of the costuming and some of the routines of the minstrel show were first suggested by Dan Emmett, its definitive form was finally realized by Ed Christy when the Christy Minstrels made their debut in New York on April 27, 1846. In the next half dozen years, Christy's minstrels gave over 2,500 performances in New York and were acclaimed in England, where they were responsible for initiating a vogue for this American kind of stage entertainment.

The pattern devised by Christy is the one to which minstrel shows were henceforth to adhere. There were three distinct parts to the entertainment. The most significant was the first, a variety show called an "olio." Blackface performers were seated in a semicircle, dressed in frock coats, striped trousers, and white gloves and with large flowers in their lapels. Mr. Interlocutor sat in the middle of the row, serving as a go-between for the end men, Mr. Tambo (so named for his proficiency with the tambourine) and Mr. Bones (performer on the clappers, or bones). Mr. Interlocutor would ask questions, and Mr. Tambo and Mr. Bones would respond with puns, double-entendres, and other amusing answers. In between this gay exchange of repartee, would come solo songs, choral numbers, and dances.

The second part of the show was a free fantasia with no set format. Here individual performers were given freedom of activity. The third and concluding section burlesqued some of the procedures and activities of the first two parts.

It was not long after Christy had crystallized this format for the minstrel show that other companies sprouted throughout the country providing shows like Christy's. Some of these troupes were headed by Cool White (John Hodges), considered one of America's leading minstrels behind only Christy himself. White headed such renowned organizations as the Virginia Serenaders, the Ethiopian Minstrels, and the New York Minstrels. Among the other well-loved groups were the Harrington Minstrels organized in or about 1848, the Ordway Minstrels, who appeared in 1850, and the celebrated Bryant Minstrels for which Dan Emmett wrote "Dixie."

The minstrel show provided the fertile soil out of which grew many of the nation's most popular songs. Dan Emmett's songs, all written for minstrel shows, have already been mentioned. Others which, like Emmett's, are now permanent fixtures in the repertory of American popular music, also came out of the minstrel show—Cool White's "Lubly Fan" (now sometimes called "Buffalo Gals"), which he introduced with the Virginia Serenaders; the nonsense song, "Polly Wolly Doodle," of unknown authorship; and Bobby Newcomb's "The Big Sunflower," made popular by Billy Emerson.

Of the many composers drawn to the minstrel show to write gay or sentimental songs about the Negro and the South, the most significant was Stephen Foster (1826-1864), America's greatest composer in the era preceding the Civil War.

Foster's significance rests almost exclusively upon his spontaneous and imaginative and emotionally compelling lyricism. He was a voice of his times, the foremost musical spokesman for Northern sentiments about Southern slavery. It is no accident, then, that his greatest songs are those which speak with sentimentality about the Southern Negro and with nostalgia about the Southland. It is also no accident that he should have achieved his greatest successes as a composer for the minstrel show, since this was the form of entertainment most receptive to such songs.

One of the paradoxes about Stephen Foster is that he came from a family of Democrats who were all slave owners and all passionate foes of abolition. Another Foster paradox is that he had so little contact with the South, the subject of so many of his songs. But if he knew little about the territory below the Mason-Dixon line, he did know a great deal about Negro songs, which were a dominant musical influence in his life.

Born to a middle-class family in Lawrenceville, near Pittsburgh, Pennsylvania, he was only seven when a household slave took him to a Negro church. The effect of Negro religious music on him was such that some years later he freely borrowed some of it for songs like "Hard Times, Come Again No More" and "Oh! Boys, Carry Me 'Long." As a youngster he was raised on tunes like "Zip Coon," "The Coal Black Rose," and "Jump Jim Crow," which he sang frequently while imitating the styles and mannerisms of famous blackface entertainers. Later, when he resided in Cincinnati, he loved to idle along the banks of the Mississippi and watch Negroes load and unload the river boats to the accompaniment of poignant work songs.

He was an exceptionally musical child who early learned by himself to play the flute and the piano. But he was completely indifferent to academic study while attending the Allegheny Academy, the Athens Academy in Tioga Point, and, for a few weeks, Jefferson College in Canonsburg. "I regret extremely," his father wrote when Stephen suddenly dropped his academic schooling for good by leaving Jefferson College, "that Stephen has not been able to appreciate properly . . . the advantages of a college education which will cause him much regret before he arrives at my age. . . . He does not appear to have any evil propensities to indulge . . . and all his leisure hours are all devoted to music for which he possesses a strange talent."

Freed of academic schooling, Foster could now give free rein to his musical inclinations. He began writing songs. The first to be published was "Open Thy Lattice, Love," written probably in 1842 and issued in 1844 by a Philadelphia firm. The lyrics, by George P. Morris, had appeared in the *New York Mirror* and had in 1840 been set to music by Joseph Philip Knight. In "Open Thy Lattice, Love" there was not much to indicate Foster's future creative development. The piano technique in the accompaniment and the harmonic writing are clumsy (though much less so in the published version than in the original manuscript), and the sentimental melody is nondescript.

Some of Foster's songs at this time were written for a men's club that regularly met at Foster's home and that sometimes sang at its meetings. For them Stephen one day produced "Lou'siana Belle," for which he wrote lyrics as well as music. The club members were so enthusiastic over this song that Foster was encouraged to write several more for their next meeting. Among them was "Old Uncle Ned," Foster's first attempt at sentimentalizing the Negro. It is also probable that Foster's first song success, "Oh, Susanna!" was likewise written for this club.

Late in 1846, or early in 1847, Stephen went to Cincinnati to work as bookkeeper in his brother's commission house. There Foster found a publisher for "Lou'siana Belle" in 1847, and for "Old Uncle Ned" and "Oh, Susanna!" in 1848. For the first two songs he received no payment whatsoever, and the third brought him a flat fee of $100. Meanwhile, on September 11, 1847, "Oh, Susanna!" was sung publicly for the first time by a group of minstrels at a Pittsburgh ice-cream parlor and proved so successful that it was immediately appropriated by minstrel shows throughout the country. In 1849 the song was adopted by the "forty-niners" en route to California.

By 1850 Foster seems to have realized that he was no more suited for the business world than for the academic. He returned to Pittsburgh to devote himself entirely to song writing. His hopes for the future were bolstered by a new arrangement with a powerful New York publisher—Firth, Pond and Company—whereby he was to receive a royalty on the sale of sheet music, giving him an assurance of some kind of continuous income. On July 22, 1850, he married Jane Denny McDowell—the "Jeanie" for whom he wrote "Jeanie with the Light Brown Hair"—and one year later their daughter, Marion, was born. This proved to be no ideal marriage. As the years passed, it grew increasingly intolerable. Jane was a religious woman with little tolerance for her husband's partiality for alcohol. As a practical woman she was continually upset by his shiftless way of living and by his insistence on trying to make his living from music rather than business. In due course they started drifting farther and farther apart, with Foster seeking and finding a refuge in his solitary reveries and introspection and in the creation of music.

He was increasingly prolific as a composer. In the first half year of 1850 he published eleven songs, two in the light and quasi-nonsensical style of "Oh, Susanna!": "Nelly Bly" and "Camptown Races," the latter originally issued as "Gwine to Run All Night." It was with "Camptown Races" that Foster initiated his fruitful association with the famous minstrel, Ed Christy. "I wish to unite with you in every effort to encourage a taste for this style of music so cried down by opera mongers," Foster wrote to Christy on February 23, 1850. Christy introduced "Camptown Races" early in 1850, and soon after that the song was featured by major minstrel troupes.

It was for Ed Christy that Foster wrote his greatest Negro ballads, all of which Christy introduced and some of which he issued as original compositions. There is considerable dispute as to whether Christy paid a flat sum of $500 for the right both to introduce "The Old Folks at Home" (or "Swanee River"), written in 1851, and to have his name appear as the author on the sheet music. In the first draft of this song, Foster used "Pedee River" rather than "Swanee." When he came to the conclusion that the name "Pedee River" did not sound euphonious enough, he went hunting through an atlas for another two-syllable name for a river in the South. Thus he came upon "Suwanee," which emptied into the Gulf of Mexico. He liked the sound of that name, contracted it to "Swanee," and used it instead of "Pedee."

"Old Folks at Home" was published in the fall of 1851, its title page reading, "Ethiopian Melody as Sung by Christy's Minstrels, Written and Composed by E. P. Christy." It was a triumph. A year later, as was reported in *The Musical World*, it was "one of the most successful songs that has ever appeared in any country. The publishers keep two presses running on it, and sometimes three; yet, they cannot supply the demand. The sale has already reached over forty thousand copies, and at the present rate will soon come up to a hundred thousand." The *Albany State Register* remarked that it was "on everybody's tongue, and consequently in everybody's mouth. Pianos and guitars groan with it, night and day; sentimental ladies sing it; sentimental young gentlemen warble it in midnight serenades; volatile young bucks hum it in the midst of their business and pleasures; boatmen roar it out stentorially at all times; all bands play it; amateur flute players agonize over it every spare moment; the street organs grind it out at every hour; and singing stars carol it on the theatrical boards and at concerts." The song was widely imitated and parodied in numbers like "The Old Folks Are Gone" by George F. Root, Hattie Livingston's "Young Folks at Home," and H. Craven Griffith's "Young Folks from Home," the last of which was also introduced by the Christy Minstrels.

Such a formidable success led Foster once and for all to drop the practice of permitting his songs to appear as Christy's, and he made his intentions clear to Christy in a letter dated May 25, 1852. "I find I cannot write at all unless I write for public approbation and get credit for what I write." Under his own name he now issued "Massa's in de Cold, Cold Ground" in 1852, "My Old Kentucky Home" and "Old Dog Tray" in 1853, and "Jeanie With the Light Brown Hair" in 1854. His Negro songs were his best, most of them still carried to success by Ed Christy and his minstrels. Late in 1854, Foster's publishers announced that the sales for "Old Folks at Home" had reached 130,000; for "My Old Kentucky Home," 90,000; and for "Massa's in de Cold, Cold Ground," 74,000. Foster himself computed that by 1857 he had earned almost $10,000 in royalties, a considerable figure for that period.

Foster's last Negro classic was "Old Black Joe," inspired by a kindly old slave in his wife's family. It was published late in 1860. After that Foster concentrated on sentimental ballads, producing an abundant library. Regrettably, only rarely do we find in these ballads any of the fresh melody and poignant feeling that stir us so vitally in his Negro songs.

In the fall of 1860, Foster brought his family to New York, where the last chapter of his life unfolded grimly. Extraordinarily prolific, he produced in New York more than half of the total number of his compositions, but the quality did not keep step with the quantity. Much of it was hack work, hastily conceived and completed for a quick sale.

His greatest successes were now behind him, and his popularity with the public was in a rapid decline. His royalties had dwindled to pennies; the only way he could keep from starvation was to write a song and dispose of it hastily for a few dollars. His family soon refused to share with him the squalor into which he had allowed himself to descend and returned to Pittsburgh. Tormented by loneliness, frustration, and despair, Foster found increasing solace in drink, for which he had always had a weakness. For days he would live in a state of total inebriation in his sordid room in a Bowery hotel.

A chambermaid found him there one day in January, 1864, bleeding and unconscious. He was hurriedly transferred to the Bellevue Hospital, where he died on January 13, 1864. After his death there were found in his pockets three pennies, thirty-five cents in Northern scrip, and a slip of paper on which he had hastily written "dear friends and gentle people," possibly a subject for a sentimental ballad.

4—Civil War Songs

From the Civil War there emerged a rich song literature reflecting the varying shades of emotion aroused in both war camps—the ardor and the bitterness, the exaltation and the despair, the hopes and the frustrations, the nostalgia and the loneliness.

The first Civil War songs were calculated to inflame the patriotism of the belligerents, to inspire them to battle. The South appropriated the melody of Dan Emmett's minstrel-show tune, "Dixie," dressed it up with new martial lyrics, and adopted it as its war song. The fact that "Dixie" had been written by a Northerner was conveniently forgotten; and a report was allowed to circulate that this music was actually the composition of a Negro speaking of his inextricable bond to his master and to the Southland. Throughout the war "Dixie" remained the South's favorite song. Just before General Pickett made his charge at Gettysburg, he ordered that it be played to lift the morale of his troops. After Appomattox, Abraham Lincoln remarked that since the North had conquered the South it had also acquired "Dixie" as one of the spoils of war. As testimony to his own enthusiasm for "Dixie" he asked the band outside the White House to play it for him.

Because "Dixie" was so closely identified with the South, its composer—Dan Emmett—became an object for attack by several Northern newspapers, even though he had been merely the innocent victim of confiscation. To counterbalance the influence of his song in the South, Emmett wrote a new set of lyrics for his melody, exhorting the North to remember Bunker Hill and to "meet those Southern traitors with iron." But even with these new verses "Dixie" never caught on in the North.

"Maryland, My Maryland" was another war song strongly favored by the South. The lyrics were written by James Ryder

Randall, Professor of English Literature at Poydras College, Louisiana. Reading a newspaper account of how Northern troops, passing through Baltimore, had been fired upon, Randall immediately recognized in this episode a valuable source of propaganda to help carry Maryland into the camp of the South. One sleepless night in 1861, he wrote a fiery poem, "Maryland, My Maryland," and had it published in a Baltimore newspaper. Soon thereafter, at a meeting to rally the people of Baltimore to the Southern cause, the poem was sung by Jennie Cary to the familiar German Christmas tune, "O Tannenbaum." It created such an outburst of enthusiasm that people outside the auditorium flocked to the windows to see what was happening. Jennie Cary repeated her performance—and her success—at a concert for the men of Beauregard's army. In 1862 the song was published with the music and achieved at once a wide distribution.

"The Bonnie Blue Flag" was a third song popular in the South, credit for which was claimed by Henry Macarthy, a stage entertainer. His lyrics traced the events leading up to the secession; for his melody he borrowed the tune of a popular Irish ditty, "The Jaunting Car." He introduced "The Bonnie Blue Flag" in his act in New Orleans in 1861, then repeated his performance throughout the South, where it was heard and adopted by Confederate soldiers.

But, as on the field of battle, it was the North which had the upper hand in the exchange of war songs. For it was the North, rather than the South, that produced the two leading composers of such music: George Frederick Root and Henry Work.

George Frederick Root (1820-1895) was born in Sheffield, Massachusetts, and received a thorough training in music in Boston and Paris. After being active in the field of music education in Boston and New York, he turned to the writing of popular music—apparently with a certain amount of condescension since he issued such efforts under the pen name of Wurzel (*Wurzel* is the German word for Root). Several songs published between 1853 and 1855 were successful: "The Hazel Dell," "Rosalie, the Prairie Flower," "There's Music in the Air" (later popular in many colleges), and the Evangelical hymn, "The Shining Shore."

In 1859, Root went to Chicago. There he became a member of the publishing establishment, Root and Cady, which his older brother had helped to found a year earlier. When the Civil War broke out, Root directed his song writing activity to the war effort, writing lyrics as well as music. His first war song "The First Gun Is Fired" was stimulated by Lincoln's second call for volunteers in 1863 and was a failure, but his second song, "The Battle Cry of Freedom," published that year by Root and Cady, proved to be his masterpiece. A singing duo, Frank and Jules Lombard, introduced the song so impressively at a rally at the Chicago Court House Square that the audience spontaneously joined in singing one of the refrains. After that, the Hutchinson Family performed it throughout the North. The song became a particular favorite with Union soldiers. As one of them wrote at the time: "A glee club which came down to the battlefield from Chicago brought with it the brand-new song, and it ran through the camp like wildfire. The effect was little short of miraculous. It put as much spirit and cheer into the army as a splendid victory. Day and night you could hear it by every campfire and in every tent. Never shall I forget how these men rolled out the line, 'And although he may be poor, he shall never be a slave.'"

Root continued producing war songs—some martial, some sentimental—until the end of the conflict. The best were: "Just Before the Battle, Mother" in 1863; "Tramp! Tramp! Tramp!" in 1864; and, in 1865, "On, On, On, the Boys Came Marching" and "The Vacant Chair," the last inspired by the death of a lieutenant in the 15th Massachusetts Infantry.

Henry Clay Work (1832-1884) was fired by his profound abolitionist and Unionist sentiments to write some of the North's most eloquent war songs. Like Root, he wrote both the lyrics and the music. He was the son of an active abolitionist, whose home was a station in the Underground Railway through which over 4,000 slaves escaped.

Work was born in Middletown, Connecticut. While serving as a printer's apprentice in Hartford, he discovered a melodeon in a room above the printer's shop and soon used it for the writing of songs. His first was "We Are Coming, Sister Mary," which the Ed Christy Minstrels are said to have bought for $25 and performed successfully for ten years following its first publication. In 1854, Work moved to Chicago to work as a printer. There he became a friend of George Root, at whose urging he began writing war songs as soon as the Civil War broke out. The first was "Kingdom Coming," a spirited folk melody to lyrics in Negro dialect. It proved so successful immediately after its publication by the firm of Root and Cady that Work was encouraged to give up the printing trade and concentrate on composition. After General Lee's invasion of Pennsylvania, Work wrote "The Song of a Thousand Years," and as a consequence of his apprehension over the fate of the North he produced "God Save the Nation." He also wrote delightful comedy songs, "Grafted into the Army" in 1862, "Babylon Is Fallen!" in 1863, and "Wake Nicodemus!" in 1864. The song with which his name will always be associated came in 1865, in the last months of the war. It was "Marching through Georgia," inspired by General Sherman's historic march to the sea. (Many years later, Princeton University borrowed the melody for a football song.)

After the first gun was fired, Stephen Foster also began channeling his musical energy into war songs. But, unlike those of Work and Root, these efforts were weak—among the weakest Foster had written. None of his war songs was particularly popular, and none has survived. The following are some of Foster's Civil War songs: "We Are Coming, Father Abraam," with words by James Sloan Gibbons, which had already been set to music by Luther Orlando Emerson, among others, "We've a Million in the Field," and "Was My Brother in the Battle?", all in 1862; and in 1863, "When This Dreadful War Is Ended," "My Boy Is Coming from the War," "Nothing but a Plain Old Soldier," and "For the Dear Old Flag I Die."

Three more Northern Civil War songs are remembered today. "The Battle Hymn of the Republic" was a poem by the famous suffragette and poetess, Julia Ward Howe, set to a melody of William Steffe long familiar at camp meetings of Negro congregations and known as "Say Brothers, Will You Meet Us?" Early in the Civil War this same melody had been used for "John Brown's Body," a song supposed to taunt a naive, hapless soldier of the 12th Massachusetts Regiment. As Northern soldiers marched to battle, they kept in step singing this brisk tune. Julia Ward Howe heard them sing it one day, in December, 1861, and that very night in her hotel room she wrote for it an eloquent poem, "The Battle Hymn of the Republic." It was first published in *The Atlantic Monthly* in February, 1862, and soon thereafter was reprinted in various newspapers, magazines, and army hymn books. The song was issued by three different sheet-music publishers. The chaplain of the 122nd Ohio Regiment of Volunteers taught it to his soldiers. It is said that when Lincoln first heard it he was so moved that he asked it to be sung a second time.

"Tenting on the Old Camp Ground," in which the soldier's terrible loneliness finds poignant expression, was written by Walter Kittredge in 1862. On the eve of being drafted, he wrote the somber lyrics and music to express his own suffering in having to leave wife and home. Since, however, he had once had an attack of rheumatic fever, he was turned down by the army. He now tried marketing his song but without much success, since publishers everywhere considered it too depressing for mass appeal. But the Hutchinson Family liked it and presented it frequently at its concerts. It was through their influence that the song was finally published by Oliver Ditson in 1864, with rewarding results. The song continued to be sung long after the war had ended, a favorite at rallies, meetings, and all kinds of martial gatherings.

"When Johnny Comes Marching Home," by Patrick S. Gilmore, actually became famous in another and later war, but since it was written for the Civil War, and enjoyed its initial success then, it deserves mention here. Patrick S. Gilmore (1829-1892) became famous after the Civil War as the leader of the celebrated Gilmore Band, which gave concerts throughout the United States and helped establish the American concert band. He was also the organizer of monumental festivals and jubilees employing Gargantuan musical forces. Gilmore founded his first band just a year before the Civil War. In 1860 he attached this group to the 24th Massachusetts Volunteers, and eventually he achieved the title of Bandmaster General with the rank of Colonel. In 1863 he wrote the words and music of "When Johnny Comes Marching Home" and published it under the pseudonym of Louis Lambert. His band introduced it and helped to popularize it among Union soldiers. Even in the South, the melody was so well liked that it was used for a set of comic verses, "For Bales!" But the greatest popularity of "When Johnny Comes Marching Home" belongs to a later period. Successfully revived during the Spanish-American

War, it became one of its leading songs; to this day it is only with the later war that the tune is usually associated. Since the turn of the century, "When Johnny Comes Marching Home" has appeared in various versions—as a fox-trot during World War I and as a symphonic composition in ambitious adaptations by Roy Harris and Morton Gould.

5—The Flourishing Ballad

After the Civil War the sentimental ballad again dominated the song-writing activity of American popular composers. With the cessation of hostilities, Henry C. Work abandoned martial tunes for sentimental ones. He had already proved his aptitude for this kind of song in 1864 with a temperance ballad, "Come Home, Father." Often performed in the Timothy Shay Arthur melodrama, *Ten Nights in a Barroom*, it was destined to become a potent propaganda weapon for the temperance movement. Such a talent for mawkish lyrics and lachrymose melody made it possible for Work to produce other ballads. Among the best were "The Lost Letter," "The Ship That Never Returned," and, in 1876, "Grandfather's Clock," which sold almost a million copies of sheet music in an era when a million-copy sale was truly a rarity.

Other composers besides Work, active before and during the Civil War, were fertile in creating sentimental ballads after 1865. William Shakespeare Hays (1837-1907), who was born and who lived for most of his life in Louisville, Kentucky, where for many years he worked on the staff of the *Louisville Courier-Journal*, had achieved his first recognition during the war with "The Drummer Boy of Shiloh," published in 1862. Only one year after the end of hostilities, he wrote two song hits, each a ballad, and each boasting a sale of over a quarter of a million copies—"Write Me a Letter Home" and "We Parted by the River Side." In all, his more than three hundred ballads had a combined sheet-music sale of over fifteen million copies. The most popular was "Mollie Darling," in 1871, but others were also well liked, including "Nora O'Neal," "The Little Old Cabin in the Lane," "Susan Jane," and "Angels Meet Me at the Cross Roads." Hays also wrote several effective songs in Negro dialect, among them "Early in de Mornin'," "Roll Out! Heave Dat Cotton," and "Walk in de

Middle of de Road," the last long thought really to be a Negro spiritual.

Septimus Winner (1826-1902), who published his ballads under the pseudonym of Alice Hawthorne, was a Philadelphian who owned and managed a music store in that city, taught music, and published valuable instruction books on various instruments. He also wrote music articles for *Graham's Magazine*, then edited by Edgar Allan Poe. During the Civil War, Winner wrote several war songs, none of them distinguished. In "Give Us Back Our Old Commander" he gave voice to the prevailing sentiment for the return of General McClellan. The song was considered so subversive that Winner was briefly imprisoned. Nevertheless, during the Presidential campaign of 1868, the song returned with new lyrics to advance the cause of General Grant. Ironically, the only Civil War effort of Winner to survive is a set of non-sensical verses which he adapted to the German folk song "Lauterbach": "Oh, Where, Oh, Where, Has My Little Dog Gone?"

However, in the field of the sentimental ballad Winner first met success before the Civil War—in 1854 with "What Is Home without a Mother?" A year later he published "Listen to the Mocking Bird," which in half a century sold over twenty million copies in America and Europe and which is still known and loved; but Winner had disposed of his song outright for $5.00 and thus never enjoyed the fruits of this formidable success, which he never managed to repeat. Nevertheless, after the war he did write some successful ballads. The most notable of these was "Whispering Hope," in 1868, which retained its popularity to the end of the century.

One year after the publication of "Whispering Hope" there appeared another sentimental ballad whose appeal was both immediate and permanent. It was called "Sweet Genevieve," and its composer was Henry Tucker, who, during the Civil War, had written several other topical songs including "Weeping, Sad and Lonely," or "When This Cruel War Is Over." In 1869, Tucker purchased the lyric of "Sweet Genevieve" from its author, George Cooper. Cooper—a prolific lyricist, whose verses were set by

many composers including Stephen Foster—had written "Genevieve" as an emotional release after the sudden death of his wife
soon after their marriage. Tucker's melody was written and the
complete song published in 1869, and performed extensively by
many minstrel-show companies.

"I'll Take You Home Again, Kathleen" and "Silver Threads
Among the Gold" were two of the most popular ballads of the
1870's. The first was written by a Virginian, Thomas Paine
Westendorf. For a long time it was believed that the inspiration
for both the words and the music came to Westendorf in 1875
from his wife's serious illness caused by the death of their son.
But recently uncovered information is much less poetic. The
song was merely Westendorf's expression of loneliness when his
wife was visiting her folks. It is also fact, and not legend, that
the composer's immediate stimulus had been another song highly
popular at that time, "Barney, Take Me Home Again," by Arthur
W. French and George W. Brown.

Hart Pease Danks (1834-1903), born in New Haven, Connecticut, had been an apprentice builder and carpenter before adopt-
ing music as a profession. In this field he earned his living as a
conductor, choirleader, bass singer, and composer. Before the
Civil War he wrote an excellent hymn, "Lake Street," and two
fine ballads, "Anna Lee" and "The Old Lane." But success did
not come until 1870, after he had settled in New York; and it
came with "Don't Be Angry with Me, Darling." Soon after that,
Danks happened to read a poem by Eben E. Rexford, a Wisconsin
farm-journal editor. He offered Rexford $3.00 for the rights to
set that poem to music—a price that Rexford apparently considered so generous that he dispatched to Danks several other
lyrics for his use. One of these was "Silver Threads Among the
Gold," which Rexford had written as a sentimental gesture to
his wife. Danks wrote and published his song in 1873. Before
the end of the century it sold over a million copies. (Ironically,
Danks divorced his wife one year after the ballad was published.) Then, in 1907, it was revived by the minstrel, Richard
J. José, and entered into a new period of popularity; it now rose
to even greater heights of commercial success than before. To
this day it is a favorite of barbershop quartets. Once again, as had
been the case with so many other composers of the time, Danks

had sold his song outright for a few dollars. He died in a drab rooming house in Philadelphia soon after the beginning of the twentieth century, leaving behind him over a thousand published songs—religious hymns as well as ballads. Among these were "Not Ashamed of Christ," "Allie Darling," and "Little Bright Eyes, Will You Miss Me?".

One of the most significant composers of sentimental ballads in the 1870's was James A. Bland (1854-1911), a Negro. Bland's father was the first member of his race to hold the post of examiner in the Patent Office in Washington, D.C. As a boy, while serving as page in the House of Representatives, James often entertained Washington notables with songs to his own banjo accompaniment. Before becoming a professional entertainer, however, he completed his education at Howard University. He then joined an all-colored minstrel troupe touring the country, and it was for these performances that he began writing songs, which he himself introduced. Two of his earliest efforts were among his best, "Carry Me Back to Old Virginny," in 1878, and "In the Evening by the Moonlight," one year later. Between 1878 and 1879 he also wrote "Oh, dem Golden Slippers" and "Hand Me Down My Walking Stick," both exceedingly popular in minstrel shows of the time and both still remembered.

In 1881, Bland went to Europe with an all-Negro minstrel troupe. For a number of years he was such a favorite in England that he was summoned to give a command performance for the Prince of Wales. He returned to the United States in 1901 to find that during his absence he had been forgotten, and, because he had freely squandered his huge earnings, he was completely destitute. When he died in Philadelphia in 1911, no newspaper noticed his passing and he was assigned a humble and unmarked grave. But, almost thirty years later, his grave was located, and a headstone was erected by ASCAP. Finally in 1940, "Carry Me Back to Old Virginny" was officially designated by the Legislature of Virginia as the song of that state.

While it is impossible to say authoritatively just how many songs Bland wrote, since so many of them were not copyrighted and were taken over outright by performers of his day, the general belief is that they numbered several hundred. Besides the four already mentioned, his best efforts included "De Golden

Wedding," "Close dem Windows," "Pretty Little Carolina Rose," and "Listen to the Silver Trumpets."

Neither Joseph P. Skelly nor Harry Kennedy were of Bland's creative stature, nor did they ever produce a ballad to equal "Carry Me Back to Old Virginny." Both, however, were prolific writers of sentimental ballads. Skelly was a shiftless plumber who was continually impoverished and usually drunk, despite which he managed to complete more than four hundred songs. His initial successes came with "My Pretty Red Rose" in 1877, and "The Gentleman from Kildare," "If My Dreams Would All Come True," and "Pride of the Kitchen," in 1879. In 1880 he published "Why Did They Dig Ma's Grave So Deep?" for many years thereafter a favorite with boy sopranos in vaudeville theaters. In 1883, he issued what is perhaps his best song, "Strolling on the Brooklyn Bridge," lyrics by George Cooper.

Kennedy was a ventriloquist who appeared extensively in minstrel shows and for whom song writing was a hobby. His first two successes were both in the current tradition, "A Flower from Mother's Grave" in 1878 and "Cradle's Empty, Baby's Gone" in 1880. He continued writing not only ballads but also comic and dialect songs. His most popular numbers were written towards the end of his life, "Molly and I and the Baby" in 1892 and "Say Au Revoir but Not Goodbye" in 1893. The latter, a favorite with barbershop quartets, was sung over his fresh grave by Helene Mora, after Kennedy had succumbed to tuberculosis.

The heyday of the sentimental ballad came in the 1890's and continued well into the new century. If any single composer can be said to have ushered in this era it is Paul Dresser (1857-1906), probably the most famous and the most successful ballad composer of his time. Brother of the famous novelist, Theodore Dreiser, Dresser was born in Terre Haute, Indiana, near the river which he immortalized in "On the Banks of the Wabash." Son of a deeply religious man, Paul was destined for the church, but his own inclinations drew him ineluctably to music. As a boy he learned to play the guitar and the piano and to accompany himself in song. When he was sixteen, he ran away from home and joined a traveling medicine show where he sang parodies of the day's popular tunes. In 1885 he became a member of the

Billy Rice Minstrels with whom he appeared as end man and for whom he wrote songs, some of which were published, the first being "Wide Wings." His first success—the sentimental ballad, "The Letter That Never Came," 1886—was also written for the Minstrels. One outstanding song now followed another in rapid succession—"The Outcast Unknown," in 1887; "The Convict and the Bird," in 1888; and one of his greatest successes up to that time, "The Pardon Came Too Late," in 1891. "He was," wrote his brother Theodore, "ever full of melodies of a tender . . . nature—that of a ballad-maker of a nation. . . . [His ballads] bespoke . . . a wistful seeking . . . tender and illusioned, with no practical knowledge of any side of life, yet full of true poetic feeling for the mystery and pathos of life and death, and wonder of waters, the stars, the flowers, accidents of life, success and failure."

After Dresser had become a partner in the New York publishing house of Howley and Haviland, in 1894, he produced a number of songs that realized a fortune for both himself and his firm—"The Blue and the Gray," "Just Tell Them That You Saw Me," "The Curse of the Dreamer," "My Mother Told Me So," and, in 1899, his masterpiece, "On the Banks of the Wabash."

Max Hoffman, an orchestrator, has recalled the circumstances under which Dresser wrote the last-named ballad in his Chicago hotel room. "It was summer. All the windows were open and Paul was mulling over a melody that was practically in finished form. But he did not have the words. So he had me play the full chorus over and over again at least for two or three hours, while he was writing down the words, changing a line here and a phrase there until the lyric suited him. . . . When Paul came to the line, 'through the sycamores the candlelights are gleaming,' I was tremendously impressed. . . . I have always felt that Paul got the idea from glancing out of the window now and again as he wrote, and seeing the lights glimmering on Lake Michigan. . . . The song was published precisely as I arranged it. . . . During the whole evening we spent together Paul made no mention of any-one's having helped him with the song."

The last years of Dresser's life might have served him well as material for one of his own sentimental ballads. In 1905 he found himself penniless, even though his past earnings exceeded half a million dollars. He had always lived in the grand manner, had always been extravagant in showering his money on those around him, but now his published songs stopped selling and his new ones failed to find a publisher. His own publishing house had gone bankrupt. His old-time friends and associates, many of whom had profited from his generosity, avoided him. His health and spirit broke—but not his creative gift. The last of his ballads, "My Gal Sal," which he himself managed to publish in 1905, proved to be one of the greatest triumphs of his career, but he did not live to enjoy it. He died suddenly in Brooklyn in 1906.

6—Show Business

The minstrel show had been the first significant type of stage production for which American composers wrote popular songs and which served as the springboard from which these songs leaped into popularity. A second important stage presentation to serve a similar function for our popular music was vaudeville. Vaudeville (originally called variety) developed out of the fantasia section of the minstrel show, in which individual performers strutted their stuff in song, dance, and humorous skits. Eventually vaudeville superseded the minstrel show, even as it, in turn, was finally replaced by other media of entertainment.

The first known use of the term "vaudeville" for variety entertainment occurred in Weisiger's Hall, Louisville, Kentucky, on February 23, 1871, when a troupe headed by H. J. Sargent billed itself as "Sargent's Great Vaudeville Company from Chicago." One person above others, however, is responsible for establishing vaudeville as a popular form of stage entertainment—Tony Pastor.

Pastor was a graduate from minstrel shows where he had appeared as a blackface minstrel and where he performed on the tambourine and sang songs to his own banjo accompaniment. From the minstrel show he progressed to the circus, extending his versatility by appearing in turn as a clown, singer, ringmaster, comedian, bareback rider, and tumbler. Just prior to the Civil War, Pastor appeared in variety entertainment, and, when the war broke out, he initiated a routine by which his act was identified for many years thereafter—the presentation of topical songs, some of his own invention, some the work of others, and some parodies. One of the songs he hastily concocted for the mayoralty campaign in New York in 1886 included a catch phrase said to have been significant in carrying its candidate into City Hall, "What's the matter with Hewitt? He's all right."

Greater even than his success as a performer in variety were his achievements as the manager of such entertainment. He is, indeed, sometimes called the father of American vaudeville. On March 21, 1865, in Paterson, New Jersey, he opened the first theater in America devoted exclusively to variety entertainment. His aim was to present such wholesome shows that women and children might for the first time be drawn inside a theater. Though that venture was a failure, Pastor was not discouraged. A year later he opened another variety theater, this time at 199-201 Bowery in New York City, calling it the Tony Pastor Variety Theatre, or Pastor's Opera House. In order to lure women as patrons, he offered pots, pans, dress patterns, and groceries as door prizes. The women succumbed to the bait, came into the theater, and were so completely won over to Tony Pastor's clean entertainment that they returned again and again, often bringing their children with them. "I am quite serious," wrote James L. Ford in *Forty-Odd Years in the Literary Shop*, "that the most important moment in the history of the development of the theater in this country was that in which Tony Pastor first gave away his coal, flour, dress patterns to secure the patronage of respectable women."

Pastor produced his variety shows at 201 Bowery through March, 1875, then for another six years, beginning on October 4, set up shop a bit further uptown, at 585 Broadway. In 1883 he became the first showman to tour the country with a vaudeville troupe. Meanwhile, in 1881, he opened the house that for the next quarter century remained the temple of vaudeville entertainment—Tony Pastor's Music Hall, in Union Square. It was on this stage that many stars of the musical stage were first swept to success—Lillian Russell (a stage name devised by Tony Pastor for Helen Louise Leonard), the Four Cohans, Pat Rooney, May Irwin, Gus Williams, Weber and Fields, Billy Jerome, Eddie Foy, Emma Carus, and others. And it was on this stage that these and other stars (often assisted by song pluggers strategically placed in the audience) introduced songs that came out of Union Square to conquer the country. A number of these songs will be treated in later chapters, but a few should be mentioned now in passing—J. W. Kelly's "Throw Him Down, McCloskey," dynamically presented by Maggie Cline to backstage noises devised by the stagehands; "Kaiser, Don't You Want to Buy a Dog?", popularized by Gus Williams; the Stern and Marks ballads, "Mother Was a Lady" and "The Little Lost Child"; and

Ben Harney's piano rags, with which ragtime first became a vogue in commercial music.

A second branch of the musical theater to develop from the minstrel show was burlesque. Through the years the term "burlesque" has been used to designate different types of entertainment. In the 1820's and 1830's burlesque referred to satires and travesties. Near the end of the century burlesque was applied to stage productions emphasizing bawdy skits, double-entendres, hoochee-coochee dances, and strip teases. But in the years immediately following the Civil War, burlesques referred to shows filled with broad humor and slapstick, whose principal characters were caricatures of Negroes, Germans, or Irishmen.

Some of the most successful of these burlesques were written and produced by Ed Harrigan and Tony Hart in New York between 1879 and 1885. They were known as the *Mulligan Guard* plays—the Mulligans being a New York family who, with their friends and neighbors, were carried through such ordinary episodes as an election, a picnic, a chowder, or a wedding anniversary and who were usually involved in all kinds of humorous accidents, mishaps, and coincidences.

The embryo of this series of plays was a one-act vaudeville skit called *The Mulligan Guard* which Harrigan and Hart wrote in 1873 and presented at the Academy of Music in Chicago. The skit satirized the many organizations then popular in the United States that enjoyed parading about in various military uniforms. Outfitted with absurd costumes, Harrigan and Hart made such a mockery of this practice that most of these groups were quickly laughed out of existence.

The success of this skit led Harrigan and Hart to write the full-length stage satires *The Mulligan Guard Picnic* and *The Mulligan Guard Ball*, presented in New York in 1878 and 1879 respectively. These were the first of a long series of burlesques using he same principal characters: *The Mulligan Guards' Chowder*, *The Mulligan Guards' Christmas*, *The Mulligan Guards' Surprise*, *The Mulligans' Silver Wedding*, and so forth, ending with *Dan's Tribulations*, in 1884. They provided a wealth of merriment through their detailed and at times penetrating depiction of Irish, German, or Negro characters within a familiar New York setting, and their problems and complications were those of everyday people. These burlesques became the first productions in our musical theater to provide a realistic picture of New York City life and people, their customs, manners, and speech. When Isaac Goldberg wrote that these musicals marked "an important epoch in the development of the American song and dance show," he was placing considerable emphasis on the word "American."

All the music for the Harrigan and Hart burlesques was written by David Braham (1838-1905). Braham, of English birth, had come to America as a young man and found employment first as a violinist in the Pony Moore Minstrels and after that in the pit orchestras of most of New York's better musical theaters. His first success as a composer came with several songs patterned after English music-hall tunes; these included "The Bootblack" and "Over the Hill to the Poorhouse." In 1873 he wrote in Chicago the music for the Harrigan and Hart skit, *The Mulligan Guard,* the title song being an especial favorite. From then until Harrigan and Hart separated in 1884, Braham contributed all the songs for the Mulligan productions, many of the songs being as rich and colorful in racial interest as the characters themselves. The most important songs from these productions were "The Babies on Our Block," "My Dad's Dinner Pail," "The Pitcher of Beer," and "The Skidmore Fancy Ball."

After the dissolution of the partnership of Harrigan and Hart, Braham continued writing music for Harrigan's plays. For *Old Lavender* he wrote one of his most effective songs, "Poverty's Tears Ebb and Flow." Later Harrigan productions yielded several more significant Braham numbers, notably "Maggie Murphy's Home" (a waltz made famous by Ada Lewis), "Taking in the Town," and "Danny by My Side" (the last sung by Al Smith in 1933 to celebrate the 50th anniversary of the opening of the Brooklyn Bridge).

It should be noted as a footnote to Braham's biography that his relationship with Harrigan was closer than merely that of a collaborator, for in 1876 Braham had married Harrigan's daughter. Braham's death in New York in 1905 preceded that of Harrigan by half a dozen years.

The most successful burlesque produced in America in the nineteenth century was Charles Hoyt's *A Trip to Chinatown.* The basic musical score was by Percy Gaunt, though many songs by other composers were interpolated, including Charles K. Harris' famous ballad, "After the Ball." *A Trip to Chinatown* toured the country for more than a year before it arrived in New

York on November 9, 1891, to begin the longest run of any musical up to that time, 650 performances. Like the plays of Harrigan and Hart, *A Trip to Chinatown* placed everyday Americans in recognizable situations and settings. The play was spiced with amusing and at times satirical references to topical subjects, such as woman's suffrage and the temperance crusade. From Gaunt's music came three hit songs: "Reuben and Cynthia," "Push dem Clouds Away," and the still celebrated "The Bowery." Each of these sold several hundred thousand copies of sheet music, thus giving to *A Trip to Chinatown* the added distinction of being the first American musical production to derive a sizable income from its published music.

Between 1896 and 1903, Joe Weber and Lew Fields presented a series of highly successful burlesque productions at their Music Hall in New York. The series began with *The Art of Maryland*, with book and lyrics by Joseph Herbert. Weber and Fields were cast as two Dutchmen, the one short and fat, the other tall and thin. Their exchange of broad humor was couched in a thick German-English dialect as they were helplessly tossed about in all kinds of ridiculous situations. The best of these burlesques were *Hurly Burly*, *Whirl-i-Gig*, *Fiddle-Dee-Dee*, and *Twirly Whirly*. Each proved the step on which some performer or performers began the climb to success—David Warfield, Fay Templeton, Bessie Clayton, Cecilia Loftus, and the McCoy Sisters, to name only a few.

Like the Harrigan and Hart burlesques those with Weber and Fields employed a single composer up to his death—John Stromberg (1853-1902). Stromberg was raised in Tin Pan Alley, where he worked as arranger for the house of Witmark. His first success came in 1895 with "My Best Girl's a New-Yorker [Corker]," which brought him the assignment to write the music for *The Art of Maryland*. During the next half dozen years, Stromberg produced the shows from which came "Dinah" (also known as "Kiss Me Honey, Do"), "When Chloe Sings a Song," "Come Back, My Honey Boy, to Me," "Dream On, Dream of Me," and one with which Lillian Russell will always be identified, "Come Down, Ma' Evenin' Star." The last of these was Stromberg's valedictory, for he died, perhaps by his own hand, in his New York apartment in 1902. When Lillian Russell introduced it in *Twirly Whirly* she broke down and could not finish it.

The score for the 1903 Weber and Fields production, *Whoop-*

Dee-Do, was written by William T. Francis. With that burlesque the collaboration of Weber and Fields ended. Each henceforth went his separate way in the theater until their respective deaths, that of Fields in 1941, and that of Weber in 1942.

A third species of musical theater to become popular after the close of the Civil War was the extravaganza. That term, however, made its appearance four years before the war, with *Novelty, with the Laying of the Atlantic Cable,* a handsomely mounted production featuring a European ballet company. *Novelty* was a failure, but extravaganzas were here to stay.

The first successful extravaganza also became the most successful musical production seen in America up to that time. It was *The Black Crook,* introduced at Niblo's Gardens in New York on September 12, 1866. The initial run extended to 474 performances and earned a profit of over a million dollars. With a book by Charles M. Barras and music mainly by Giuseppe Operti, *The Black Crook* consisted of a breath-taking succession of ballets, spectacles, transformations, and enchantments within a complex and often confused story involving a black crook who sells his soul to the devil in return for supernatural powers. Utilizing the most advanced stage techniques then known and the last word in spectacular sets, costumes, and stage effects, *The Black Crook* was a five-hour feast for eye and senses. Not the least of its many attractions were the ballet sequences in which appeared girls dressed in pink tights—the reason why *The Black Crook* was so vigorously denounced in the press and from the pulpit. Sex insinuated itself also into several of its songs, particularly into "You Naughty, Naughty Men," by T. Kennick and G. Bicknell, provocatively sung by Milly Cavendish as she directed her charms, attention, and a wagging forefinger at the men in the audience.

Because of its advanced stage methods, its girls in the pink tights, and its show tunes, *The Black Crook* is sometimes described as America's first musical comedy. Actually it was nothing of the sort. The formula for musical comedy, as we know musical comedy today, was not realized for another half century. Extravaganzas continued to dominate the New York stage until they were finally displaced by the comic opera and the operetta.

7—Where Tin Pan Alley Was Born

Between 1890 and 1930, Tin Pan Alley was a dominant force in our music. The name "Tin Pan Alley" refers not so much to a specific geographical location—an alley, street, or vicinity in which many song publishers were concentrated, even though such a concentration actually did exist—but rather, more accurately, Tin Pan Alley refers to a way of life in American popular music—a way of life in which the American popular song became a big business, subject to the tried methods and techniques used by big business to reap huge financial rewards. In short, Tin Pan Alley was a way of writing songs to established patterns and a science of marketing and popularizing them.

Long before the song industry was christened Tin Pan Alley, it had arrived at, perfected, and refined some of the procedures by which it would eventually become what might be termed a "Song Trust." The name "Tin Pan Alley" was concocted soon after the turn of the twentieth century to identify a specific street in New York where many powerful publishers transacted their business. But as a *modus operandi* in popular music Tin Pan Alley existed in spirit, if not yet in name, some years before 1900.

Something of the spirit of Tin Pan Alley could be found in Milwaukee in the 1880's, in a cramped office on Grand Avenue rented by a young composer, Charles K. Harris, for $7.50 a month. Outside his door he hung the sign, "Songs Written to Order." That phrase was to denote a standard practice of Tin Pan Alley. During the same period, but in Chicago, something of Tin Pan Alley could also be found with Will Rossiter, a young publisher. Rossiter was one of the first to suggest that the success of a song need not be left exclusively to chance. Rossiter tried publicizing his songs by singing them in retail stores, and he brought his songs to the attention of performers through advertisements in a theatrical trade journal.

Most of the practices and aspirations of Tin Pan Alley could be found in New York's Union Square between the middle 1880's and the end of the century. At that time Union Square was the entertainment Mecca of New York, if not of the whole country. The Academy of Music, home of grand opera, was located there, as were Tony Pastor's Music Hall (leading vaudeville theater of the time), the Union Square Theater (for legitimate plays and musicals), and various burlesque houses, dance halls, penny arcades, restaurants, and saloons.

It was inevitable that several far-sighted publishers would become aware of the rich market such an area of concentrated entertainment provided for songs and that they would consequently decide to open offices near to such a market. Early in the 1880's the house of Willis Woodward & Co. opened up shop in the Star Theater Building on Broadway and 13th Street, only a stone's throw from Union Square. In 1888, the then young firm of Witmark moved to East 14th Street, and in 1894 a newcomer to the industry, Jos. W. Stern & Co. appeared on the same street. By the time Howley, Haviland & Co., Charles K. Harris Company, and Shapiro-Bernstein shifted to Union Square in the middle 1890's, this neighborhood boasted the largest representation of song publishing houses the country had known. Before then, publishers had been scattered not merely in many different parts of New York City, but even throughout many different cities.

The younger, newer firms appeared with hardly more than a song and a prayer. They had no financial resources to speak of. Howley and Haviland opened on a capital of $200, and Joseph W. Stern did not even have that when he and Edward Marks formed their company. About all that these newcomers possessed was a desk, a chair, a filing cabinet, some songs—and a mountain of drive and initiative. They sensed that the method existing up to that time to promote and sell songs was obsolete. A song, they sensed, could not only be manufactured but could also be sold to the public like any other commodity—through continual and unrelenting exposure. Once the song was written, it became a commodity for the song plugger to handle. Upon his charm, talent for salesmanship, and personal contacts often rested the ultimate fate of a song. The plugger had to persuade managers, music section heads of department stores, orchestra leaders, stage stars,

singing waiters—in short anybody who had access to an audience
—to use his latest products.

Varied methods were devised in Union Square for plugging a
song. Pluggers would invade a local music shop or department
store and spend the day with their latest songs playing them on
the piano or singing them. Pluggers sometimes traveled by truck
to congested parts of the city. The truck would then become the
platform from which songs would be introduced to curious
passers-by. Pluggers even induced the managers of sports arenas
to permit them to sing their songs during major events.

Another important method of song plugging was devised in
1893. Gus Edwards (later a distinguished vaudevillian and song
composer, but then only a boy of fourteen) was hired by a publisher to sit in the balcony of Hurtig and Seamon's Theater in
New York. After a performer on the stage had sung the publisher's latest number, it was Gus' job to rise, as if spontaneously,
from his seat and repeat the refrain of the song several times.
The boy scored such a success with this innovation that song
publishers made it a practice to plant singers in theaters. Long
before he became famous as a composer, Irving Berlin worked in
this capacity in Union Square for the firm of Harry von Tilzer.

Another highly efficacious method of song plugging was
devised in 1892 by George H. Thomas, an electrician. He produced a series of magic lantern slides which told the story of a
song pictorially. Under each picture the lyrics of the song were
reproduced. Motion-picture audiences were thus able to learn
a new song quickly and enjoy a community songfest. First widely
used in 1894 for the Stern and Marks ballad, "The Little Lost
Child," the song slide became an accepted form of entertainment
in motion-picture theaters everywhere, enjoyed equally by the
theater owner (who was given an attraction free of charge),
the publisher (who found a powerful new medium for spreading
his songs), and the audience (who loved singing). An entertainer on the stage would introduce the number and then lead
the audience in the singing as the slides flicked on and off. As
boys, Eddie Cantor and Georgie Jessel earned their first pay as
performers singing the songs of the day in front of these slides.

Usually the head of a publishing house served as his own
plugger. "Sixty joints a week I used to make," wrote Edward B.
Marks. "Joe Stern, my partner, covered about forty. What's more

we did it every week." Julie Witmark was the plugger for the house of Witmark, Patrick Howley for Howley and Haviland. But there were also pluggers who were hired. Meyer Cohen was one, employed by Stern and Marks, and he was one of the most famous song pluggers in Union Square. Cohen was responsible for lifting the Stern and Marks ballad, "Mother Was a Lady" to commercial triumphs, introducing it himself at Tony Pastor's Music Hall and then getting Lottie Gilson to sing it in vaudeville houses throughout the country. Mose Gumble, from Shapiro-Bernstein, was another influential plugger. Gumble's persuasive powers convinced leading stars of the stage such as Nora Bayes, George M. Cohan, and Weber and Fields that they ought to use his numbers. The fabulous success of Jean Schwartz's "Bedelia" in 1903 was mainly due to his supreme selling efforts.

Union Square perfected not merely the methods by which songs were introduced to the public and marketed but even the ways in which they were written. Song styles were set, established, and rigidly followed as created from a convenient matrix; and whatever the style of the song, the thirty-two-bar chorus became an inflexible pattern.

There was the sentimental ballad, still the country's favorite kind of song. In Union Square the sentimental ballad attained the heights of its popularity. Indeed, it was on the foundation of the sentimental ballad that several new firms erected the solid framework of their establishments.

The house of Jos. W. Stern & Co., for example, was firmly established as a result of the success of its first song, "The Little Lost Child," one of the most celebrated ballads of the 1890's. The music was by Joseph W. Stern, formerly a necktie salesman; Edward B. Marks, a salesman of buttons, notions, and novelties, wrote the lyrics. One day, Marks happened to read the newspaper account of a child found wandering in the streets by a policeman, who turned out to be the child's long lost father. Since writing verses had long been his avocation, Marks enlarged upon this incident in a song lyric and asked his friend Stern (who could play the piano "with one hand and fake with the other") to set it to music. When the song was written, Stern and Marks decided to publish it themselves, for which purpose they founded the firm of Jos. W. Stern & Co. in a cubicle on 14th Street. Della

Fox, star of stage extravaganzas, wandered into their office in search of new material and was completely won over to their song. After she had introduced it in vaudeville, song slides in motion-picture theaters helped to make the ballad a nationwide sensation.

Stern and Marks published "The Little Lost Child" in 1894. Two years later they had a second triumph in "Mother Was a Lady." Like its predecessor, this ballad was inspired by an actual incident—this time witnessed by the authors in a Union Square restaurant. There a waitress, insulted by two brash male patrons, exclaimed proudly, "My mother was a lady." Marks extended this idea into a song lyric, and Stern provided a suitable melody. Meyer Cohen introduced it on the stage of Pastor's Music Hall, after which Lottie Gilson sang it with phenomenal results. So successful did this ballad become that the sheet music sold several million copies, and the phrase "my mother was a lady" became a pet saying of the times.

Though the house of Witmark was originally established in 1886 with "President Grover Cleveland's Wedding March" by Isidore Witmark, it did not achieve financial stability until it, too, published a sensational sentimental ballad in Union Square. Their song was "The Picture That Is Turned toward the Wall," with words and music by Charles Graham. Graham's inspiration had been a scene in a play, *Blue Jeans*, in which a farmer turns the picture of his wayward daughter to the wall. Graham wrote his ballad in 1891 and sold it to Witmark for $15.00. Willard Mack, an Irish tenor in vaudeville, came upon it in the Witmark offices and popularized it in theaters everywhere, after which Julie Witmark plugged it indefatigably in theaters, restaurants, and department stores. The ballad spread rapidly, and the formerly humble and ignored publishing establishment of Witmark was suddenly regarded with the highest esteem by the trade, as Isidore Witmark himself pointed out in his autobiography, *From Ragtime to Swingtime*. Graham composed several more hits, the best being "Two Little Girls in Blue" and "My Dad's the Engineer." His life ended sordidly in Bellevue Hospital in New York, in 1899, after many years of helpless addiction to gambling and alcohol.

A real episode provided still another composer with the material for his most famous ballad. This composer was Charles K.

Harris (1865-1930). Harris appeared as a boy performer in vaudeville theaters in Milwaukee, singing minstrel-show tunes and accompanying himself on the banjo. He began writing songs during his teens and even succeeded in placing one of them in *The Skating Rink,* a musical in which Nat Goodwin starred in Milwaukee. Having written several songs that failed to find a publisher, Harris decided to start a publishing firm of his own. It was soon after he had opened his office on Grand Avenue in Milwaukee that he wrote and published the ballad that made him wealthy and famous.

When he was visiting Chicago, he happened to overhear a young couple at a dance quarrel and go their separate ways. "Many a heart is aching after the ball," he thought. This incident seemed to him tailor-made for a sentimental ballad, and he wrote both the lyrics and the music immediately after his return to Milwaukee. "After the Ball" was sung for the first time by Sam Doctor in a Milwaukee vaudeville house in 1892 and was a dismal failure, probably because midway in his performance Doctor forgot his lines. But soon after that, J. Aldrich Libby interpolated the ballad into Charles Hoyt's *A Trip to Chinatown* in which he was at the time starred. "After the Ball" was such a sensation there that, as the composer later recalled, "the entire audience arose and, standing, applauded wildly for five minutes." One year later, John Philip Sousa performed it with his band at the World Exposition in Chicago to such acclaim that for the next decade or so he rarely performed a concert without including it either on the program itself or as an encore. Five million copies of the song were sold within a few years.

Although Charles K. Harris never again attained a triumph of such magnitude, he did manage to write several more ballads that were popular in their day and are still remembered in ours. Three deserve special mention—"Break the News to Mother" (a favorite during the Spanish-American War), "I've Come to Say Good-bye," and "Hello, Central, Give Me Heaven" (one of the earliest examples of the "telephone song").

James Thornton (1861-1938) was a singing waiter in New York's East Side and then toured the vaudeville circuit with Charles B. Lawlor, the composer of "The Sidewalks of New York." Thornton's first song success came in 1892 with "My Sweetheart's the Man in the Moon," which his wife, Bonnie Thornton, a successful performer in her own right, helped make famous. During the next decade he wrote several more ballads, among them "On the Benches in the Park," "It Don't Seem Like the Same Old Smile," and "The Bridge of Sighs."

One day, when Thornton's wife asked him whether he still loved her, he answered, "I love you like I did when you were sweet sixteen." Thus the idea for the song "When You Were Sweet Sixteen" was born. Thornton wrote both the lyrics and the music and sold his song for $15.00 to Witmark, who, after its publication in 1898, realized a fortune from it through the sale of a million copies of sheet music. In 1944, this ballad was effectively revived in the Bing Crosby motion picture, *The Great John L.*

Thornton's last successful song, "There's a Mother Always Waiting for You at Home Sweet Home," was published in 1903. Though he lived for another thirty-five years, his career as a successful songwriter ended that year. Except for occasional appearances in vaudeville he spent the rest of his life in obscurity, greatly embittered by the fact that the kind of songs with which he grew up and which he once wrote had lost favor with the public.

Other types of songs besides the sentimental ballad enjoyed high esteem in Union Square. There were the sweet, gentle songs of nostalgia and sentiment—Harry Dacre's "Daisy Bell" (or "A Bicycle Built for Two"), in 1892; "The Sidewalks of New York," by Charles B. Lawlor and James W. Blake, in 1894; and Charles B. Ward's "The Band Played On," 1895, which enjoyed a successful return in 1941 in the motion picture *The Strawberry Blonde*. "Daisy Bell," inspired by the then national passion for cycling, became a hit in London before it struck New York. "The Sidewalks of New York" was first sung by Lottie Gilson on the Bowery and soon thereafter was industriously plugged by its composer, Charles B. Lawlor, in vaudeville. "The Band Played On" was the first song ever to be successfully promoted by a newspaper, the *New York World*.

There were also many dialect songs of German or Irish interest. One of the best of these was the waltz, "Sweet Rosie O'Grady," in 1896, with words and music reputedly by Maude Nugent, a singer who appeared regularly in a saloon on Eighth Avenue.

Since Maude Nugent never again wrote a good song and since her husband, Billy Jerome, was a professional song writer, the long-held suspicion that the song was actually his refuses to die.

Also very popular were nonsense songs in the style of "Ziggy, Ze, Zum, Zum," in 1898, with words by Karl Kennett and music by Lyn Udall, and the still familiar "Ta-ra-ra-boom-der-é," of unknown authorship. The latter is believed to have come out of Babe Connors' dive in St. Louis. In 1891, Willis Woodward & Co. issued it with new gibberish verses by Henry J. Sayers. Lottie Collins scored a sensation with it in vaudeville, and since that time this song has served as one of those identifying and characterizing the gay '90's.

Some of the current "rowdy" songs demanded an athletic presentation by their performers. "Drill Ye Tarriers, Drill," in 1888, was probably the work of Thomas F. Casey, one-time driller turned vaudevillian. It first became popular in *A Brass Monkey*, a musical extravaganza by Charles Hoyt. Of a similar nature was "Down Went McGinty," by Joseph Flynn, in 1889, about an accident-prone Irishman. Flynn himself introduced it in a Brooklyn theater before it made the rounds of vaudeville. A third popular rowdy song concerned a boxer named McCloskey, "Throw Him Down, McCloskey," by J. W. Kelly, in 1890. This was successfully introduced in vaudeville in a vigorous presentation by Maggie Cline.

Perhaps the most successful of all song styles in Union Square, other than the sentimental ballad, was the "coon song." Negro dialect songs had been popular since the first days of the minstrel show, but in the 1880's, in Union Square, there emerged a new kind of Negro dialect song, vitalized and energized by syncopation. In all probability the designation of "coon song" came from the first successful song in this new genre, "New Coon in Town," by Paul Allen, originally presented by the composer in vaudeville in 1883. Coon songs flourished in Union Square for the next two decades. Ernest Hogan, a Negro, wrote and popularized "All Coons Look Alike to Me," in 1896. Later in his life Hogan deeply regretted writing this hit, since the label "coon song" was by then being deeply resented by his race.

Probably the most famous of all coon songs was "My Gal Is a High Born Lady," by Barney Fagan. Fagan was a vaudeville buck-and-wing performer and had received his stage apprentice-

ship in the minstrel show. He himself disclosed that his syncopated tune came to him while he was bicycling along Lake
Michigan in Chicago, suggested by the sound produced by a
broken pedal on a wheel. Witmark bought the song for $100
and realized a fortune from it after publishing it in 1896 in an
effective arrangement by Gustav Luders.

If the coon song has any significance in American popular
music it is because it was the first to contain elements of ragtime.
Ragtime would soon inundate Union Square and Tin Pan Alley.
Ragtime, however, was not born there but further south—in New
Orleans, home of jazz.

(The word "jazz" is believed to have been coined in Chicago in 1914, long after the music it named had sprung into being.) It is not clear just from where this word came. Some say it is a corruption of a bawdy Elizabethan term, "jass." Others maintain that it is a bastardization of the name Charles contracted to "Chas" or "Jas"—Charles having probably been some popular Negro musician. Still others insist it comes from "jasbo," a word bandied about for a long time in minstrel shows.

In any event, in 1915, an ensemble named the Original Dixieland Band performed at the Boosters Club in Chicago. The audience was particularly receptive one evening and kept demanding encores by calling out for "more jass." Soon after this episode, the Original Dixieland Band added the word "jass" to its name, and many similar groups in Chicago followed suit. *Variety* recognized this trend on October 27, 1916, by stating: "Chicago has added another innovation to its list of discoveries in the so-called 'jazz bands.' The Jazz Band is composed of three or more instruments and seldom plays regular music. The College Inn and practically all the other high-class places of entertainment have a Jazz Band featured, while the low cost makes it possible for all the smaller places to carry their jazz orchestras." "Jazz," both the word and the music, appeared on a record label for the first time in March, 1917, when Victor released the "Livery Stable Blues" and "Tiger Rag" in a recording by the Original Dixieland Jazz Band.

(The origin of the word "jazz" may be obscure. Not so that of the music itself, which sprang from the songs and dances, the religious shouts, and the sorrow and work songs of the Negro people.) This Negro music, in turn, had been derived from that of West Africa—from complex and varied African rhythms, strong accents, and marked syncopations. Even the tonality of the blues the "break," and the "call and response" technique—all basic to jazz—find their source in West African music.

The American Negro combined some of these primitive elements of West African music with the more sophisticated European approaches to music that he encountered in the New World. A new form of song was evolved, into which the Negro brought his profound religious feeling, immense sorrow, and extraordinary vitality. A musical people, Negroes made up songs for work and play, for religious worship, as a solace to pain, and as an escape from oppression.

The innovations introduced by the Negro into his songs were often the result of accident rather than design. When he sang at work, he not only created lyrics describing the conditions under which he was laboring, but as a result of his special aptitude for improvisation, he also gradually developed new melodies for these lyrics. The melodies that his fancy thus spontaneously embroidered were influenced by the conditions under which they were created. With no musical instrument at hand to set an exact pitch, the Negro indulged in a curious type of deviating intonation, in which he allowed his voice to ascend and descend to tones foreign to the basic scale and in intervals sometimes smaller than the traditionally accepted quarter-tone interval. He also interpolated grunts and groans in his melody—in rhythm with his taxing physical labors in the fields, mines, and tunnels.

When the Negro graduated from singing to playing a wind instrument, he acquired his performing proficiency entirely through a haphazard method of trial and error. He arrived at altogether unorthodox techniques, sounds, and timbres, not found in any instruction book or printed music. Since he could not read a note of music, he had to indulge his natural bent for improvisation further by weaving fanciful figurations and tunes around familiar melodies, guided only by instinct and emotion. In his playing he tried to imitate the harsh, guttural quality of singing toward which he was so partial. In doing this, he managed to produce a kind of throaty tone since come to be identified as "dirty" and found in no other kind of performance.

If any single place can be said to have been the birthplace of jazz it is New Orleans. There is good reason why jazz, in its infancy, should have flourished there. In the closing decades of the nineteenth century, New Orleans was a free and easy city, since 1857 the only one in America to have legalized prostitution. Brothels flourished and with them gambling houses, saloons, barrel houses, and all kinds of honky-tonks, most of them concentrated in a district known as Storyville, where pleasure was king and vice queen. New Orleans was a gay town tolerant of illicit love affairs between white gentlemen and quadroons, the latter, fair-skinned daughters of mulattos. It was a place where on Saturday night the Negroes danced the primitive bamboula in Place Congo, a colorful city where a varied population contributed to it the warm, the inflammable spirit of the Spanish and the Creole, the voodoo superstition and restless temperament of the Negro, and the tolerance of the Latin.

Since New Orleans was tolerant of Negroes, it became the city to which many were drawn after their emancipation. The city also happened to be a center for the manufacture of wind instruments, which were both cheap and plentiful. Negroes soon acquired some and discovered them to be an inexhaustible medium for making music. Once they learned to play these instruments, New Orleans Negroes began forming bands that performed in the streets, at carnivals, parties, excursions, bargain sales, and prize fights, on river boats, and for funeral processions. But most of all they played during the night in the pleasure domes of Storyville, at the 101 Ranch, at the Tuxedo Hall, or at Pete Lala's.

The kind of music that the Negro could coax from his musical instrument was what habitués of these vice palaces could respond to instinctively. It was music of kinesthetic appeal—loud and barbaric, full of strange impulses and emotional thrusts. It was music without discipline or inhibition. It was music that made the pulse beat fast, the feet become restless, and the blood turn hot. It was a new kind of music. It was jazz.

Jazz, evolved in New Orleans, was not a style of composition but a style of performance. It was not written; it was played. Jazz was, moreover, not only the strange, feverish sounds and sonorities produced on musical instruments. It was also the spontaneous and often elaborate improvisations of melodies old and new. Sometimes these improvisations appeared in solo passages, as one musician in the band took the spotlight and allowed his musical fancy to wander. Sometimes these improvisations were performed by the entire ensemble in a complex contrapuntal network of rhythm and melody; each man in the ensemble was permitted to pursue his own direction, but without losing contact with the basic rhythmic and melodic structure.

In these jazz improvisations, two stylistic elements predominated—ragtime and the blues. The word "ragtime" itself is believed to have come from "ragging," a term applied to Negro clog-dancing. The music consisted of pronounced syncopation in the treble against a rigid and even rhythm in the bass. Syncopation—that is, making a weak beat strong or the expected strong beat weak—had appeared often in the popular songs and dance music of the minstrel show, in cakewalk music, and in such familiar numbers as "Zip Coon" and "Old Dan Tucker." But when syncopation was set against a steady bass rhythm, as happened in New Orleans, ragtime came into existence.

The second important element of jazz improvisations in New Orleans, the blues, was an outgrowth of the sorrow songs of Negro folk music. Soon after the end of the Civil War, Negro performers began improvising a new type of sorrow song on street corners and in saloons, in which they lamented their lot in an unfriendly world. Slowly a form of composition came into being. The lyric was made up of three-line stanzas, usually in iambic pentameter, and the second stanza repeated the first. The melody was made up of three four-bar phrases. Other distinguishing features slowly began to intrude into these songs, henceforth known as "the blues"—flatting of the third and seventh notes of the diatonic scale, henceforth known as "blue notes"; dissonant harmonies in the accompaniment when blue notes were absent; breaks in the melody to allow at first the interjection of such exclamations as "Oh Lawdy" or "Oh Baby," and later in New Orleans to provide jazz musicians with an opportunity for spontaneous improvisation. As vocal music, the blues found its interpreters in such artists as Ma Rainey and Bessie Smith. As instrumental music, its high priests were the jazz players of New Orleans.

•

The first of the outstanding jazz performers was Buddy Bolden, a cornettist. He was by profession a barber and in his spare time edited a scandal sheet, but essentially he was a musician who sent Storyville rocking with his ragtime and his blues. Bolden formed his own band in the middle of the 1890's and from the

first was an idol of Storyville. His was one of the most powerful
cornets in New Orleans and his pure, clear, ringing tones could
be heard for miles around. "He'd turn his big trumpet toward
the city and blow his blues," recalled the New Orleans jazz
pianist, "Jelly Roll" Morton, "calling his children home, as he
used to say. The whole town would know Buddy Bolden was at
the Park, ten or twelve miles from the center of town. He was the
blowingest man ever lived since Gabriel." His gift at the cornet
was exceeded only by his gift for improvisation, particularly in
such rags as "The Idaho Rag," "Make Me a Pallet on the Floor,"
"Careless Love," and "Maple Leaf Rag." Buddy was called "the
King"—no one ever bested him in a jazz session—until he lost his
mind, one day in 1907, while performing in a street parade. Until
his death in 1931 he lived in an asylum.

Almost as legendary in the early history of jazz was the
trumpeter Joe "King" Oliver. Though strongly influenced by
Bolden, whom he studied and imitated, Oliver was a jazz stylist
in his own right. In the end the designation of "king," which
Bolden had so long assumed, became Oliver's, particularly after
a memorable night in Storyville. On that occasion, Oliver walked
up and down Iberville Street playing on his trumpet the most
varied and fanciful improvisations and defiantly pointing the
mouth of his trumpet towards cabarets and honky-tonks in which
such favored musicians as Freddie Keppard and Emanuel Perez
held sway. They say that on that night, lovers of jazz began
drifting out of all the honky-tonks and night spots to follow Joe
Oliver on his march through Storyville into the Aberdeen
Cabaret, where he was then a performer, to listen to him for
several more hours.

Oliver played with various groups, in which could be found
some of New Orleans' best loved jazz men. At one time, at
Pete Lala's, he played with the Olympia Band, which included
Freddie Keppard at the trumpet and Alphonse Picou at the
clarinet. On another occasion at the same place, he played with
"Kid" Ory's group, among whom were Ory himself (trombone),
"Miff" Mole (trombone), and, later, the young Louis Armstrong
(trumpet). At the 101 Ranch, Joe Oliver's jazz group included
Sidney Bechet (clarinet and soprano saxophone) and Emanuel
Perez (cornet). Among other popular jazz band combinations in
New Orleans at the time were the Tuxedo Band (Johnny Dodds

at the clarinet and "Zutty" Singleton at the drums), the Eagle
Band (Johnny Dodds, Freddie Keppard, and Sidney Bechet, with
"Bunk" Johnson and "Papa Mutt" Carey at the trumpets), and
the Original Creole Band organized by Keppard with several
of the members of the Olympia Band.

Rivalry was keen not merely among leading jazz figures but
also among the bands. Bands performing in the streets often
suddenly became involved in a free-for-all competition that
would sometimes last for hours. "They used to have 'cutting
contests' every time you'd get on the streets," wrote "Kid"
Ory. "Freddie Keppard's band whipped us good because he was
a stronger trumpet player than we had at first. Then we started
whipping everybody." "Bunk" Johnson has written: "Bands in
those days fighting all the time. During the Mardi Gras and
parades, bands got taken around in wagons, and they'd back
them, tail gate to tail gate, and play each other down." "Kid"
Ory also recalls the way "when the other band finished, they'd
tie the wagons together. The crowd tied them to keep them
from running away from us."

Soon after 1910, jazz began traveling north. In 1911, Freddie
Keppard toured the vaudeville circuit with the Creole Band,
and in 1914 Tom Brown formed the Brown Band from Dixieland, a white ensemble performing first in vaudeville and later
at the Lambs' Café in Chicago. Other white and Negro jazz
bands sprouted in various Chicago night spots—the Original
Dixieland (a white group), for example, and a Negro five-man
ensemble formed by Emanuel Perez for the De Luxe Café.

As a capital of jazz, New Orleans went into rapid decline after
1917, the year in which Storyville was closed down by government order. For several years thereafter, jazz flourished in
Chicago. Freddie Keppard and Sidney Bechet were heard at
the De Luxe Café, "King" Oliver at the Dreamland Café and
Royal Gardens. The Original Creole Band played at the Royal
Gardens and the New Orleans Rhythm Kings at Friars' Inn. These
and many other performers and jazz groups kept the New Orleans
tradition alive—not merely at formal performances in cafés and
nights spots, but also informally at The Three Deuces where
they would meet when the night's work was done to engage in
cutting contests, soon to be known as "jam sessions."

While New Orleans musicians dominated the jazz scene in Chicago, other and younger men rose to prominence in that city to carry on the Dixieland tradition and to create one of their own. The most significant was Louis Armstrong. Armstrong was born in New Orleans, where he received his apprenticeship, but it was Chicago where he achieved maturity as an artist and where he became famous. Armstrong's strongest influence was Joe "King" Oliver, whose jazz style and approaches he imitated unashamedly. On Oliver's recommendation, Armstrong replaced Oliver as trumpet with the "Kid" Ory band in New Orleans when Oliver set off for Chicago. Then, in 1922, Oliver asked Armstrong to join him in Chicago. Together they made incomparable music, as each inspired in the other unparalleled flights of musical fancy. They went through a "break" with stunning virtuosity and a beautiful sense of coordination. They synchronized as no two jazz trumpets had heretofore done, understanding each other's most subtle aims with a seemingly infallible instinct.

After marrying the jazz pianist, Lil Hardin, in 1924, Armstrong left the Oliver ensemble to set out for himself. He organized his own jazz group, the Hot Five, for the Dreamland Café. There and in other Chicago night spots—with the Hot Five, the Hot Seven, and the Quintet—he reached a pinnacle of fame equaled by few and surpassed by none. His trumpet virtuosity was electrifying—the dazzling succession of high C's, the breathtaking glissandos, the piercing sonorities. His art at improvisation was so formidable that even as serious a music critic as Virgil Thomson was led to remark that it combined "the highest reaches of instrumental virtuosity with the most tensely disciplined melodic structure and the most spontaneous emotional expression, all of which in one man you must admit is pretty rare." In addition, he was a born showman, with a flamboyant style all his own.

From Chicago, Armstrong went on to conquer the world in every possible medium—an undisputed king of jazz music. But he was not the only fabulous musician produced by Chicago. Another was the cornettist, "Bix" Beiderbecke. "Bix" was a contrast to Armstrong, restrained and disciplined and subdued where Armstrong was uninhibited and gaudy. "Bix" was the classicist— in the purity and sweetness of his cornet tone, the artistry of his phrasing, and in his indefatigable experimentation with beautiful sound. He first began attracting attention in 1922 in Chicago's smaller hot spots. One year later he organized The Wolverines, one of the most significant jazz ensembles arising in Chicago, and with this group he helped make jazz history. He later moved on to New York, where excessive drinking and dissipation brought him to a premature and unhappy end in 1931. After his death his career inspired Dorothy Baker's novel, *Young Man With a Horn,* from which a fine motion picture was made in 1950 starring Kirk Douglas as "Bix."

Among the other prominent jazz groups to come to the fore in Chicago in the 1920's were the Blue Friars, with Jimmy McPartland, trumpet, Frank Teschemacher, clarinet, and Bud Freeman, tenor sax; the Chicago Rhythm Kings, led by Teschemacher; and the Chicagoans, formed by guitarist Eddie Condon. Other important new jazz performers in Chicago were Coleman Hawkins (tenor sax), "Muggsy" Spanier (cornet), Earl Hines (piano), "Fats" Waller (piano), Jess Stacy (piano), Gene Krupa (drums), and Mezz Mezzrow (clarinet and saxes).

An important style of jazz performance and music born in Chicago's South Side in the 1920's was "boogie-woogie." The name was derived from the phrase "pitchin' boogie," often heard in Chicago to describe monthly parties to help raise money for the rent. The music itself consisted of piano improvisations on the blues that were often presented at these parties. A brief rhythmic figure, usually with eight beats to the bar repeated without variation, furnished the background for a blues melody. One of the first leading exponents of this style of piano jazz was "Pinetop" (Clarence) Smith, composer of among other pieces, "Pinetop's Boogie-Woogie." Others who distinguished themselves in this art were Jimmy Yancey, composer of "Yancey Stomp" and "State Street Special," and Meade Lux Lewis, composer of "Honky Tonk Train Blues," "Bear Cat Crawl," and "Whistlin' Blues."

Swing was a second significant new jazz style to appear in Chicago, its high priest being Benny Goodman. Goodman was a native Chicagoan and received his musical training in Chicago's night spots, where he had the opportunity to study and assimilate the styles of Joe "King" Oliver, Louis Armstrong, and Freddie Keppard. Before long he was playing the clarinet in jam sessions with Bud Freeman, Teschemacher, and Jimmy McPartland. When he was sixteen, Goodman became a member of Ben Pollack's jazz ensemble, made up entirely of white performers, and it was with this group that he made his first recording in 1926. After leaving Pollack, Goodman played in or near Chicago with various groups. In 1934 he formed a Dixieland band of his own, with which he made some excellent records for Columbia, appeared over the radio, and toured the country, popularizing such numbers as "King Porter Stomp" and "Sugar Foot Stomp." On November 6, 1935, Benny Goodman and his band began a sensational engagement at the Congress Hotel in Chicago. It was on this occasion that his own brand of Dixieland jazz—baptized "swing" in advertisements and in a report in *Time* Magazine— became famous. In swing, group-notated improvisation displaced spontaneity, the harmony was often enriched and dramatized by dissonance, and the melody retained a clear and precise beat. Goodman popularized swing music with various small groups that he organized expressly for jazz performances—the Benny Goodman Trio, one of the first interracial jazz ensembles ever formed, with Teddy Wilson at the piano and Gene Krupa at the drums; then the Quartet, in which Lionel Hampton (vibraharp and piano) joined the other three; and, after that, the Sextet, with Charlie Christian, guitar, and Artie Bernstein, bass.

Swing invaded New York on May 24, 1936, at a concert at the Imperial Theater in which the Clambake Seven, led by Tommy Dorsey, and the Artie Shaw String Ensemble were among the performers. In 1937, Benny Goodman came to New York, first with a sensational engagement at the Paramount Theatre and then with a concert in Carnegie Hall. He himself was lionized, and his music achieved such a vogue that on May 29, 1938, a Carnival of Swing was held at Randall's Island in the East River, New York, at which twenty-six bands performed for seven hours before an audience of over 25,000.

Boogie-woogie also came to prominence in New York, beginning with a Carnegie Hall concert on December 23, 1938, featuring Meade Lux Lewis among others.

But long before swing and boogie-woogie caught on in New York, jazz in the true Dixieland and Chicago styles had become a fixture in the musical life of the metropolis. In 1915, the Louisiana Five, led by Alcide Nunez, rocked Bustanoby's Restaurant, and on January 16, 1917, the Original Dixieland Band, headed by Nick La Rocca (cornet), started a successful engagement at Reisenweber's Restaurant. In 1920, New York had a major jazz ensemble of its own in the Fletcher Henderson Orchestra. Fletcher placed greater emphasis on formal orchestrations than on improvisations and ad-lib solos, but in its colors, nuances, and techniques his music was deeply imbued with the traditions of Dixieland jazz. Many outstanding jazz artists played with the Fletcher Henderson orchestra until it was disbanded in 1924, including Coleman Hawkins, Louis Armstrong, Buster Bailey (clarinet), and Don Redman (saxophone).

Another important jazz ensemble that arose in New York and was even truer to the basic style of New Orleans and Chicago than Henderson's orchestra was the group organized and led by Duke Ellington for the Kentucky Club in the early 1920's. Ellington was born in Washington, D.C., in 1899. There he played in various jazz bands, organized his own ensemble, and wrote his first popular number, "The Soda Fountain Rag." After coming to New York in 1923, he played with several bands, including the Wilbur Sweatman Jazz Band in Harlem. He then founded a five-piece group of his own called "The Washingtonians" and played in a night spot originally known as the Hollywood but soon renamed the Kentucky Club. With jazz virtuosos such as Joe "Tricky Sam" Nanton at the trombone, "Bubber" Miley at the trumpet, and Rudy Jackson at the clarinet, this combination started to experiment with a new kind of jazz that would soon become identified with the name of Ellington. It was a kind of swing music that Ellington himself described as "stark and wild and tense. . . . We tried new effects. . . . We put the Negro feeling and spirit in our music." Expanded into an orchestra of fourteen members, Ellington's ensemble began making records and in 1927 launched a historic five-year engagement at the Cotton Club in Harlem. From this time on, the name of Duke Ellington, as Leonard Feather has written, "became internationally synonymous with the highest qualities of both orchestral and improvised jazz." Ellington's enormous reputation in popular music, however, rests on his achievements not only as a performer and orchestra leader but also as a prolific composer of songs and piano pieces, the most famous being "Sophisticated Lady," "Solitude," "Mood Indigo," and "East St. Louis Toodle-oo," the last of which he adopted as his radio theme music.

Many other important swing groups came into prominence in New York in the 1930's. Among them were those founded and directed by such apostles of swing as Artie Shaw, Tommy Dorsey, Woody Herman, Cab Calloway, Count Basie, and Glenn Miller.

Indicative of the importance jazz men were beginning to assume in New York was the fact that in the middle 1920's most of the exponents of true jazz left Chicago for New York—Louis Armstrong, "Bix" Beiderbecke, Sidney Bechet, "Jelly Roll" Morton, Jimmy McPartland, Gene Krupa, Eddie Condon, and Frank Teschemacher. Their activity helped make New York the third capital of jazz music as the successor to New Orleans and Chicago.

In the wake of the spread of jazz came argument and controversy. John Roach Straton, the eminent Baptist clergyman, denounced jazz from his pulpit as "savage" and "utter degradation," and the distinguished musical educator, scholar, and composer, Daniel Gregory Mason, called it "sterile cleverness—an epilepsy simulating muscular action." In 1921, a city ordinance in Zion City, Illinois, banned jazz "along with smoking and other sinful practices."

On the other hand there was a heated defense of jazz, sometimes from completely unexpected quarters. The famous violinist, Fritz Kreisler, and the conductor of the Philadelphia Orchestra, Leopold Stokowski, both spoke for its musical vitality. H. L. Mencken heaped editorial praise on it in *The American Mercury*, and another eminent journalist, Hiram K. Motherwell, considered it "the perfect expression of the American city. . . . Its resourcefulness continually surprises me."

More and more important institutions of learning, musical organizations, and scholars began to give serious consideration to jazz. In the 1920's, Harvard University held a jazz symposium, conducted by one of its renowned professors of music, Edward Burlingame Hill; the League of Composers in New York, dedicated to serious activity in modern music, held a jazz conference; and the New School for Social Research in New York instituted a course on jazz. In 1925, Alfred Frankenstein published one of the earliest critical evaluations of jazz in *Syncopating Saxophones*, the vanguard of many other valuable analytical and historical volumes on jazz to be issued in the United States and Europe in the succeeding years, among them, studies by Rudi Blesh, André Coeuroy, Ralph de Toledano, Robert Goffin, Wilder Hobson, Hugues Panassié, and Marshall Stearns.

Through the establishment of annual jazz festivals from as far east as Newport, Rhode Island, to as far west as Monterey, California, through the publication of scholarly journals like *The Jazz Review* and *Jazz,* through valuable historical anthologies of phonograph records, through the syndication of critical jazz columns in newspapers, and through the establishment of courses on jazz in leading American colleges and universities, through all these the respectability of jazz has been repeatedly confirmed.

9—Ragtime and the Blues
in Tin Pan Alley

The strongest impact of real jazz on commercial music took place through the infiltration of such styles as ragtime and the blues into the Tin Pan Alley song.

In New Orleans, ragtime had been improvised, and it was some time before ragtime music was put down on paper. This happened in Tin Pan Alley in 1897 with "At a Georgia Camp Meeting," by Kerry Mills, born Frederick Allen Mills (1869-1948). For many years Mills had been a serious student of the violin, and for one year he served on the music faculty of Princeton University. His conversion from serious to popular music became official with his cakewalk, "Rastus on Parade," in 1895, in which he first disclosed his strong bent for syncopation and with which in 1896 he launched his own Tin Pan Alley publishing firm of F. A. Mills. A year later he wrote and issued "At a Georgia Camp Meeting," described on the sheet music as a "two-step march." (Mills added lyrics to it in 1899.) In 1904, Mills achieved another major hit with "Meet Me in St. Louis," with lyrics by Andrew B. Sterling; this song enjoyed a highly successful revival in 1944 in the motion picture of the same name starring Judy Garland. But Mills made his major contribution to popular music not half so much by writing any hit song as by introducing ragtime into Tin Pan Alley.

As a commercial product, ragtime received another strong boost with Scott Joplin's "Maple Leaf Rag," published as a piano solo by a Missouri firm in 1899. Joplin (1868-1917) was a Negro pianist whose ragtime performances in various St. Louis night spots made him a significant pioneer in that style. In the early 1900's he came to be known as the "king of ragtime." He was improvising his rags at the Maple Leaf Club in Sedalia,

70

Missouri, when he attracted the interest of John Stark, a publisher. Stark issued Joplin's "Original Rag" in 1899 and followed
it in the same year with the publication of what has since
become a jazz classic, "Maple Leaf Rag." After that Joplin wrote
and had published many more excellent piano rags including
"Sunflower Rag," "Sugar Cane Rag," and "Magnetic Rag." He
also issued an instruction volume entitled *The School of Ragtime,*
and wrote music for a stage production, *A Guest of Honor,* which
he called a "ragtime opera."

The most important composer of piano rags after Joplin was
Ben Harney (1872?-1938), credited with being the man who
made this kind of music popular in New York. Harney received
his apprenticeship as ragtime pianist in vaudeville theaters in
the Midwest and West in the middle 1890's, where one of his
attractions was ragging the scale. In 1895 he joined a minstrel-
show act, doing a specialty "stick dance" and singing his own
songs. One of these was a dynamic syncopated number entitled
"Mister Johnson, Turn Me Loose," sung by May Irwin in the
stage musical, *Courted into Court.* In 1897, Witmark published
Ben Harney's *Rag-Time Instructor,* the first such instruction book,
preceding Scott Joplin's by several years. Harney here empha-
sized that ragtime was not a specific kind of music but a specific
way of playing music. To prove his point he frequently played
semi-classics in ragtime style—"Annie Laurie," Mendelssohn's
"Spring Song," Rubinstein's "Melody in F," and the "Intermezzo"
from Mascagni's *Cavalleria Rusticana.* He was thus probably the
first to indulge in a practice that later became habitual for Tin
Pan Alley, that of giving a popular musical dress to classical
melodies.

Harney scored his greatest success at Tony Pastor's Music Hall.
In his act, Harney employed a colored performer, Strap Hill,
who would sit in the audience and then mount the stage and
seemingly improvise a ragtime tune based on one previously
played by Harney.

Harney helped establish the position of ragtime in Tin Pan
Alley. So popular did ragtime become by the end of the nineteenth century that it was attacked in the editorial columns of
the *Musical Courier* in 1899. "A wave of vulgar, filthy and sug-

gestive music has inundated the land. . . . Nothing but ragtime prevails." Two years later, the American Federation of Musicians passed a resolution to do everything in its power to "suppress and discourage the playing and publishing of such musical trash." But ragtime also found a stout defender in Rupert Hughes, who wrote in the *Musical Record* on April 1, 1899: "Ragtime will find its way gradually into the works of some great genius and will thereafter be canonized." In 1901, the famous prima donna, Emma Nevada, told an interviewer for the *Boston Herald* that she was enthusiastic about ragtime and hoped that nobody would suppress it.

Piano rags continued to flourish through the 1910's. One of the most significant composers of ragtime during that period was Felix Arndt (1889-1918), whose best known composition is "Nola," published in 1916. It later became famous as Vincent Lopez' signature, and in 1958 it acquired for the first time a lyric and thus a new lease on popularity. Among other ragtime pieces by Arndt were "Soup to Nuts" and "Marionette." It was through Arndt's influence that the young and still unknown George Gershwin wrote a piano rag number with Will Donaldson in 1916, "Rialto Ripples," published a year later by Remick; it was first recorded in 1959 in a Decca album entitled *The Gershwin Years.*

Other distinguished piano rags of the period include "Twelfth Street Rag" by Euday L. Bowman, written in 1914 but published in 1916, and Domenico Savino's "Indianola," published in 1917. But the most significant composer of piano rags after Arndt was Zez Confrey (1895-   ), born Edward E. Confrey. Confrey was a student at the Chicago Musical College and then played the drums in various theater and jazz orchestras. His aim of translating the rhythm of the drums into piano music first stimulated him to write music, and he produced such popular piano rags as "Kitten on the Keys," "Stumbling," and "Dizzy Fingers."

While essentially a piano style, ragtime soon made its presence felt in popular song. Syncopation, after all, had existed for a long time in the songs of the minstrel show and in the coon songs of the 1880's and 1890's. Harney wrote an outstanding ragtime song in 1896 with "Mister Johnson, Turn Me Loose" and followed this effort immediately with other ragtime songs including "You've Been a Good Old Wagon, But You've Done Broke

Down," "I Love My Little Honey," and "The Cakewalk in the Sky." "Hello Ma Baby," by Joe Howard was a leading ragtime song of 1899 and is not yet forgotten.

A notable career in ragtime music began in 1911 with "When Ragtime Rosy Ragged the Rosary," by Lewis F. Muir. Little is known of Muir's early life (even the place and date of his birth are unknown) except that in the early 1900's he was popular in St. Louis as a ragtime pianist. His first published song hit was "Play That Barber Shop Chord" in 1910, a success after its introduction into the *Ziegfeld Follies* of that year by Bert Williams. This was succeeded by one of the most highly regarded ragtime songs of that period, "Waiting for the Robert E. Lee," with lyrics by L. Wolfe Gilbert. Published in 1912, this song was soon heard on the stage throughout the length and breadth of the country, in renditions by such popular performers as Al Jolson and Belle Baker. Muir also wrote "Ragtime Cowboy Joe," "Hitchy-Koo," and "Mississippi River Steamboat," among other ragtime favorites.

Among the ragtime hit tunes of the early 1910's one song stands out prominently. More than any other it helped make ragtime the vogue that it became at the time. The song was "Alexander's Ragtime Band," by Irving Berlin, published in 1911. Berlin's career, both preceding and following the writing of his ragtime classic must be reserved for a later chapter. Here it is merely necessary to outline the details surrounding "Alexander's Ragtime Band," the work with which Berlin achieved the first of his many song triumphs. He wrote it in 1910 as a piano rag without lyrics. When, a year later, he became a member of the Friars Club in New York and was asked to appear in the *Friars Frolics,* he decided to use his rag melody in his act, but to dress it up with a set of his own lyrics. On that occasion, the song attracted little interest. A few months later, however, Emma Carus sang it in a Chicago vaudeville theater with dynamic results. "If we were John D. Rockefeller or the Bank of England," wrote one Chicago newspaperman, "we should engage the Coliseum and get together a sextet including Caruso. . . . After the sextet sang it ["Alexander's Ragtime Band"] about ten times we should, as a finale, have Sousa's Band march about the building tearing the melody to pieces in all kinds of variations."

The song now went on to conquer. Within a few months it sold over a million copies of sheet music. It was the song heard most frequently in theaters in 1911 and 1912. Since social dancing had just become a national craze mainly through the influence of ragtime, the song was also the one most often danced to. With ragtime now one of Tin Pan Alley's most valuable commodities, Berlin, now one of its foremost exponents, continued writing songs in that style—"Ragtime Violin," "Everybody's Doin' It," and "That Mysterious Rag," in 1911, always to his own lyrics and, after that, "At the Devil's Ball" and "International Rag." The last of these was written in 1913 for his appearance at the Hippodrome Theatre in London, where he was billed as "The Ragtime King." On that occasion, after his formal act was over, he asked his audience to name any other of his ragtime songs they would like to hear him sing, and the audience began shouting the titles of songs by many other composers. "They thought," Berlin remarked at the time, "I wrote every ragtime song they'd ever heard." In 1914, Charles Dillingham asked Berlin to write the music for a Broadway ragtime revue, *Watch Your Step*, starring Irene and Vernon Castle, for which Berlin wrote "The Syncopated Walk."

But Berlin was by no means the only one writing significant ragtime numbers. Louis A. Hirsch's "The Gaby Glide"—written for Gaby Deslys, who introduced it in *Vera Violetta*—and Theodore F. Morse's "Another Rag" were hits in 1911. In 1912, "That Daffydill Rag" by Bill and Frank Mueller and Morse's "When Joe Plays a Ragtime on His Banjo" were popular. In 1913 came Chris Smith's "Ballin' the Jack," and in 1917, Shelton Brooks' ragtime gem, "The Darktown Strutters' Ball." (Brooks was also the composer of the notable ballad, "Some of These Days," with which Sophie Tucker has been identified for almost half a century.) Among the leading ragtime songs in 1919 was "Dardanella," with music by Felix Bernard and Johnny S. Black.

W. C. Handy (1873-1958) was the man responsible for carrying the blues into Tin Pan Alley, for it was he who wrote the first blues song to be published. The son of a minister, Handy was born in Florence, Alabama, where he learned to play the trumpet on a one-dollar instrument sold him by a visiting circus musician. Handy soon ran away from home, because his father objected to his musical activities, and joined a traveling minstrel-show company. Later on he came to St. Louis, where for seven years he served first as a cornettist and then as a bandleader for a minstrel-show troupe. After that he formed his own band with which he performed jazz throughout Mississippi.

Handy wrote his first blues song in 1909 for a mayoralty campaign in Memphis, Tennessee. He was hired to advance the campaign of the since then notorious Boss Crump, then running on a reform ticket. In order to gain the Negro vote for his candidate, Handy wrote a song about Crump in the musical idiom that Negroes knew and appreciated. That song, "Mr. Crump," proved a powerful influence in carrying its namesake into office. In 1912, this piece was published in Memphis as a piano composition and renamed "The Memphis Blues." One year later a New York publisher bought all the rights for $50.00 and reissued it with lyrics by George A. Norton. It proved a tremendous commercial success— the first published composition to use the term "blues" and the work that established the blues as a profitable commodity for exploitation by Tin Pan Alley.

In order to capitalize on the success of his first blues song, Handy decided to write another one in the same style with the hope it might equal the popularity of its predecessor. As he worked in his room in Beale Street, as he later revealed, "a flood of memories filled my mind. First there was a picture I had of myself, broke, unshaven, wanting even a decent meal, and standing before the lighted saloon in St. Louis without a shirt under my frayed coat. There was also from that same period a curious and dramatic little fragment that till now seemed to have little or no importance. While occupied with my own miseries during the sojourn, I had seen a woman whose pain seemed even greater. She had tried to take the edge off her grief by heavy drinking, and it hadn't worked. Stumbling along the poorly lighted street, she muttered as she walked, 'My man's got a heart like a rock cast in the sea.' . . . By the time I had finished all this heavy thinking and remembering, I figured it was time to get something down on paper, so I wrote 'I hate to see de evenin' sun go down.' If you ever had to sleep on the cobbles down by the river in St. Louis you'll understand the complaint."

Handy called his new song the "St. Louis Blues." When every publisher to whom it was submitted turned it down, he decided to issue it himself, formed a company with Harry Pace, and published the song in Memphis in 1914. The sale at first was slow, nor did it begin to pick up until Handy had transferred his publishing establishment to New York. Then Sophie Tucker sang it in vaudeville, and Victor issued a successful recording. Other record companies followed suit, and so did piano roll manufacturers. The "St. Louis Blues" finally caught on; what followed was a veritable conflagration. It was the inspiration for a motion picture and lent its name to several other movies. It was featured in a Broadway revue. Forty years after its publication the sheet music and recordings were selling so well that Handy was still earning a yearly royalty of $25,000.

Handy's most successful blues songs after the "St. Louis Blues" were "Beale Street Blues," "John Henry Blues," "Joe Turner Blues," and the "Harlem Blues," but it was the "St. Louis Blues" that made him an immortal in American popular music. It was because of that classic that a public park in Memphis was named after him and that the New York World's Fair in 1938 called him one of America's foremost contributors to world culture. It was no accident that in 1958 the motion-picture biography of Handy was called *The St. Louis Blues.*

However, not all successful published blues were by Handy. He set the example, but others followed his lead with profit, for example, Fred Meinken in the "Wabash Blues" and Gus Mueller, Buster Johnson, and Henry Busse in "The Wang, Wang Blues."

10—A New Century—
A New Era for Popular Music

The twentieth century brought the dawn of a new day for the United States. Everywhere there were expansion and vital growth—in foreign affairs, industry, invention, construction, education, and the arts. Americans became conscious of their own country as never before. Beginning in the 1890's, novelists like Jack London, Edith Wharton, and Frank Norris explored American backgrounds and experiences. The Metropolitan Opera produced an American opera for the first time in 1910, Frederick Converse's *The Pipe of Desire*. Native American drama received an impetus and direction with William Vaughan Moody's *The Great Divide* in 1906. Florenz Ziegfeld began glorifying the American girl in 1907, and during the same period George M. Cohan started to drape the American flag around himself in musical comedies based on American backgrounds and filled with American characters.

A new wave of patriotism swept the country and found expression in our popular music and ballads. In 1893, Katherine Lee Bates, professor of English at Wellesley College, wrote the poem, "America, the Beautiful" ("O beautiful for spacious skies"). Her immediate stimulus had been the sight of Pike's Peak but, undoubtedly, the aroused national consciousness of the time, already asserting itself in the closing years of the nineteenth century, had much to do with the writing of this stirring tribute to her native land. The words found their musical mate in a song written in 1888 by Samuel A. Ward, "Materna." Though words and music had been written separately, they were combined into a stirring anthem and published in 1895.

Perhaps nothing in American popular music of this period voiced more eloquently the swelling national ego than the Sousa march. John Philip Sousa (1854-1932) was born in Washington, D.C., where he early received a comprehensive musical training. At fourteen he enlisted in the Marine Corps and played in its band. After leaving the Corps, he served as violinist in various orchestras (including one conducted by Jacques Offenbach during his American tour) and led several theater ensembles. In 1879, Sousa wrote the first of his ten comic operas, *The Smugglers*. One year later he became the leader of the United States Marine Band. He held this post with distinction for twelve years, a period in which he wrote his first famous marches—"Semper Fidelis" in 1888, and, in 1889, "The Thunderer" and "The Washington Post." In 1892 he formed his own band, with which he toured the world for many years, giving over ten thousand concerts. He continued writing marches, earning for himself the sobriquet of "The March King." "The Liberty Bell" came in 1893, "King Cotton" in 1895, "El Capitan" in 1896, "The Stars and Stripes Forever" in 1897, and "Hands Across the Sea" in 1899.

"The Stars and Stripes Forever" is surely the most celebrated march by an American. Sousa conceived it aboard the liner *Teutonic* while returning from a trip to Italy. During that trip the strains of a melody kept haunting him, and, when he put it down on paper after arriving in New York, it became the main theme of his most famous march. In all probability this dramatic music spoke for Sousa's own nostalgia for home and his aroused feelings in returning to his native land. In any event, it is American music to its very bone and marrow, as eloquent a patriotic utterance as has yet been written.

Sousa was also responsible for the popularity of a song identifying a major branch of the Armed Forces the "Field Artillery March" known also as "The Caisson Song." In 1918 he made an effective band arrangement of the melody and presented it at the Hippodrome Theatre in New York during a Liberty Loan drive, when he brought down the house. For many years Sousa was identified as the composer of this march, but later research has disclosed that both the words and the music had been written in 1908 by Edmund L. Gruber, lieutenant with the 5th Artillery in the Philippines.

Of the other songs intimately associated with our Armed Forces, that of the Navy, "Anchors Aweigh," was first published in 1906, with words by A. H. Miles and R. Lovell and music by Charles A. Zimmerman. The "Marines' Hymn," was first issued in 1918 in an uncopyrighted version and a year later was copyrighted by the Corps. The author of its lyrics has never been authoritatively identified, though the Marine Corps copyright edition gives the credit to L. Z. Phillips. The music was borrowed from an aria in a forgotten opéra comique by Offenbach, *Geneviève de Brabant*. The "Army Air Corps Song" was written by Robert Crawford, a teacher at Princeton University, for a song contest sponsored by the Air Corps in 1939; it won first prize. A song now often identified with the Infantry came during World War II, Frank Loesser's "What Do You Do in the Infantry?".

This was a new day not merely for our marches and our patriotic music but also for every other facet of our popular musical expression. Tin Pan Alley was enjoying such unprecedented prosperity that a million-copy sale of sheet music, formerly a phenomenon, became quite frequent. Between 1900 and 1910 almost a hundred songs sold over a million copies each. The decade began with Harry von Tilzer's sentimental ballad, "A Bird in a Gilded Cage," which sold two million copies, and ended with Tell Taylor's "Down by the Old Mill Stream" and with "Let Me Call You Sweetheart" by Beth Slater Whitson and Leo Friedman, which sold four million and eight million copies respectively.

The young century brought to Tin Pan Alley many new composers and publishers. Gus Edwards, Harry von Tilzer, Albert von Tilzer, and Theodore F. Morse were perhaps the most successful of those who filled the dual role of composer and publisher.

Gus Edwards (1879-1945) was born in Germany and came to this country when he was only eight. Both his academic and musical education were haphazard. The former began and ended in New York's elementary public schools and the latter consisted only of solitary experiments at the piano. As a boy, Edwards started earning his living by working in a cigar factory. At the same time he began his musical career in the evenings by singing at lodge meetings, in saloons, and on boats, and later by working as a song plugger at Tony Pastor's and other theaters. Before long he helped devise a vaudeville act with which he toured the circuit— *The Newsboy Quintet*, in which the performers wore tattered clothing, appeared with dirty faces, and sang popular ballads. For this act, Edwards wrote his first popular song, "All I Wants Is My

Black Baby Back," which May Irwin later used in her vaudeville act.

While entertaining troops at Camp Black, during the Spanish-American War, Edwards met a lyricist, Will D. Cobb. They formed a song writing partnership that eventually proved so successful that they were often referred to as "Words and Music." Their first hit was a ballad, "I Can't Tell Why I Love You, But I Do" in 1900. Other successes were "I'll Be with You When the Roses Bloom Again," in 1901, and "Good-bye, Little Girl, Good-bye," in 1904

In 1905, Gus Edwards formed his own publishing firm in Tin Pan Alley, placing it on solid footing with several of his own songs, including "I Just Can't Make My Eyes Behave" (piquantly introduced by Anna Held in *A Parisian Model*) and "Sunbonnet Sue," both in 1906, and "School Days," in 1907. The last of these was first heard in 1907 in a vaudeville sketch which Edwards produced and in which he starred. Through the years he was to produce different variations of the same act with undiminished success. It consisted of a group of youngsters over whom Edwards presided as a teacher and who were featured in song and dance routines. This sketch became the nursery in which many a subsequent star of stage and screen was first raised, including Eddie Cantor, Georgie Jessel, Ray Bolger, Georgie Price, Eleanor Powell, Bert Wheeler, Lila Lee, and Ann Dvorak. This act also provided Edwards with a convenient showcase for his songs, the best being "By the Light of the Silvery Moon," with lyrics by Edward Madden, introduced by Georgie Price in 1909.

Two more songs by Gus Edwards deserve mention—"In My Merry Oldsmobile" and "Tammany," both written in 1905 to lyrics by Vincent P. Bryan. "Tammany" is of particular interest, since it has survived as the quasi-official song of the New York Democratic Party. For a gala affair conducted by the National Democratic Club of New York at which Edwards served as a master of ceremonies, he wrote a song about the Democratic Party, parodying popular Indian songs of the time. Though it commented facetiously on some of the less creditable practices of their party, "Tammany" was an immediate hit with the New York Democrats, and it went on from there to further success in the Broadway musical extravaganza, *Fantana*.

Like that of Gus Edwards, the publishing house of Harry von Tilzer owed its first successes to the songs of its founder. Harry von Tilzer (1872-1946) was born Harry Gumm in Detroit. When he was only fourteen he ran away from home and joined a circus. After that he was a member of a traveling theatrical troupe, for which he wrote songs and played the piano. It was on this occasion that he changed his name to von Tilzer, Tilzer being the maiden name of his mother and the "von" being added to give the name distinction. In 1892, while performing in a Chicago burlesque house, von Tilzer met the vaudeville star, Lottie Gilson, who persuaded him to consider a song writing career in New York. After he had arrived there, he achieved his first song success with "My Old New Hampshire Home," in 1898, with lyrics by Andrew B. Sterling; it sold over two million copies. Such a formidable success brought von Tilzer a partnership in the publishing firm of Shapiro-Bernstein. In less than two years, von Tilzer justified his firm's faith in him by creating a second monumental success, "A Bird in a Gilded Cage," with lyrics by Arthur J. Lamb, one of the most celebrated sentimental ballads of the 1890's.

In 1902, von Tilzer formed his own publishing organization. Hardly had this firm opened its doors on 28th Street when it issued three major von Tilzer successes—"The Mansion of Aching Hearts" (Arthur J. Lamb), "Down Where the Wurzburger Flows" (Vincent P. Bryan), and "On a Sunday Afternoon" (Andrew B. Sterling). Two of von Tilzer's best sentimental ballads after that were "Wait 'Til the Sun Shines, Nellie" (Andrew B. Sterling) and "I Want a Girl Just Like the Girl That Married Dear Old Dad" (William Dillon). Von Tilzer also wrote some excellent coon songs, the most popular being two to lyrics by Andrew B. Sterling—"Alexander," in 1904, and "What You Goin' to Do When the Rent Comes 'Round?" in 1905.

Harry von Tilzer's brother, Albert (1878-1956), also enjoyed a distinguished career in Tin Pan Alley. He came from Indianapolis, where he attended public school and managed to learn to play the piano. For a while he worked as a shoe buyer in a department store in Brooklyn, then found a job as director of a vaudeville company, and finally joined his brother's firm as staff composer. Meanwhile, in 1900, his first published composition appeared, "Absent-Minded Beggar Waltz." In 1903 he formed his own music publishing firm with still another brother, Jack, for which he wrote "Teasing" in 1904 and "Honey Boy" in 1907, the latter to lyrics by Jack Norworth. His greatest hits came shortly afterwards—"Take Me Out to the Ball Game"; "Put Your Arms Around Me, Honey"; "I'm the Lonesomest Gal in Town"; "Oh! How She Could Yacki, Hacki, Wicki, Wacki, Woo," with which Eddie Cantor made his momentous debut as a Ziegfeld star in 1916; "I May Be Gone for a Long, Long Time," an unforgettable ballad of World War I; "Oh, By Jingo! Oh, By Gee!"; "I Used to Love You But It's All Over Now"; and "I'll Be with You in Apple Blossom Time."

While few of the songs by Theodore F. Morse (1873-1924) have survived till today as many of those by Gus Edwards and the von Tilzers did, he was nevertheless in his time a prolific and highly successful Tin Pan Alley composer. Born in Washington, D.C., he ran away from the military academy he was attending to come to New York when he was fourteen. He soon found a job as clerk in a music shop, and at fifteen he had one of his compositions published. In 1897 he formed his own publishing house, but five years later he became an associate of Howley, Haviland and Dresser, and in 1904 a full partner in the then newly founded organization of F. B. Haviland. Morse's first success as composer came in 1902 with "In the Moonlight with the Girl You Love," introduced by Christie MacDonald in *The Toreador*. Two big hits followed in 1903—"Dear Old Girl" and "Hurray for Baffin's Bay," the latter interpolated into the extravaganza *The Wizard of Oz* for Montgomery and Stone. Some of Morse's song hits were written to lyrics by Edward Madden, among these being "Blue Bell," "I've Got a Feelin' for You," "Daddy's Little Girl," "Starlight," and "Down in Jungle Town." To lyrics by Jack Drislane he wrote "Keep on the Sunny Side" and "Arrah Wanna." With Howard Johnson he wrote "M-O-T-H-E-R," one of the earliest spelling songs. He also frequently collaborated with a lyricist who used the pseudonym of Dorothy Terriss, but who in private life was his wife, Theodora. Theodora Morse was destined to become a partner in several solid song hits, but none to her husband's music. Two worth mentioning are Ernesto Lecuona's "Siboney" and Julian Robeldo's "Three O'Clock in the Morning."

Paradoxically, the one achievement by which Morse is most often remembered today is not one of his own songs, of which he wrote several hundred, but a set of breezy and unconventional lyrics he wrote to the "Pirates' Chorus" of the Gilbert and Sullivan operetta, *The Pirates of Penzance*, beginning with the rousing line, "Hail, Hail, the Gang's All Here!"

The forte of composers like the von Tilzer brothers and Theodore Morse was the sentimental ballad. One of the most important writers of such songs in the early part of the new century was Ernest R. Ball (1878-1927), who came from Cleveland, Ohio, where he attended the Conservatory and composed his first opus, a march. In the early 1890's he arrived in New York and worked first as a pianist in a Union Square theater and later as a demonstration pianist for Witmark. In the latter capacity he wrote his first popular songs, of which "In the Shadow of the Pyramids" had a moderate vogue after May Irwin introduced it in vaudeville.

His first substantial success appeared in 1905, "Will You Love Me in December as You Do in May?" with lyrics by James J. Walker, then a state senator and subsequently the dapper mayor of New York. Walker gave Ball his lyrics on a scrap of paper that Ball carried around with him for two months before he went to work on the melody. The song was an instantaneous success. As Ball himself recalled: "I awoke one morning to find that I had written a piece of music that was being sung from one end of the country to the other." Because of this achievement, Ball received a twenty-year contract with Witmark.

Having achieved fame with a sentimental ballad, Ball continued in the same vein for the next few years. In 1906 he wrote "Love Me and the World Is Mine"; in 1910, in collaboration with Chauncey Olcott, star of Irish musicals, he wrote what is still one of the most famous Irish ballads, "Mother Machree." Ball's later successes included "Till the Sands of the Desert Grow Cold," "When Irish Eyes Are Smiling," for which Chauncey Olcott helped write the lyrics, "A Little Bit of Heaven," "Turn Back the Universe," and "Let the Rest of the World Go By."

Chauncey Olcott, who occasionally helped Ball write his melodies and sometimes collaborated on the lyrics, was in his own right an esteemed composer of sentimental ballads. His most celebrated song was "My Wild Irish Rose," to his own lyrics, written in 1899 and introduced in the Irish musical, *Romance of Athlone*. Other Olcott ballads were prominently featured in the Irish musicals in which Olcott starred after the turn of the century, the most outstanding being "Old Fashioned Mother" and "Sweet Iniscarra" from *Sweet Iniscarra,* "Olcott's Home Song" from *The Minstrel of Clare,* "Olcott's Lullaby" from *Romance of Athlone,* and "Voice of the Violet" from *Old Limerick Town.*

Many others in Tin Pan Alley were writing ballads. Egbert van Alstyne (1878-1951), who had attended the Chicago Musical College and had toured the West as concert pianist and vaudeville entertainer, came to New York in 1900. Three years later he produced a hit song in "Navajo," one of the first Tin Pan Alley creations to use Indian names and subjects, first sung by Marie Cahill in the Broadway musical, *Nancy Brown.* Van Alstyne's greatest success came in 1905 with "In the Shade of the Old Apple Tree." His list of successes continued with "Won't You Come Over to My House?" "I'm Afraid to Come Home in the Dark," and "Your Eyes Have Told Me So."

Harry Armstrong was the composer of what is undoubtedly the prime favorite of all barbershop quartets, "Sweet Adeline." In its initial form it dates back to 1896 when it appeared as a melody without lyrics. Eventually Richard Gerard Husch provided appropriate verses, and the song was called "You're the Flower of My Heart, Sweet Rosalie." When publisher after publisher turned it down, the authors decided that the song needed a new title. Happening to see a poster advertising the world-famous prima donna, Adelina Patti, Husch suggested to Armstrong that they use the name Adeline instead of Rosalie. Now renamed "Sweet Adeline," the song was immediately accepted and published by Witmark, and a year after that—in 1904—was introduced at the Victoria Theater in New York by the Quaker City Four with such acclaim that its success became assured.

"I Wonder Who's Kissing Her Now?" another of the pre-eminent sentimental ballads of the early 1900's was written by Joe Howard in 1909 to lyrics by Will M. Hough and Frank R. Adams. Though Howard lived to write hundreds of other songs and ballads, this remained the one to keep his name alive, and it was this song that lent its title to the screen biography of Joe Howard produced by 20th Century-Fox in 1947. It first appeared in the Broadway musical, *The Prince of Tonight.* Apparently Howard profited from the collaboration of Harold Orlob, for, though Orlob's name never appeared on the published music, a court ruling in 1948 credited him with being co-composer.

Fred Fisher (1875-1942) arrived in Tin Pan Alley with a coon song, "If the Man in the Moon Were a Coon." But it was with sentimental lyricism rather than syncopation that Fisher achieved his greatest success. "Peg o' My Heart," in 1913, inspired by the Broadway play starring Laurette Taylor; "Ireland Must Be Heaven For My Mother Came from There," in 1916; and "Daddy, You've Been a Mother to Me," in 1920, were among the most frequently sung ballads of their respective years. Fisher also possessed a nimble touch for songs in a lighter vein, as "Come, Josephine, in My Flying Machine, "Who Paid the Rent for Mrs. Rip van Winkle When Rip van Winkle Went Away?", "Oui, Oui, Marie," the last a humorous ditty of World War I revived in 1948 in the Betty Grable screen musical, *When My Baby Smiles at Me*.

Jean Schwartz (1878-1956) soared to Tin Pan Alley fame in 1903 with the ballad "Bedelia." Profiting from the effective song plugging techniques of Mose Gumble and the stage allure of Blanche Ring in *The Jersey Lily*, "Bedelia" rolled up a sheet-music sale of three million copies. Schwartz had received his musical apprenticeship in Tin Pan Alley as a song plugger for Shapiro-Bernstein. By the close of the 19th century he had published a piano rag, "Dusky Dudes." In 1901 he found a valuable collaborator in William Jerome, already a highly esteemed lyricist. They wrote "When Mr. Shakespeare Comes to Town" (interpolated into the Weber and Fields burlesque, *Hoity-Toity*) and "Rip van Winkle Was a Lucky Man," both in 1901; "Mister Dooley," in 1902, introduced in *A Chinese Honeymoon;* in 1903, "Hamlet Was a Melancholy Man" (made popular by Eddie Foy in his Chicago extravaganza, *Mr. Bluebeard*) and the already-mentioned "Bedelia." After 1903 their best songs included "Chinatown, My Chinatown," "When the Girl You Love Is Loving," and "Where the Red, Red Roses Grow." During this period they also wrote the scores for numerous Broadway musicals.

After the dissolution of his partnership with Jerome in 1914, Schwartz began writing music with various other lyricists. Among his greatest successes were two songs triumphantly introduced by

Al Jolson in *Sinbad* in 1918, both of them with lyrics by Sam M. Lewis and Joe Young—"Rock-a-bye Your Baby with a Dixie Melody" and "Hello, Central, Give Me No Man's Land."

It was inevitable that the outbreak of World War I should have exerted a profound effect on Tin Pan Alley. By 1917, Tin Pan Alley had become extremely sensitive to public taste and public demand. It had developed into a well-oiled machine capable of manufacturing songs for every need. Not only was Tin Pan Alley cognizant of the way in which the war had changed the lives, thoughts, and emotions of the American people, but it was also in a position to give direct expression to such thoughts and emotions.

Americans were sentimental about their boys leaving for war in a foreign land, and the soldiers were equally sentimental about the home and the girls they left behind. Reflecting such poignant feelings were Richard A. Whiting's "Till We Meet Again," perhaps the most eloquent ballad of the war, and Albert von Tilzer's "I May Be Gone for a Long, Long Time" and "Au Revoir But Not Good-bye, Soldier Boy"; also, Al Piantadosi's "Send Me Away with a Smile," written in collaboration with Louis Weslyn, Pete Wendling's "Oh How I Wish I Could Sleep Until My Daddy Comes Home," and Jean Schwartz' "Hello Central, Give Me No Man's Land."

Americans fed their patriotic ardor and stirred their martial spirit with "Just Like Washington Crossed the Delaware, General Pershing Will Cross the Rhine" and Billy Baskette's "Good-bye, Broadway, Hello France," the latter featured in *The Passing Show* of 1917, and with tunes like "We're Going Over" and "We Don't Want the Bacon—What We Want Is a Piece of the Rhine." Americans sang hymns of praise to the various services in songs like "Rose of No Man's Land" and "The Navy Took Them Over and the Navy Will Bring Them Back."

Americans spoke their hatred of the Kaiser in over a hundred songs in which he was caned, whipped, kicked, shot, or hanged, such as "We're Going to Hang the Kaiser Under the Linden Tree" and "I'd Like to See the Kaiser with a Lily in His Hand," the latter from the 1918 Broadway musical, *Doing Our Bit*, and Americans spoke their love of the their ally, France, in "Joan of Arc, They Are Calling You," Fred Fisher's "Lorraine—My Beautiful Alsace Lorraine," and Robert A. King's "Lafayette, We Hear You Calling."

There was humor in army life and in some aspects of the war, and many songs reflected this lighter mood—"K-K-K-Katy," "I Don't Want to Get Well," Con Conrad's "Oh! Frenchy!", Fred Fisher's "Oui, Oui Marie," Walter Donaldson's "How Ya Gonna Keep 'Em Down on the Farm?", and Irving Berlin's "Oh! How I Hate to Get Up in the Morning" and "They Were All out of Step but Jim."

"Oh! How I Hate to Get Up in the Morning" originated in the all-soldier show, *Yip, Yip, Yaphank*, which Irving Berlin wrote and produced while stationed at Camp Upton, New York, in 1918. The purpose of this production was to raise $35,000 for a new service center at the camp, but by the time its run and tour had ended, following its première at the Century Theater in New York, it brought to Camp Upton $150,000 and to Irving Berlin two outstandingly successful songs. The first was "Oh! How I Hate to Get Up in the Morning," which Berlin himself sang in a scene where he was wearily dragged from his cot to reveille, and the second was "Mandy," which Marilyn Miller revived in the *Ziegfeld Follies of 1919* and made into a formidable hit.

Undoubtedly the most famous World War I song of all is George M. Cohan's "Over There." He wrote both the lyrics and the music in one morning at his home in Long Island after reading the news that America had declared war on Germany. The song was introduced by Charles King at a Red Cross benefit at the New York Hippodrome in the fall of 1917. Nora Bayes helped to popularize it further by singing it in vaudeville. Before the war had ended, "Over There" had sold over two million copies of sheet music and a million records. Because it had been "a genuine inspiration to all American manhood," as President Wilson wrote, the song brought Cohan—though many years later—a Congressional Medal, bestowed by President Franklin D. Roosevelt under a special Act of Congress.

11—The Changing Musical Theater

A new era was also at hand for the musical theater, and that era produced the theater's first significant composers.

The extravaganza was followed by the operetta and the comic opera. Operettas came into vogue with the importation from Europe of opéra-bouffes by Offenbach, Planquette, and Lecocq and the German-speaking operettas of Franz von Suppé and Johann Strauss the Younger, beginning in the 1860's. Comic opera captured the hearts of American theatergoers when *H.M.S. Pinafore*, by Gilbert and Sullivan, became a triumph following its première in Boston in 1878. Such was the appeal to Americans of *Pinafore* that soon after its introduction to this country it was produced by over ninety companies, five of them in New York.

Imitation was the flattery that American writers paid to this foreign type of stage entertainment. In 1879, John Philip Sousa, then just a young composer searching for a métier, wrote the music for *The Smugglers*. This was not only Sousa's first comic opera, but one of the first written by an American. Sousa wrote many more comic operas, none of them either significant or successful. One that is remembered is *El Capitan* (1896), because one of its choral sections was adapted by the composer into a famous march, also named "El Capitan."

The first successful American operetta was written by a Philadelphian, Willard Spencer. It was *The Little Tycoon,* which had a five-hundred-performance run in Philadelphia before coming to New York in 1887; it finally totalled a greater number of performances than any American musical production up to its time. Spencer wrote the book, lyrics, and music. With both his eyes on *The Mikado* of Gilbert and Sullivan, Spencer disguises his principal character, an American young man, in the robes of the "great tycoon" of Japan. It seems that General Knickerbocker is partial to titled nobility, and the young American is trying to win the hand of the General's daughter. The amusing book, with its gentle ribbing of social snobbery, was enhanced by a few pleasing melodies, the best being "On the Sea," "Love Comes Like a Summer Night," and "Sad Heart of Mine."

Undoubtedly spurred on by the immense returns of *The Little Tycoon,* American composers and librettists set themselves industriously to the writing of operettas. Willard Spencer himself achieved another phenomenal hit with *Princess Bonnie* (1895), which had a run of over a thousand performances in Philadelphia before it came to New York. *Wang*—once again derived from *The Mikado*—was a highlight of the 1891 New York theatrical season, Wang being the Regent of Siam acted by De Wolf Hopper; the book was by J. Cheever Goodwin and the music by Woolson Morse. In 1892 came *The Isle of Champagne*—book by Charles A. Byrne and Louis Harrison, and music by William Wallace Furst; several of its songs became popular, among them "There's a Land in the Shimmery Silver Moon," "Fly Sweet Bird," and a topical number called "Old King Mumm Could Make Things Hum."

If Willard Spencer was America's first successful composer of operettas, Reginald De Koven (1859-1920) was its first significant one, certainly the first whose name still has meaning for us. Though born in Middletown, Connecticut, De Koven received his academic education at St. John's College, Oxford, and a comprehensive musical training in Germany and Paris, notably with Léo Delibes. Returning to the United States in 1882, he worked in Chicago first in a bank and then in a stock-brokerage firm. Marriage to the daughter of a wealthy merchant, followed by his own successful operations in Texas real estate, made him financially independent. He was now able to return to his first love, music. Forming a collaborative arrangement with a young writer, Harry B. Smith, he wrote in 1887 his first operetta, *The Begum,* also strongly influenced by *The Mikado.* This comic opera and the one that followed were failures, but the authors had a dashing winner with their third work, *Robin Hood* (1890), the most significant comic opera by an American before Victor Herbert and the only one of the pre-Herbert period that is still occasionally revived.

Perhaps the principal reason why *Robin Hood* has not passed into the complete oblivion that has engulfed all the other comic operas of its days is the song "Oh, Promise Me," which has become an almost indispensable adjunct to American weddings. "Oh, Promise Me" (lyrics by Clement Scott) was not in the original score of *Robin Hood,* having been written some years earlier. When *Robin Hood* was in rehearsal, a need was felt for a sentimental number. De Koven tried unsuccessfully to get several members of his cast interested in "Oh, Promise Me." One day, Jessie Bartlett Davis, who played the role of Alan-a-Dale, hummed this tune in her dressing room, but an octave lower than written. She was overheard by the producer, who persuaded her to sing it in the play in the same key in which she had hummed it in her room. As it turned out, "Oh, Promise Me" became the most successful song of the production. Two lesser numbers have been obscured by its fame, but they also deserve mention—"Brown October Ale" and "The Armorer's Song."

After *Robin Hood,* De Koven and Smith wrote comic opera after comic opera, hardly a year passing without one of their shows being on Broadway. Among the most successful were *The Knickerbockers* (1893), *Rob Roy* (1894), *The Highwayman* (1897), *The Little Duchess* (1901), *Maid Marian* (1902), and *The Golden Butterfly* (1907). None of the songs from these operas approach the fame of "Oh, Promise Me," but a few are not without interest—"My Home Is Where the Heather Blooms," from *Rob Roy;* "Moonlight Song," from *The Highwayman;* "The Only Girl," from *The Little Duchess;* and "True Love Is Not for a Day," from *Maid Marian.*

De Koven's last comic opera was *Her Little Highness* (1913), with book and lyrics by Channing Pollock and Rennold Wolf. Seven years later he died in New York City. For two decades thereafter his palatial home on Park Avenue served as a museum, with his bedroom and study left intact.

With Victor Herbert (1859-1924) the American theater acquired its first outstanding musical figure, and American popular music its most significant creator since Stephen Foster.

Herbert was born in Dublin, Ireland, and received his first piano instruction from his mother and an intensive musical education at the Stuttgart Conservatory in Germany. He completed studying the cello with Bernhard Cossmann in Baden-Baden, after which he played in German and Austrian orchestras for several years and wrote two major works for cello and orchestra, a *Suite* and a *Concerto*.

In 1886, Herbert married Theresa Foerster, a German prima donna who had just been engaged by the Metropolitan Opera. The Herberts came to the United States in the fall of that year, when Theresa Foerster made her American debut in the title role of Karl Goldmark's *The Queen of Sheba*. Herbert became a cellist in the Opera orchestra.

America now became Herbert's adopted country, in whose musical life he was to play a vital role. As a cellist, he played in several major orchestras, including the New York Philharmonic. As a conductor, he was the head of the renowned 22nd Regiment Band, from 1898 to 1904 of the Pittsburgh Symphony, and after 1904 of his own orchestra. As a composer, he produced several serious American works, such as the *American Fantasia*, for orchestra, and in 1911 the opera, *Natoma*.

His greatest contribution to his adopted land was, of course, his music for the stage. His first produced operetta, *Prince Ananias*, came four years after De Koven's *Robin Hood*. A satire on the theater by Francis Neilson, it had been commissioned by the Boston Light Opera Company. One year later, in 1895, *The Wizard of the Nile*, with book and lyrics by Harry B. Smith, was an outstanding success in New York.

Herbert now assumed a ruling position in both the musical theater and Tin Pan Alley. His most significant operettas were *The Serenade* (1897), *The Fortune Teller* (1898), *Babes in Toyland* (1903), *It Happened in Nordland* (1904), *Mlle. Modiste* (1905), *The Red Mill* (1906), *Naughty Marietta* (1910), *Sweethearts* (1913), and *Eileen* (1917). For these and many other lesser musical productions, he wrote some of the greatest songs ever heard on the American stage. He had a seemingly inexhaustible fund of melody; and the range of his style extended from laughter to sentiment. His songs also had an irresistible charm, freshness, and spontaneity, together with an unusual technique in composition and orchestration. In short, he was, as Deems Taylor once wrote, "a genius. . . . He wrote upwards of forty operettas and musical-comedy scores, the least successful of which are alive, *as music,* just as much as on the day they were written.

. . . Today . . . there is no composer, serious or light, living or dead, whose music is more in demand." In speaking such words, Taylor was undoubtedly thinking of the long procession of Victor Herbert songs whose survival in the repertory seems assured—"Star Light, Star Bright," from *The Wizard of the Nile*; "I Love Thee, I Adore Thee," from *The Serenade*; "Gypsy Love Song" (or "Slumber On, My Little Gypsy Sweetheart"), from *The Fortune Teller*; "March of the Toys" and "Toyland," from *Babes in Toyland*; "Kiss Me Again," from *Mlle. Modiste*; "The Isle of Our Dreams" and "Moonbeams," from *The Red Mill*; "Ah, Sweet Mystery of Life," "I'm Falling in Love with Someone," "Italian Street Song," and " 'Neath the Southern Moon," from *Naughty Marietta*; "Sweethearts," from the operetta of the same name; and "Thine Alone," from *Eileen*.

Three of these songs warrant some explanatory comment. "I Love Thee, I Adore Thee" is not only the principal love song of *The Serenade*, but a recurring melody that changes its personality throughout the operetta. It becomes a parody of grand opera, a chant of monks, a call of parrots, a song of brigands, and, of course, a sentimental love song. This melody assumes such importance in the development of the plot that it has been said that it is the real hero of the operetta.

Since "Kiss Me Again" is surely one of Herbert's best loved sentimental waltzes, it is amusing to remark that in the operetta, *Mlle. Modiste,* it was originally intended as an amusing parody. In the first act, the heroine, Fifi (unforgettably portrayed by Fritzi Scheff) wants to exhibit her vocal gifts. In a sequence entitled "If I Were on the Stage" she proves her versatility by singing several different kinds of song—a gavotte, a polonaise, a waltz, and so on. For each of these types of vocal composition Herbert wrote a caricature, and for the waltz he intended his melody to be a take-off on all similar music. The audience, however, demonstrated such enthusiasm for the waltz that Herbert decided to add a new verse to the melody and to find an important place for it in his play as a sentimental number.

"Ah, Sweet Mystery of Life" is one of the two greatest commercial successes achieved by Herbert (the other being "Thine Alone"). A legend has long existed that Herbert originally wrote this as an instrumental number but that the star of *Naughty Marietta* prevailed upon him to rewrite it as a tenor air. The truth, however, is that the song was in the production as a major tenor number from the very beginning.

Though Herbert continued to write for the stage prolifically after 1917—indeed, up to the last day of his life—his reign as a king of operetta may be said to end with *Eileen*. As this writer had occasion to remark elsewhere:[*] "His romantic, tender, sentimental music belonged to an epoch that died with World War I. In the newer, frenetic period of the fox trot and the Charleston, of ragtime and jazz, his songs sounded almost like an anachronism. 'My day is over,' he told a friend. 'They are forgetting poor old Herbert.' "

Nevertheless, "poor old Herbert" was not forgotten, not even after his sudden death from a heart attack in New York in 1924. The radio, just beginning to invade the American household, was pouring out his music more plentifully than that of any other composer. His best operettas have been frequently revived; the return to Broadway of *The Red Mill* in 1945 resulted in an impressive run of more than a year, and *Babes in Toyland* was given a spectacular television production in 1960. Many of his operettas have been turned into motion pictures, and in 1949 Paramount released *The Great Victor Herbert*, a screen biography of the composer.

During Herbert's long reign on Broadway, his productions were supplemented by those of many other gifted composers. Gustave A. Kerker (1857-1923) came to the United States from Germany when he was a child of ten. For many years he was the conductor of The Casino in New York (home of operettas), where he made his debut as a Broadway composer with *The Pearl of Pekin* in 1888. His success began two years later with *Castles in the Air*, adapted from the French, in which De Wolf Hopper was assigned his first starring role. Most of Kerker's later operettas were produced at The Casino. The most significant of these were *The Belle of New York* (1897), in which Edna May became an overnight singing star in "She Is the Belle of New York" and "They All Follow Me"; *The Girl from Up There* (1899); *A Chinese Honeymoon* (1902); *Winsome Willie* (1903);

---

[*] David Ewen, *Complete Book of the American Musical Theater* (New York: Henry Holt & Co., 1958), p. 132.

The Social Whirl (1908); and *The Two Little Brides* (1911). "In Gay New York" from the operetta of the same name, "Baby, Baby" from *The Lady Slavey*, "The Good Old Days" from *The Whirl of the Town*, and "You're Just the Girl I'm Looking for" from the *Social Whirl* were some of his best songs.

Another composer associated with The Casino early in the twentieth century was Ludwig Englander (1859-1914). Englander was born in Vienna and in 1882 came to New York, where he became conductor at the Thalia Theater. His first attempt at writing music for the stage was *The Princess Consort*, a failure. In 1893 he was engaged by George W. Lederer to write the music for *The Passing Show* at the Casino Theatre, the production with which the revue came into existence. In 1899 Englander enjoyed a moderate success with *The Rounders*. His most significant scores appeared in the early 1900's—*The Casino Girl* and *Belle of Bohemia*, both with books and lyrics by Harry B. Smith, and both produced in 1900; *The Strollers* (1901); *A Madcap Princess* (1904); *The Rich Mr. Hoggenheimer* (1906), starring Sam Bernard; and *Miss Innocence* (1908). A few of the more memorable songs from these productions were "Mam'selle" and "New York" from *The Casino Girl*, "When Shall I Find Him?" from *Belle of Bohemia*, "Strollers We" from *The Strollers*, and "Don't You Want a Paper, Dearie?" and "This World Is a Toy Shop" from *The Rich Mr. Hoggenheimer*.

Gustav Luders (1866-1913), of German origin, came to the United States in 1885 and found employment in Tin Pan Alley, with Witmark. In 1899 he wrote his first operetta score, *Little Robinson Crusoe*. One year later he found a sympathetic collaborator in Frank Pixley, editor of the *Chicago Times-Herald*, to whose libretto and lyrics he wrote the music for *The Burgomaster*, a production for which Luders wrote his first song hit, "The Tale of the Kangaroo." This was followed by Luders' crowning success, once again with Pixley, *The Prince of Pilsen* (1903), which enjoyed a substantial success in its initial run in New York and then toured the country for five seasons, returning to New York during that time for three additional engagements. The gaiety and charm of the text, set on the Riviera, were greatly enhanced by the most inventive score Luders ever wrote, its principal numbers being "The Message of the Violet," "Pictures in Smoke," and two rousing choral numbers, "The Heidelberg Stein Song" and "The Tale of the Seashell."

Other Luders operettas to texts by Pixley included *King Dodo* (1902), *Woodland* (1904), and *The Grand Mogul* (1907). With George Ade, Luders wrote *The Sho-Gun* (1904) and *The Fair Co-Ed* (1909). Luders' last operetta was *Somewhere Else* (1913), his thirteenth stage work and as it turned out his unluckiest. The critics were so devastating that the show closed down after the third performance. This defeat affected Luders so profoundly that he suffered a fatal heart attack one day after the show left the boards.

Karl Hoschna (1877-1911) was the composer of *The Three Twins* (1908) and *Madame Sherry* (1910), for both of which Otto Hauerbach (later Harbach) wrote the text and the lyrics. The first production elevated Bessie McCoy to stardom in the song, "The Yama-Yama Man," and from then on Bessie McCoy was referred to as "the Yama-Yama girl." Another outstanding number was "Cuddle Up a Little Closer." In view of the importance of both these songs to the success of the production as a whole, it is interesting to note that neither one was originally intended for this play. Hauerbach & Hoschna had written "Cuddle Up a Little Closer" for a vaudeville act long before they started working on *The Three Twins,* and "The Yama-Yama Man," with lyrics by Collin Davis, was interpolated into the operetta while it was being tried out in Chicago.

Hoschna's *Madame Sherry* was one of the most celebrated American operettas before World War I. To the editor of *Theater Magazine,* Hoschna's music was "the best native score since *Mlle. Modiste.*" The most important song was a provocative number, "Every Little Movement," and two other melodic delights were found in the waltzes, "The Girl of My Dreams" and "The Birth of Passion."

Ivan Caryll (1861-1921) came to America in 1911. Born in Liège, Belgium, he first became a successful operetta composer in England. In the year of his arrival in New York he achieved a triumph with *The Pink Lady,* an operetta that smashed all attendance records for the New Amsterdam Theatre where it was presented. Other box-office records were subsequently broken during its extensive countrywide tour. It was because of the popularity of this operetta that the color pink came into fashion in women's clothes in 1911. Hazel Dawn was "the pink lady," and to her Caryll assigned his biggest numbers, the infectious waltz, "My Beautiful Lady," and "The Kiss Waltz."

After *The Pink Lady*, Caryll's operettas were frequent visitors to the American stage. Those particularly successful were *Oh, Oh, Delphine* (1912), *Chin-Chin* (1914), *Jack o' Lantern* (1917), *The Girl Behind the Gun* (1918), and *Tip Top* (1920). "Wait Till the Cows Come Home" from *Jack o' Lantern* and "There's a Light in Your Eyes" from *The Girl Behind the Gun* were two of his most popular songs.

If any one composer can be said to have inherited the mantle of Victor Herbert, it is Rudolf Friml (1879-   ), and it was because of Victor Herbert that Friml was given his first opportunity to write for the New York stage. In 1911 Herbert had contracted to write a new operetta for Emma Trentini, who had previously starred in his *Naughty Marietta*. But, after the run of the latter production, Victor Herbert and his star were no longer on speaking terms, and he refused to work with her. During the search for a composer to replace Herbert, the publishers Max Dreyfus and Rudolph Schirmer suggested the little known name of Rudolf Friml to the producer, Arthur Hammerstein. Hammerstein was willing to take a chance on a novice and was bountifully rewarded with one of the most enchanting scores of the 1910's, that for *The Firefly*.

Born in Prague, Friml received his musical training at the Prague Conservatory. Following his graduation, he toured Europe as a pianist in joint concerts with the violinist, Jan Kubelik. When the latter was engaged to tour America 1901, Friml came with him. In the fall of 1904 he appeared as soloist with the New York Symphony in a performance of his own piano concerto, and in 1906 he decided to remain in the United States and to further his career in serious music. After taking up residence in the United States, Friml devoted himself to teaching the piano, giving concerts, and writing piano pieces, songs, and various instrumental numbers. The melodic interest in these compositions led Dreyfus and Schirmer to consider him a potentially significant operetta composer even though up to that time Friml had written nothing for the stage.

The Firefly, book and lyrics by Otto Harbach, was first produced in 1912. Emma Trentini was cast as an Italian street singer who becomes a famous prima donna. Herself a one-time opera star, Trentini could be counted upon to do full justice to Friml's melodies, some of which have a concert-hall spaciousness—"Giannina Mia," "Love Is Like a Firefly," "When a Maid Comes Knocking at Your Heart," and "The Dawn of Love." A fifth outstanding number was the sentimental duet, "Sympathy."

Several lesser Friml successes followed in the next decade before he was able to surpass the triumph of *The Firefly.* He did so with *Rose-Marie* (1924), which had a New York run of over five hundred performances while four companies toured the road. *Rose-Marie* was described by its authors—Otto Harbach and Oscar Hammerstein II—as a "musical play," and they made a special point of explaining in the program that each musical number was an integral part of the action. Nevertheless, several numbers do stand out prominently—the duet, "Indian Love Call," the title song, and "Totem Tom-Tom."

Two noteworthy operettas followed *Rose-Marie.* For *The Vagabond King* (1925)—which had for its principal character the 15th century vagabond-poet, François Villon—Friml wrote the rousing chorus, "Song of the Vagabonds," and several unforgettable lyrical pieces including "Huguette Waltz," "Only a Rose," and "Love Me Tonight." *The Three Musketeers* (1928), adapted from Dumas' novel, also combined virile and romantic music with songs like "March of the Musketeers," "With Red Wine," "Ma Belle," and "Heart of Mine."

Friml wrote the music for two operettas early in the 1930's, both of them failures. He then worked for a time in Hollywood, where, since World War II, he has lived in comparative retirement.

Sigmund Romberg (1887-1951) was the last of the American composers of operetta, and in some respects he was the best. He was born in Hungary, but his spiritual roots were deeply embedded in the soil of Vienna, where he spent his early manhood. Romberg came to the United States in 1909 and began earning his living by playing the piano in cafés and orchestras. By 1912 he was directing his own salon orchestra at Bustanoby's Restaurant in New York, for which he made his own arrangements. At this time he also began writing popular music; two one-steps and a waltz were published in Tin Pan Alley and became popular with dance orchestras.

In 1913, J. J. Shubert, the Broadway producer, engaged Romberg as staff composer, his first assignment being to write the score for *The Whirl of the World*, starring Eugene and Willie Howard at the Winter Garden in 1914. Between 1914 and 1917, Romberg wrote the music for seventeen Shubert musicals, including three editions of *The Passing Show* and *Robinson Crusoe, Jr.*, a Winter Garden extravaganza starring Al Jolson. More important by far is the fact that during this period he also wrote the nostalgic and sentimental waltz, "Auf Wiedersehn," lyrics by Herbert Reynolds, interpolated in the operetta, *The Blue Paradise* (1915).

For many years Romberg divided his activity between American revues and extravaganzas produced by Shubert, and operettas of the European type. It was for the latter that he wrote his finest music, for his heart, spirit, and sentiment always belonged to Vienna. Several of his operettas were among the most successful productions of the American musical stage—*Maytime* (1917), such a box-office attraction that before its first year's run ended a second company had to open in a nearby theater, the first time any musical had two productions running simultaneously in the Broadway area; *Blossom Time* (1921), freely based on the life and music of Vienna's great composer, Franz Schubert; *The Student Prince* (1924), set in the romantic city of Heidelberg, Germany, in the middle nineteenth century; *The Desert Song* (1926), with its exotic background of French Morocco; and *The New Moon* (1928), which had one of the longest Broadway runs of any Romberg operetta and which brought from Hollywood the highest price for screen rights paid up to that time for Broadway musicals. Such a formidable caravan of stage hits carried a treasure of never-to-be-forgotten melodies—the nostalgic waltz, "Will You Remember?" from *Maytime;* "Song of Love," from *Blossom Time*, based on the beautiful main theme from the first movement of Schubert's *Unfinished Symphony;* "Serenade," "Drinking Song," "Deep in My Heart," and "Golden Days," from *The Student Prince;* "One Alone" and "Blue Heaven," from *The*

Desert Song; "One Kiss," "Wanting You," "Lover Come Back to Me," "Stout-Hearted Men," and "Softly, As in a Morning Sunrise" from *The New Moon.*

After the close of his career in operetta Romberg turned to musical comedy with *Up in Central Park* (1945), a huge success, and *The Girl in Pink Tights,* produced posthumously in 1954, a failure. But the writing of the kind of music demanded by the American extravaganza, revue, and musical comedy never came easily to Romberg, whose natural bent was for the romantic, escapist, nostalgic sort of music that suited the world of the operetta so naturally. When the story of Romberg's life was told on the screen in *Deep in My Heart,* produced and released posthumously, it was his beloved operetta songs alone that gave the picture its musical distinction.

Out of Romberg's activity in Hollywood—which began in 1930 with the score for *Viennese Nights*—a single song stands out—the sentimental waltz, "When I Grow Too Old to Dream," from *The Night Is Young.*

Even while Friml and Romberg were producing their best works and scoring their greatest successes, the operetta was slowly being pushed into oblivion by the musical comedy. Whereas the operetta was a foreign importation even when it was created by Americans, musical comedy was a native product. The operetta was partial to foreign or exotic settings, to plots far removed from the real and the contemporary, to stock characters involved in stock situations, and to music that borrowed its three-quarter lilt or two-quarter and four-quarter pulses as well as its sweet lyricism from the Continental stage. On the other hand, musical comedy usually had an American background, American characters, and an American flavor in the brisk rhythms and breezy melodies of its music. The emergence of the American musical comedy at the beginning of the twentieth century was an event of first importance in the American theater.

The term "musical comedy" was first used in conjunction with *Evangeline,* a burlesque produced in 1874. At that time, Edward E. Rice, the composer of its musical score, expressed the hope that his production would "foster a taste for musical comedy relieved of the characteristic and objectionable features of the opéra-bouffe." Nevertheless, *Evangeline* was no musical comedy by any stretch of the imagination. It was a broad travesty on Longfellow's poem in the burlesque style so popular in the American theater at the time.

When musical comedy was evolved early in the 1900's, it took over some of the approaches, methods, and techniques of earlier species of our musical theater. The large production numbers and lavish sets came from the extravaganza. Satire, slapstick, and travesty were borrowed from burlesque. The occasional irrelevant interpolation of songs, dances, comedy routines, and large scenes within the plot was a heritage from the operetta. To these familiar elements, however, musical comedy added something new: a native identity. In 1900, our musical theater began drawing its settings from American backgrounds and its characters from the American people more freely than heretofore. At the same time, a new vigor, a new freshness and brashness, and an accelerated tempo entered the writing of dialogue, lyrics, and music. This represented a divorce from European influences and practices.

We find the first flowering of American musical comedy with George M. Cohan (1878-1942). He was the Pooh-Bah of the American theater. He wrote not only his own plays, but also the lyrics and the music. He frequently starred in them as well and at times even produced them. He was not equally endowed in all the departments in which he functioned and was probably at his best as a performer. With his peculiar kangaroo-step dancing, his inimitable strutting up and down the stage, his nasal singing, his saucy way of bandying a bamboo cane and cocking a hat over one eye, and his way of addressing an audience with an improvised speech or a prepared monologue, he was a showman to the tips of his agile toes, an incomparable song-and-dance man. He knew how to create a bond between himself and his audience, how to put over a number, and how to project a dynamic and at times brash characterization.

But his stature as a dramatist and composer was not quite so impressive. He was ever partial to a cliché and a stereotype, and the range of his invention was limited. He himself realized his shortcomings when he said, "As a composer I could never find use for over four or five notes in any musical number . . . and as a playwright, most of my plays have been presented in two acts for the simple reason that I could never think of a third act."

Even when we recognize his limitations, we must also acknowledge that at the beginning of the twentieth century he brought into the musical theater an excitement and vibrancy it had not often encountered before. Even when he did not drape the American flag around himself—a favorite routine for a climactic scene—he was American in everything he said, wrote, and did—a "Yankee Doodle Dandy." He was the personification of the new century in America, with its energy, versatility, chauvinism, and self-assurance.

Cohan was the son of vaudevillians. He was still a child when he made his stage debut in his parents' act in Haverstraw, New York, billed as "Master Georgie." Before long, his little sister also joined the act, bringing into existence the "Four Cohans," who for many years toured the vaudeville circuit as headliners. It was not long before George M. Cohan started writing dialogue and songs for the act. He produced sketches and songs for other vaudeville performers as well. His first published song was "Why Did Nellie Leave Home?" in 1894. A year later, May Irwin sang his coon song, "Hot Tamale Alley," and in 1898 he had a substantial hit in "I Guess I'll Have to Telegraph My Baby."

He soon began reaching towards horizons beyond the vaudeville sketch. Between 1901 and 1903 he expanded two of his skits into full-length musical comedies and brought them to Broadway as *The Governor's Son* (1901) and *Running for Office* (1903), neither one a success. In 1904 he wrote the text, lyrics, and music for a completely new musical, *Little Johnny Jones,* which he himself produced at the Liberty Theater in conjunction with Sam H. Harris and in which he starred as an American jockey come to London to ride in the Derby. *Little Johnny Jones* established some of the routines that Cohan henceforth would exploit to the full. He delivered his sprightly songs in the infectious style that was uniquely his—strutting up and down the stage and then breaking into a kangaroo dance step. Two of the songs from this show have become Cohan classics, "Yankee Doodle Boy" and "Give My Regards to Broadway." He also delivered a sentimental monologue to his audience in "Life's a Funny Proposition After All." He dominated the stage so completely that everyone and everything else about the production was thrown into the background.

His next musical was *Forty-Five Minutes from Broadway* (1906), a mild little comedy starring Fay Templeton and Victor

Moore. For this production Cohan wrote two more songs that have survived, "So Long, Mary" and "Mary's a Grand Old Name." In *George Washington, Jr.* (1906), Cohan introduced still another popular Cohan routine—draping the American flag around his body and cavorting across the stage while hymning the praises of his flag and his country. He did this to "You're a Grand Old Flag." Cohan originally entitled this song "You're a Grand Old Rag," quoting a phrase spoken to him by a G.A.R. veteran who had been color-bearer during Pickett's charge at Gettysburg, but the day after the première patriotic societies condemned Cohan for referring to the American emblem as a "rag," and as a consequence he changed the controversial word to "flag."

Until the outbreak of World War I, Cohan's musical comedies, in some of which he starred, continued to brighten the corners of the American theater. *The Talk of the Town* and *The Honeymooners* came in 1907; *The Yankee Prince* and *Fifty Miles from Boston* in 1908; *The Man Who Owns Broadway* in 1909; *The Little Millionaire* in 1911; and *Hello Broadway* in 1914. The leading songs from these productions included "Harrigan," "I'm a Popular Man," "You Remind Me of My Mother," "Little Nellie Kelly," "When a Fellow's on the Level with a Girl That's on the Square," and "Barnum Had the Right Idea."

By the end of World War I, Cohan's day in the American musical theater was almost over. New writers of texts, lyrics, and music appeared and introduced a wit and sophistication of which Cohan had never been capable. In comparison to the newer musical comedies, those by Cohan appeared as old-fashioned as a Model-T Ford. The only two of his later plays that had even a moderate success were those without music, *The Tavern* (1923) and *The Song and Dance Man* (1927). The six musicals he wrote between 1918 and 1928 were failures in varying degrees. "I guess people don't understand me any more and I don't understand them," he remarked ruefully. "It's got so that an evening's entertainment just won't do. Give an audience an evening of what they call realism, and you've got a hit. It's getting too much for me, kid." What he failed to realize was that both the American theater and American popular music had been moving forward swiftly and that he had failed to keep pace with that advance.

Still another thing embittered him after World War I. In 1919 he was the spearhead against the attempt of Actors Equity to gain recognition as the bargaining agent for its members. The fact that so many of his friends and associates were in the camp of the "enemy"—and the fact that his battle against Actors Equity was a losing cause—was so searing to his sensibilities that he dissolved the prosperous producing firm of Cohan and Harris and withdrew his membership from the Friars and Lambs clubs.

But he was not through by any means. Near the end of his life he scored triumphs as a performer in the Rodgers and Hart musical *I'd Rather Be Right*, in which he played the role of President Franklin D. Roosevelt, and in Eugene O'Neill's heart-warming comedy, *Ah, Wilderness!* In 1940 he received a Congressional medal from President Roosevelt. Just before Cohan's death the screen paid him homage with a magnificent motion-picture biography, *Yankee Doodle Dandy*. There were not many to say that Gene Buck overstated the case when in his eulogy on Cohan he called him "the greatest single figure the American theater has produced." Certainly Cohan's influence can hardly be overestimated, for it is on the foundation of his homespun and sentimental texts, lyrics, and music that the structure of American musical comedy rests.

While the musical comedy was slowly acquiring its identity, another form of musical theater was taking shape—the revue. The revue grew out of the fantasia section of the minstrel show, in which individual performers did their specialties, and out of the variety entertainment then being seen in vaudeville theaters. But the song, dance, and comedy acts of minstrel shows and vaudeville found a more ambitious frame than heretofore in the revue—with spectacular sets, costumes, and production numbers.

The revue came into existence on May 12, 1894, with *The Passing Show*, not to be confused with later revues of the same name produced by the Shuberts. The 1894 *The Passing Show* was presented at the Casino Theater by George W. Lederer and featured acrobatics, amusing travesties, and burlesques of prominent actors and actresses, female beauty in the form of "living pictures," and spectacles in sumptuously mounted "dance divertissements." The completely original musical score was the work of Ludwig Englander, with lyrics by Sydney Rosenberg.

The Passing Show gave birth to a new idea which other producers quickly adopted. *The Merry World* came in 1895; *In Gay*

New York, All of the Town, and *Yankee Doodle* (all three to music by Gustave Kerker) were seen in 1896, 1897, and 1898 respectively; *In Gotham* appeared in 1898; and *Round New York in Eighty Minutes* was produced in 1899.

Florenz Ziegfeld made the revue an institution on Broadway. The first *Ziegfeld Follies* was produced in 1907, a comparatively modest affair costing only $13,000 to mount, and carrying a weekly overhead of $3,800. But already Ziegfeld's weakness for beautiful scenes and girls was evident. The former could be found in several eye-winning numbers, and the latter in the appearance of the Anna Held Girls. Ziegfeld continued presenting his *Follies* until 1931 (except for 1926, 1928, and 1929) and became one of the foremost showmen of his generation. Unsparing of expense, he continued mounting his productions with ever greater lavishness and extravagance, providing a dazzling background for his beautiful girls, and the *"Follies* girl" became a synonym for the ultimate in feminine beauty. Out of the ranks of the Ziegfeld chorus line came such later stars of stage and screen as Mae Murray, Ann Pennington, Marion Davies, and Lilyan Tashman, to mention only a few.

To his various productions Ziegfeld brought a long procession of stars, some whose reputation was already established when he brought them into the *Follies* and others whom he lifted from complete obscurity. Some of the most brilliant names in the American musical theater lighted the marquees of the New Amsterdam Theater, where the *Follies* were seen—Fanny Brice, W. C. Fields, Eddie Cantor, Will Rogers, Sophie Tucker, Nora Bayes, Leon Errol, Bert Williams, Marilyn Miller, and Ed Wynn.

Several composers devoted their principal activity to the demands of the *Follies.* One was Dave Stamper (1883-   ), whose first song for Ziegfeld was "Daddy Has a Sweetheart and Mother Is Her Name," lyrics by Gene Buck, in 1912. After 1912 there was hardly an edition of the *Follies* without one or more of Stamper's songs. The most prominent of these were "Sweet Sixteen" and "Tulip Time" in 1919, "Come Back to Our Alley" and "Raggedy Ann" in 1921, "My Rambler Rose" and " 'Neath the South Sea Moon" in 1922, and "Some Sweet Day," the last three written in collaboration with Louis A. Hirsch.

Louis A. Hirsch (1887-1924) was a Ziegfeld composer for the editions of 1915, 1916, 1918, and 1922. His best numbers were

"Hello, Frisco, Hello" and "Hold Me in Your Loving Arms," in 1915, "Beautiful Island of Girls" and "I Want That Star," in 1916, "Garden of Your Dreams," "When I'm Looking at You," and "Syncopated Tune," in 1918, and "Hello, Hello, Hello," in 1922.

Raymond Hubbell (1879-1954) provided the basic scores for the editions of 1911, 1912, 1913, 1914, and 1917, with the following numbers as his main contributions: "Take Care, Little Girl," sung by Bessie McCoy, and "My Beautiful Lady," in 1911; "Romantic Girl" and "The Broadway Glide," in 1912; and "Beautiful Garden of Girls" and "Just You and Me," in 1917.

Irving Berlin was the principal composer of the editions of 1919, 1920, and 1927. He wrote "A Pretty Girl Is Like a Melody" and "You'd Be Surprised" for the 1919 edition, besides interpolating for Marilyn Miller "Mandy" from his all-soldier revue, *Yip, Yip, Yaphank*. For the 1920 edition he wrote "The Girls of My Dreams," "Tell Me, Little Gypsy," and "The Syncopated Vamp"; and for 1927, "You Gotta Have It" and "Learn to Sing a Love Song."

Besides engaging various composers to provide his main numbers, Ziegfeld also freely interpolated into his *Follies* individual songs by others, some of which became outstanding successes. "Shine On, Harvest Moon" by Jack Norworth and Nora Bayes was first made famous by Nora Bayes in 1908. (Ruth Etting revived it with extraordinary effect in the *Follies* of 1930.) Albert von Tilzer's "Oh! How She Could Yacki, Hacki, Wicki, Wacki, Woo" was the medium through which Eddie Cantor rose to fame in 1916. In "My Man," adapted by Channing Pollock from a French song in 1921, Fanny Brice showed as potent a gift for sentimentality as she had previously demonstrated for comedy, and "Mister Gallagher and Mr. Shean" was the lively patter song of their own composition for which Ed Gallagher and Al Shean were acclaimed in 1922. Other excellent songs from the *Follies* by various individual composers included "Row, Row, Row" by Jimmy V. Monaco in 1912, "Oh! Gee, Oh! Gosh, Oh! Golly, I'm in Love" by Ernest Breuer, with lyrics by Olsen and Johnson, who introduced it in 1923, and Walter Donaldson's "My Blue Heaven" in 1927.

In the presentation of lavish revues, the *Follies* found a strong competitor in *The Passing Show* which the Shuberts began producing at the Winter Garden in 1912 with a score by Louis A. Hirsch. For the 1913 edition, Jean Schwartz wrote the principal songs and between 1914 and 1924, Sigmund Romberg was the main composer. But Romberg's forte was the operetta rather than the Broadway revue, and the strongest numbers heard in this production during those years came from pens other than his. The 1917 edition had "Goodbye, Broadway, Hello France" by Billy Baskette; that of 1918 boasted two all-time Tin Pan Alley favorites in "Smiles" by Lee G. Roberts and "I'm Forever Blowing Bubbles" by Jean Kenbrovin and John William Kellette. The last edition of *The Passing Show* was in 1924.

The plush revue was in its full glory in the 1920's. In 1919 George White presented the first of his *Scandals,* music by Richard A. Whiting. White continued to produce the *Scandals* on and off until 1939. Between 1920 and 1924, George Gershwin was its composer, an assignment in which he first realized his creative identity with "I'll Build a Stairway to Paradise" in 1922 and "Somebody Loves Me" in 1924. The most important songs from 1925 to 1928 came from the team of De Sylva, Brown, and Henderson, their best score coming in 1926 with "The Birth of the Blues," "Black Bottom," "The Girl Is You," and "Lucky Day."

The Shuberts put on several editions of the *Greenwich Village Follies* from 1919 to 1928, and of *Artists and Models* in 1930. A. Baldwin Sloane was the composer for the first two editions of the *Greenwich Village Follies,* having already long since acquired a place in the theatrical sun with his music for several outstanding extravaganzas, including *The Wizard of Oz* (1903). For the inaugural edition of the *Greenwich Village Follies* he wrote a hit song in "I Want a Daddy Who Will Rock Me to Sleep." Louis A. Hirsch wrote the music for the 1922 and 1923 editions, and Cole Porter (then still unknown) for 1924.

Jean Schwartz and Al Goodman collaborated on the music for the first edition of *Artists and Models* in 1923. For the songs of the next two editions, the Shuberts called on J. Fred Coots.

Between 1923 and 1940, Earl Carroll presented nine editions of the *Vanities,* the first of which had book, lyrics, and music by Carroll himself. Among those who wrote complete scores, or the basic part of the score, for later editions were Charles Gaskill in 1925, Morris Hamilton in 1926, and Jay Gorney in 1930. The music of other editions was made up of contributions by various composers, including Harold Arlen, Burton Lane, Richard Whiting, Peter de Rose, and Charles and Henry Tobias.

The Music Box Revue, produced by Sam H. Harris at the Music Box Theater between 1921 and 1924—with book, music, and lyrics by Irving Berlin—was among the most sophisticated and at the same time elaborate revues seen in the 1920's. Several of Irving Berlin's unforgettable songs were first heard here: "Everybody Step," "Say It with Music," "Pack Up Your Sins," "Crinoline Days," "The Waltz of Long Ago," "What'll I Do?" and "All Alone."

12—The Mighty Five

Between 1910 and 1930, five composers in Tin Pan Alley and on Broadway changed the destiny of American popular music— Irving Berlin, Jerome Kern, George Gershwin, Richard Rodgers, and Cole Porter. Each carried the hallmark of greatness and rose high above the prevailing standards, techniques, and purposes of our popular music to carry it towards new horizons. It is possible that the musical historian of the future, analyzing the evolution of American music, may point to these five men as the ones producing the backgrounds and traditions from which emerged a vibrant national art.

These five composers were not members of an integrated "school," in the sense that the members of the "Mighty Russian Five" had been in the nineteenth century. The Americans never formulated a single esthetic credo, nor did they ever try to integrate their respective efforts into a unified whole as Moussorgsky, Rimsky-Korsakov, Cui, Borodin, and Balakirev had done. But in certain other respects the similarity of the Americans to the Russians is more than skin-deep. In going to folk songs and dances for their material, the Russians were reaching to the popular music of their own people. In much the same way our popular idioms provided the tools for the Americans. In possessing great talent and inventiveness, the Russian Five was able to endow a popular style with esthetic significance; the same was true of the Americans. Finally, the five Americans, like the Russians, traveled in a single direction. Their goal was genuine national art that could be produced nowhere but in their own country.

With Berlin, Kern, Gershwin, Rodgers, and Porter came a completely new concept of individualized melody, a new technique in rhythm, and a personal approach to song-form and harmony. The emancipation of the popular song from the thirty-two-bar refrain and from tonic-dominant harmonies was at hand. That these composers could write the way they did after 1910 was due partly to their own inherent musical gifts, but it was also due in a large measure to shifting social forces. Up to 1900, the singing of popular songs had been an integral part of the country's social life. Thus the greatest single market for sheet music was the American family. Since the average member was musically unsophisticated, the songs had to be conventional and simple. After 1900, however, with the rapid development of stage entertainment, the vogue for parlor singing gave way to theater-going as a favorite form of amusement. If people continued singing songs, they did so more as a personal diversion than as a social or communal practice. Their musical satisfaction now came mainly from listening to songs rather than from singing them. Popular songs, now intended for trained performers rather than untrained amateurs, could afford a greater complexity of technique and a greater subtlety of idiom.

Though Jerome Kern's first song hit preceded that of Irving Berlin by several years, it was Berlin whose impact was first felt in Tin Pan Alley, an impact that shook its world to its very foundations.

Berlin, like so many other composers in Tin Pan Alley, had no musical training. Like them, he could play the piano only with a single finger. (Later he learned to play with all his fingers, but then only in a single key.) Like them, he could not read or write a note of music. But unlike the hacks of Tin Pan Alley he possessed genuine creative power, the gift of saying in music in a fresh, new way the things others had been saying for many years.

Irving Berlin (1888-   ) was born in Russia. As a boy he came with his family to New York, where he lived in extreme poverty. He sang popular songs and ballads in the streets and saloons of the Bowery. He also worked a a song plugger for the firm of Harry von Tilzer at Tony Pastor's Music Hall. While working as a singing waiter at Pelham's Café in the Bowery, in 1906, he wrote his first song—the lyric but not the music—"Marie from Sunny Italy," with music by the café pianist, M. Nicholson. Joseph W. Stern published it, and Berlin's income from this maiden effort was thirty-seven cents in royalties.

The well-beaten path of a song writer in the early 1900's usually stretched from the Bowery to Union Square. The latter was Berlin's next stop, first as a singing waiter at Jimmy Kelly's restaurant, then as a song plugger for Leo Feist, and finally as a lyricist for the publishing house of Ted Snyder. Berlin almost immediately became one of Tin Pan Alley's most successful lyricists. "Sadie Salome, Go Home," music by Edgar Leslie, sold over 200,000 copies in 1909. By 1910, Berlin had become so well known that the New York *Journal* asked him to write a set of parodies on one of his own lyrics, and J. J. Shubert contracted with him to appear in a Broadway revue, *Up and Down Broadway*, singing his own songs.

Accident led Berlin to write his first melody. In 1909, Berlin wrote for a vaudeville entertainer a lyric named "Dorando"— Dorando being an Italian marathon runner then much in the news because he had been disqualified in an Olympics race. When the entertainer failed to use this song in his act, Berlin tried selling his lyric to Ted Snyder, who offered to buy it for $25, but only if the lyric came equipped with a melody. Berlin immediately dictated a functional tune to an arranger, and Snyder published the song. This initial attempt at composition encouraged Berlin to write other melodies to his own lyrics, though for a while he did not altogether abandon the practice of preparing lyrics for other composers. In 1909 he produced "That Mesmerizing Mendelssohn Tune" (Mendelssohn's famous "Spring Song" in ragtime) and "Yiddle on Your Fiddle."

"Oh, That Beautiful Rag" and "That Opera Rag" in 1910 were among Berlin's earliest attempts at writing ragtime songs. In 1911, Berlin introduced still another ragtime song, which soon made him one of Tin Pan Alley's leading composers—"Alexander's Ragtime Band."

"Alexander's Ragtime Band" and some of the other ragtime songs that made Berlin a "king" of that popular style have already been discussed. We have pointed out that Berlin certainly did not create ragtime but that he did succeed in endowing it with such a personal manner of writing melody and rhythm that for a long time he was believed to have been the originator of that idiom. However, there can be no doubt that he, more than anyone else, helped make ragtime songs so popular in the 1910's.

Even while he was producing ragtime, Berlin was bringing a personal lyricism and a sincere sentiment to the writing of ballads. The sudden death of his first wife, Dorothy Goetz, in 1912 (soon after their honeymoon), made Berlin express his sorrow in the first of his unforgettable ballads, "When I Lost You." Again and again, later in life, Berlin would speak his most personal thoughts in the ballad form and thus create his greatest successes—"All By Myself" in 1921, "What'll I Do?" and "All Alone" in 1924, "Always" and "Remember" in 1925, "The Song Is Ended" in 1927, and "How Deep Is the Ocean?" in 1932.

During World War I, Berlin won considerable renown for *Yip, Yip, Yaphank,* the all-soldier revue which he wrote and produced and in which he starred. His stature in the world of music continued to grow after the war's end. In 1919 he founded his own publishing firm, soon to become one of the most prosperous in Tin Pan Alley. Between 1921 and 1924 he wrote book, lyrics, and music for four editions of the *Music Box Revue,* staged at the Music Box Theatre, of which he was part owner. In 1927 he wrote the music for the *Ziegfeld Follies,* in 1931 for *Face the Music,* a musical comedy with book by Moss Hart, and in 1933 for the brilliant topical revue, *As Thousands Cheer,* once again with Moss Hart's book. It was in this last-named production that one of the most successful numbers he ever wrote was introduced—"Easter Parade." The melody itself was of earlier vintage, written in 1917 for a lyric entitled "Smile and Show Your Dimple," but it was as a first-act finale for Marilyn Miller and Clifton Webb in *As Thousands Cheer* and under a new title and with a new lyric that it became a Berlin classic.

Meanwhile, in 1925 and 1926, the much-publicized and tempestuous courtship and marriage with Ellin Mackay, daughter of the head of Postal Telegraph, led him to write some of his most celebrated love ballads, including "Always" and "Remember."

Since 1933, Berlin has written music for the following Broadway productions: *Louisiana Purchase* (1940), *Annie Get Your Gun* (1946), *Miss Liberty* (1949), and *Call Me Madam* (1950). The best song from *Louisiana Purchase* was "It's a Lovely Day Tomorrow"; "Let's Take an Old-Fashioned Walk" came out of *Miss Liberty;* and "You're Just in Love" and "It's a Lovely Day Today," from *Call Me Madam.* The greatest box-office success of Berlin's career came with *Annie Get Your Gun,* starring Ethel Merman as Annie Oakley, which amassed a formidable Broadway run of over one thousand performances. Its score was also

Berlin's richest and most versatile, a veritable cornucopia of hit songs that included "They Say It's Wonderful," "The Girl That I Marry," "Doin' What Comes Natur'lly," "You Can't Get a Man with a Gun," and "Show Business."

Mention should be made of Irving Berlin's significant contributions to the war effort during World War II. Even before America became a participant in that titanic struggle against dictatorship, Berlin had helped voice our aroused national consciousness and strengthened faith in the democratic way of life of the late 1930's in a song that soon assumed the status of a second national anthem, "God Bless America." Actually, the song predated World War II by many years, the melody having originally been written for a finale in Yip, Yip, Yaphank. Then it was completely forgotten until 1938, when Kate Smith asked Berlin for a patriotic number for one of her broadcasts. Berlin retrieved his World War I melody and wrote new lyrics for it, and the song—now named "God Bless America"—was first heard on Kate Smith's radio program on Armistice Day, 1938. Its popularity spread like a wild fire, the original spark undoubtedly provided by Kate Smith herself in further broadcasts and on records. In 1940, both political parties featured the song at their presidential nominating conventions, and in 1954 it earned for Berlin a gold medal from President Eisenhower. Meanwhile, Berlin donated its royalties—in excess of $250,000—to the Boy Scouts, Girl Scouts, and Campfire Girls.

An even more formidable war contribution by Berlin came in the form of his second all-soldier show, This Is The Army. Recognizing the hunger of American soldiers for stage entertainment, Berlin prevailed on Army officials to permit him to put on a show similar to his Yip, Yip, Yaphank of World War I. As in the earlier production, Berlin wrote all the sketches as well as the songs, finding a rich cache of material at Camp Upton where he lived for an extended period to get first-hand experiences. This Is the Army opened on Broadway on July 4, 1942—with reflections—in songs, dances, production numbers, humor, and sentiment—of army life in World War II. There was also a poignant reminder of army life in 1917, for, with his flair for showmanship, Berlin revived from Yip, Yip, Yaphank "Oh, How I Hate to Get Up in the Morning," once again sung by Berlin himself, appearing in his old army uniform.

This Is the Army played for our armed forces in all the theaters of war around the globe; it was also made into a successful motion picture. All income—over ten million dollars—was turned over to various army relief funds. A grateful country rewarded Berlin for this giant project and achievement with the Medal of Merit, which he received from General Marshall after the show had its last performance, in Honolulu, on October 22, 1945.

Irving Berlin was also richly productive in Hollywood during the 1930's and 1940's. He wrote original screen scores for several delightful musicals with Fred Astaire and Ginger Rogers. "Cheek to Cheek" was written for one of these productions—*Top Hat* in 1935—and it earned an Academy Award for Berlin. Berlin received a second Academy Award in 1942 for "White Christmas," from *Holiday Inn* with Fred Astaire and Bing Crosby. "White Christmas" is now an American classic. It has sold over twenty million records and over four million copies of sheet music. A recent newspaper poll placed it second to only "Silent Night" as a Yuletide musical favorite.

Several Berlin screen musicals consisted mainly of cavalcades of his greatest songs of the past—*Alexander's Ragtime Band, Blue Skies,* and *Easter Parade.* Other motion pictures, also named after old Berlin songs, dipped into the past for their principal numbers. Nevertheless, in these and other pictures Berlin did not fail to write and introduce important new songs for Hollywood, such as "I'm Putting All My Eggs in One Basket" in *Follow the Fleet,* "The Night Is Filled with Music" in *Carefree,* "I've Got My Love to Keep Me Warm" in *On the Avenue,* "Count Your Blessings" in *White Christmas,* and "Sayonara," the theme song from the non-musical motion picture of the same name.

Like Berlin, Jerome Kern (1885-1945) graduated into the Broadway theater from Tin Pan Alley. He was born in New York City to a well-to-do family, and first studied the piano, then attended the New York College of Music. In 1902, he published his first piece of music, "At the Casino," for piano. One year later he went to Europe, where for several months he wrote songs for productions in London by the American producer, Charles Frohman. There to lyrics by young P. G. Wodehouse, he achieved a decided hit with "Mr. Chamberlain," a topical song introduced in *The School Girl.*

Back in the United States in 1904, Kern found employment in several Tin Pan Alley houses as song plugger and staff pianist. In 1905, he was hired by Max Dreyfus of Harms to sell sheet music and demonstrate Harms songs in five-and-ten-cent stores. All this time Kern was writing songs. His first Broadway assignment was, in 1904, to adapt for the American stage the score of an English operetta, *Mr. Wix of Wickham*. A year later he scored a decisive success with "How'd You Like to Spoon with Me?", introduced in *The Earl and the Girl*. Harms published the song, beginning a composer-publisher relationship that continued until Kern's death.

Between 1904 and 1912, Kern interpolated about a hundred songs in approximately thirty Broadway musical productions. His first complete original score was *The Red Petticoat* in 1912, and his first Broadway success came with *The Girl from Utah*, in 1914. When Victor Herbert heard Kern's score for the latter production at the office of Harms, he remarked simply: "This man will inherit my mantle." Its most significant song was "They Didn't Believe Me," with lyrics by Herbert Reynolds.

After 1914 Kern was continually to tap a seemingly inexhaustible vein of wonderful melodies and flooded the Broadway stage with songs whose charm, spontaneity, and enchantment made them milestones in American popular music. Even when he utilized the basic and at times elementary structures and techniques of Tin Pan Alley, Kern was able to develop a manner of writing all his own through a fluid and graceful flow of melody and a most fastidious workmanship.

Even greater than his significance as a writer of popular songs is Kern's contribution to the American musical stage. As a composer, Kern was involved in two revolutions, whose impact on the development of American musical comedy can hardly be overestimated. The first took place between 1915 and 1918 with the *Princess Theatre Shows,* named after the theater in which they were given. Originally with the collaboration of only Guy Bolton, librettist and lyricist, and later with Bolton and P. G. Wodehouse providing the texts and lyrics, Kern wrote four musicals which introduced into the theater a new note of informality, sophistication, wit, and intimacy: *Nobody Home* (1915), *Very Good, Eddie* (1915), *Oh, Boy!* (1917), and *Oh, Lady! Lady!* (1918). *Very Good, Eddie* and *Oh, Boy!* were box-office triumphs, each with a run of over a year. For all four plays Kern contributed songs in the gay and cultured spirit of the texts. The best of these were "The Magic Melody" and "You Know and I Know," from *Nobody Home*, "Babes in the Wood" and "Nodding Roses," from *Very Good, Eddie*; "Till the Clouds Roll By" (later used as the title for Kern's screen biography), from *Oh, Boy!*, and the title song and "Before I Met You," from *Oh, Lady! Lady!*

The second time Kern helped change the destiny of the musical theater was with *Show Boat*, now an American stage classic. This production was an even more significant departure from the norm in the musical theater than the *Princess Theatre Shows* had been. Edna Ferber's novel about life on a Mississippi River show boat—and the period in which that story was set—was hardly material for musical comedy as musical-comedy material was evaluated in the 1920's. Nevertheless, Kern saw in it the basis of a new kind of musical production that placed emphasis not on chorus girls, routine situations, stock characters, or big production numbers, but on authentic backgrounds, strong characterization, and human values. With Oscar Hammerstein II adapting Ferber's novel into a libretto and providing the lyrics, *Show Boat* opened in a lavish Ziegfeld production on December 27, 1927, and made history. Robert Garland called it a "masterpiece"; Richard Watts, Jr., called it "a beautiful example of musical comedy." *Show Boat* remained on Broadway for its initial run over a year, then toured the country. Since then *Show Boat* has been frequently revived throughout the United States, and on three occasions it has been adapted for motion pictures.

Kern's score—the freshest and the most varied of his career—was unquestionably the strong suit of the play. Its principal numbers were "Ol' Man River," now often placed in the category of American folk music, "Why Do I Love You?", "Make Believe," "Can't Help Lovin' Dat Man," and "Bill." The last of these had lyrics not by Hammerstein but by P. G. Wodehouse, and is the only song not originally planned for *Show Boat*. Kern and Wodehouse had written "Bill" for a *Princess Theatre Show*, from which it was eliminated to remain in Kern's trunk until he lifted it out in 1927 for Helen Morgan, a star in *Show Boat*.

Both before and after *Show Boat*, Kern composed a considerable amount of music for productions more traditional in intent and style than either the *Princess Theatre Shows* or *Show Boat*.

In 1917, with Bolton and Wodehouse he wrote *Leave It to Jane,* based on a college town play by George Ade. It was successfully revived in 1959 in an off-Broadway production. *Sally* (1920) was a major Ziegfeld production, starring Marilyn Miller, for whom Kern conceived one of his immortal melodies, "Look for the Silver Lining," with lyrics by Clifford Grey. Also in a formal pattern were *Stepping Stones* (1923) starring Fred Stone, his wife, and his daughter; *Sunny* (1925), once again with Marilyn Miller, who helped make the song "Who?" an outstanding attraction; *Sweet Adeline* (1929), in which Helen Morgan sang "Why Was I Born?" and "Here Am I," lyrics by Oscar Hammerstein II; and *Roberta* (1933), whose great success was largely due to the triumph of its main ballad, "Smoke Gets in Your Eyes," lyrics by Otto Harbach.

But Kern did not abandon experiment. After *Show Boat,* in two musicals he made a determined effort to use fresh books, to treat settings and characterizations with consistency and credibility, and to create a strong integration between book and music. One was *The Cat and the Fiddle* (1931), whose principal songs were "The Night Was Made for Love," and "She Didn't Say Yes." The other was *Music in the Air* (1932), book and lyrics by Oscar Hammerstein II, whose score included German beer-hall songs, imitations of German folk music, and such American delights as "I've Told Every Little Star" and "The Song Is You."

Kern's last Broadway musical comedy was *Very Warm for May* (1939), a dismal failure that would long ago have been completely forgotten but for the fact that it included one of Kern's most beautiful songs, "All the Things You Are," lyrics by Hammerstein. After 1939, Kern confined his creative activity to motion pictures. On two occasions he won Academy Awards—in 1936 for "The Way You Look Tonight" from *Swingtime,* a Fred Astaire-Ginger Rogers musical, and again in 1941 for "The Last Time I Saw Paris," a song he had written with Oscar Hammerstein II as an independent number but which was interpolated into the motion picture, *Lady Be Good.* Other outstanding Kern songs for the movies included "Dearly Beloved," with lyrics by Johnny Mercer, from *You Were Never Lovelier,* "Long Ago and Far Away," lyrics by Ira Gershwin, from *Cover Girl,* and "All Through the Day," lyrics by Hammerstein, from *Centennial Summer.*

Kern had come to New York in 1945 to supervise a revival of *Show Boat* when he collapsed on a New York City street. He died a few days later without regaining consciousness.

George Gershwin (1898-1937) received his first creative stimulation from the songs of Irving Berlin and Jerome Kern. No sooner had the boy Gershwin acquired a facility at the piano than he began playing "Alexander's Ragtime Band" and other Berlin ragtime numbers. Somewhat later, at an aunt's wedding, Gershwin heard two Kern songs for the first time—"They Didn't Believe Me" and "You're Here and I'm Here." From that moment he used Kern as a model and an inspiration.

Gershwin was born in Brooklyn, New York, but most of his boyhood was spent in the streets of the Lower East Side of New York City. Several early musical experiences suggested a deep but latent love for music. One was the hearing of Rubinstein's "Melody in F" in a penny arcade, music that held him rooted to the ground. Another was the sound of real jazz from an open window of a Harlem night club. A third was a violin performance in the school auditorium by one of his schoolmates, Max Rosenzweig, who later as Max Rosen became famous as a virtuoso.

A piano came into the Gershwin household when George was twelve, and he was a slave to the keyboard from the outset. In 1912, he acquired an important teacher in Charles Hambitzer, who gave him a thorough grounding in the classics as well as an initiation into the music of some of the moderns. Hambitzer transformed the young Gershwin from a not too well informed music lover into a musician. Despite his growing appreciation of the classics, however, Gershwin did not lose his interest or faith in popular music. He continually tried to convince Hambitzer that American popular music and jazz were good music, that if the full resources of the classics were applied to our popular styles and idioms the result could very well be a vital, native art. "That boy is a genius," Hambitzer wrote to a sister, "but he wants to go in for this modern stuff, jazz or what not." Hambitzer did not discourage him from this direction, but he did intend to see to it that Gershwin first received a thorough training. For this purpose he persuaded Gershwin to take lessons in harmony, counterpoint, and orchestration with Edward Kilenyi.

When he was fifteen, Gershwin found a job as staff pianist

and song plugger for Remick's in Tin Pan Alley. In 1916, "When You Want 'Em, You Can't Get 'Em" became his first published composition; and in the same year his "The Making of a Girl" became the first of his songs to appear in the Broadway theater, in *The Passing Show of 1916*. In 1918, Nora Bayes sang his "Some Wonderful Sort of Someone" in one of her musicals. A year later Gershwin's first Broadway musical comedy, *La, La, Lucille,* was produced, and one of his songs, "Swanee," was made into a smash hit by Al Jolson.

Between 1920 and 1925, Gershwin wrote the music for five editions of George White's *Scandals,* and it was in several songs for this revue, notably "I'll Build a Stairway to Paradise" and "Somebody Loves Me," that his creative identity first asserted itself—in its remarkable virtuosity of rhythm and meter and in its use of novel harmonic colors. It was also for this revue that Gershwin made his first experiment in writing popular music in a form more ambitious than the popular song—the one-act jazz opera, *135th Street.*

Already several serious musicians were becoming aware of his immense gifts and promise. In 1922, Beryl Rubinstein, celebrated concert pianist and teacher, told a newspaper interviewer that in his opinion Gershwin "has the spark of musical genius." One year later Eva Gauthier, the distinguished concert singer, presented a serious recital in Aeolian Hall, New York, which included several Gershwin songs, and Gershwin appeared as the piano accompanist for the group of popular songs in the program. H. T. Parker, the Boston music critic, wrote: "He is the beginning of the age of sophisticated jazz."

Their faith in Gershwin became justified on February 12, 1924, when Paul Whiteman and his orchestra presented the world première of Gershwin's first large concert work, *Rhapsody in Blue,* which Whiteman had commissioned for his concert at Aeolian Hall. *The Rhapsody in Blue* made Gershwin world-famous and wealthy, and it pointed up for the first time his significance as a composer of serious music.

From 1924 until the end of his life, Gershwin followed two paths. One was that of serious concert music, about which much more will be said in a later chapter; the other was that of popular music. While rapidly rising to a place of significance among American serious composers, Gershwin did not desert the Broadway theater. He created the music for many outstanding stage successes. *Lady Be Good* (1924), starring Fred and Adele Astaire, had a remarkable score whose major items were the title song, "Fascinating Rhythm," and "So Am I." This musical is also important as the first for which George's brother, Ira, provided all the lyrics, although he and George had previously worked together on random songs, beginning with "The Real American Folk Song" in 1918. Henceforth, Ira Gershwin was to provide George's music with skillful, nimble, and sophisticated lyrics.

Tip-Toes (1925) had for its main songs "That Certain Feeling," "Sweet and Low-Down," and "Looking for a Boy." *Oh, Kay!* (1926) starred Gertrude Lawrence in her first American musical comedy. She sang one of Gershwin's most famous ballads, "Someone to Watch Over Me," in a score that also included "Do, Do, Do," "Clap Yo' Hands," and "Maybe." *Funny Face* (1927) profited from an outstanding song in "'S Wonderful." *Girl Crazy* (1930), introduced Ethel Merman to the Broadway stage in such remarkable Gershwin numbers as "I Got Rhythm," "Sam and Delilah," and "Boy, What Love Has Done to Me." A fourth Gershwin song, "Embraceable You," was sung by Ginger Rogers in what was also her Broadway debut in a principal role.

All the above mentioned musical comedies—and several not mentioned because they were failures—were traditional in content and technique. Nothing in text or production procedures pointed to a new kind of theater in the way *Show Boat* did, and their only value came from Gershwin's music.

In two Gershwin musicals, however, a new concept was explored. *Strike Up the Band* (1930), had a book by George S. Kaufman and Morrie Ryskind and lyrics by Ira Gershwin. Here was a musical comedy with a message! For *Strike Up the Band* was a satire on war and Babbittry, on big business and on international diplomacy. Gershwin's music was as trenchant as many of Kaufman's lines and Ira Gershwin's lyrics, particularly the title song (a pompous march) and a less familiar excerpt with ironic overtones, "Entrance of the Swiss Army." The scope of Gershwin's music was extended through the use of protracted choral and orchestral sequences and the interpolation of many subtle and deft touches in tonality, harmony, and orchestral color to underscore a piece of stage business or comment on some amusing episode. In the poignant ballad, "Soon," Gershwin also demonstrated that he had not forgotten how to write a memorable melody.

In 1931, the Gershwin-Ryskin-Kaufman combination presented Broadway with an even more devastating satire. *Of Thee I Sing* laughed at the foibles of Washington politics, carrying its malice to a political campaign, the White House, the Supreme Court, and the Senate. For this unorthodox text—and to some of the most scintillating lyrics of Ira Gershwin's career—George Gershwin produced his richest and most ambitious music for the popular theater. The score had hit songs in "Love Is Sweeping the Country" and in the title song, but it had much more. There were brilliant satirical numbers in the style Gershwin had uncovered in *Strike Up the Band,* in "Wintergreen for President," "I'm About to Be a Mother," and "Garçon, s'il vous plaît." The score also boasted recitatives, recitatives combined with melodies, extended choral passages, and extended instrumental sequences, all of them serving the text by accenting a mood, underlining a situation, or emphasizing an episode. Such a happy union of words and music led George Jean Nathan to describe *Of Thee I Sing* as "a landmark in American satirical musical comedy" and encouraged H. T. Parker to consider it "one of the drollest musical operettas of all time." *Of Thee I Sing* became the first musical comedy to win the Pulitzer Prize for drama.

Of Thee I Sing was Gershwin's last success on Broadway. After that came *Let 'Em Eat Cake* (1933), a sequel to *Of Thee I Sing,* with all the contrivances and disappointments that usually attend sequels. Though decidedly third-rate, *Let 'Em Eat Cake* had an asset in the song "Mine," in which delightful use is made of a choral aside sung contrapuntally to the main melody. *Pardon My English* (1933) was an even greater failure. These were Gershwin's last musical comedies for the stage. His last Broadway musical production was the folk opera, *Porgy and Bess,* in 1935.

Although *Porgy and Bess* is an opera—since it has no spoken dialogue and since its ambitious vocal and orchestral writing is in the operatic tradition—its roots reach deeply into the soil of American popular music. In fact, as this writer remarked in *A Journey to Greatness,* a biography of George Gershwin,* *Porgy and Bess* was the climactic point of the composer's career since

---

* David Ewen, *A Journey to Greatness: The Life and Music of George Gershwin* (New York: Henry Holt & Co., 1956).

it was the meeting point for the two paths in music—the serious and the popular—that he had been pursuing all his life. "The serious musician is found at his best in the musical distinguished tone-speech, in the powerful antiphonal choruses, in the expressive dissonances and chromaticisms, in the brilliant orchestration, in the effective atmospheric writing, in the skillful use of counterpoint in the duets and particularly in the last-scene trio. The popular composer emerges in the jazz background of several choruses like that in Act II, scene 1, 'Woman to Lady'; in the two songs of Sportin' Life, 'It Ain't Necessarily So,' and 'There's a Boat That's Leavin' Soon for New York'; and in Crown's sacrilegious blues ditty, 'A Red-Headed Woman Makes a Choochoo Jump Its Track.' Yet there is no feeling of contradiction, no sense of incongruity, in this mingling of the serious and popular, for the popular is as basic to Gershwin's design as the serious, with its own specific artistic function."

In our discussion of Gershwin's outstanding stage songs, "The Man I Love," has thus far not been mentioned, for the good reason that, though it had been intended for the opening scene of *Lady Be Good,* it was deleted when it was thought that it would slow up the action. After that, Gershwin tried using it in *Strike Up the Band* and once again shelved it. "The Man I Love", published as an independent number, first became famous in London after it was introduced there by the Berkeley Square Orchestra. Only after being a hit in England did the song return to America to become a staple in the repertory of jazz ensembles and blues singers.

After 1935, Gershwin lived and worked in Hollywood. This was not his first direct association with motion pictures. In 1931, he had come to Hollywood to write the score for *Delicious*, a screen musical starring Janet Gaynor. He wrote four songs, a dream sequence for voice and orchestra, and a six-minute orchestral episode describing the sounds and movements of a city. When only one of the six minutes of this last episode was used for the motion picture, Gershwin expanded the remaining musical material into a symphonic work, the *Second Rhapsody.*

Between 1935 and 1937, Gershwin wrote the music for *Shall We Dance?* a musical starring Fred Astaire and Ginger Rogers, *Damsel in Distress*, and *The Goldwyn Follies*—their principal songs being "Let's Call the Whole Thing Off," "They Can't Take

That Away from Me," "A Foggy Day," "Nice Work, If You Can Get It," "Love Walked In," and "Love Is Here to Stay." He was at work on *The Goldwyn Follies* when he collapsed. He died in a hospital following an operation for a brain tumor.

Even after his death, screen musicals with Gershwin's music continued to be produced. In 1945, Gershwin's screen biography, *Rhapsody in Blue*, was released, a sentimentalized story made memorable by Gershwin's greatest songs and concert works. *The Shocking Miss Pilgrim*, in 1947, derived its all-Gershwin score from manuscripts never before used, adapted by Kay Swift. One of these songs proved a discovery, "For You, For Me, For Evermore." *An American in Paris*, named after Gershwin's symphonic poem of the same name, used not merely the music of that composition, but also several old Gershwin songs. It received the 1951 Academy Award as the best motion picture of the year. In 1959, the Samuel Goldwyn motion-picture production of Gershwin's opera, *Porgy and Bess*, opened in major cities throughout the country.

Richard Rodgers was born in 1902 near Arverne, Long Island, the son of a successful physician. Rodgers has said that he cannot remember the time when he did not want to be a composer. He started picking out melodies on the piano when he was four, at six he began attending the Broadway theater, and at nine he attempted writing songs. When he was still a boy, he saw one of Kern's Broadway shows for the first time. Kern's songs proved a revelation. "The influence of the hero on such a hero-worshiper is not easy to calculate," Rodgers has written, "but it was a deep and lasting one. His less successful musical comedies were no less important to a listener of thirteen or fourteen. A large part of one winter most of my allowance was spent for a seat in the balcony listening to *Love o' Mike*." As a result of this stimulation, in his fifteenth year he wrote the score for an amateur production put on by a boys' athletic club at the Hotel Plaza in New York, the first of several scores he was to write for various amateur groups. In 1919, after acquiring a permanent lyricist in Lorenz Hart, he had his first song placed in a Broadway musical; it was "Any Old Place with You" in *A Lonely Romeo*. In the fall of that same year he entered Columbia College where, during his freshman year, he collaborated with Hart in writing the varsity show—the first time the work of a freshman had been accepted. Some of the songs for this production, and several new ones, were used in Rodgers' first Broadway score, *Poor Little Ritz Girl,* which opened in July, 1920.

During the next few years, Rodgers continued writing songs to Hart's lyrics for various amateur shows, none able to win the interest of either publishers or Broadway producers. Meanwhile Rodgers extended his own musical horizon by attending the Institute of Musical Art for about two years.

Success as a composer of popular music came to Rodgers in 1925 with "Manhattan" and a few other numbers for *The Garrick Gaieties,* a smart, intimate revue produced by several junior members of the Theater Guild. Later that fall, Rodgers and Hart had a second substantial success with *Dearest Enemy,* a musical comedy based on a historical episode of the Revolutionary War.

The book of *Dearest Enemy* was by Herbert Fields, and the triumvirate of Fields, Lorenz Hart, and Richard Rodgers dominated the American musical stage for the next half dozen years. Several of their musicals not only were resounding box-office successes but also helped open new channels for American musical comedy through their use of fresh, original subjects for texts, sparkling and sophisticated lyrics prepared with a virtuoso skill in versification, and music that continually tapped new veins of lyricism and sentiment. *Peggy-Ann* (1926) was the first Broadway musical to use Freudian and psychoanalytical ideas during the progress of a dream fantasy. *A Connecticut Yankee* (1927) went for its subject to Mark Twain. *Chee-Chee* (1928), an Oriental fantasy, was an early Broadway experiment in the integration of music and text. *America's Sweetheart* (1931) was a brilliant satire on Hollywood. For these and other less successful musicals Rodgers provided a rich and varied succession of song hits, whose strong musical and emotional appeal has by no means diminished with the passing years—"Here in My Arms" in *Dearest Enemy,* "Mountain Greenery" in the second *Garrick Gaieties* (1926), "The Blue Room" in *The Girl Friend,* "My Heart Stood Still" in *A Connecticut Yankee,* "You Took Advantage of Me" in *Present Arms* (1928), the title song and "With a Song in My Heart" in *Spring Is Here* (1929), "Ten Cents a Dance" in *Simple Simon* (1930), and "I've Got Five Dollars" in *America's Sweetheart.*

Between 1931 and 1935, Rodgers and Hart wrote songs for motion pictures in Hollywood, their most significant score being that for *Love Me Tonight* (1932), starring Maurice Chevalier—its main numbers being "Mimi," "Isn't It Romantic?" and "Lover."

They were back on Broadway with *Jumbo* (1935), an elaborate Hippodrome Theatre production combining extravaganza, circus, and musical comedy. Some of the songs from this play are among the most beautiful Rodgers and Hart had written up to that time —"The Most Beautiful Girl in the World," "My Romance," and "Little Girl Blue."

The pair now remained on Broadway until they broke up their partnership, proving increasingly daring in the kind of materials with which they dealt. *On Your Toes* (1936)—the first comedy for which Rodgers and Hart not only wrote the lyrics and music but also helped write the text—reached out to the world of ballet, a new field for musical comedy. Ambitious ballet sequences created by George Balanchine were used as basic elements of the plot. "Slaughter on Tenth Avenue," one of these ballets, represented Rodgers' first successful attempt at writing jazz in a large symphonic form, and it has remained a classic in jazz-symphonic literature. *On Your Toes* also contained a remarkable song in "There's a Small Hotel." *Babes in Arms* (1937)—book as well as songs by Rodgers and Hart—was a conscious attempts to make every song a "plot number," that is, a number that grew inevitably from the plot of the play. Each song contributed strongly to the action and had a specific function in the story. The best were "Where or When?", "My Funny Valentine," "The Lady Is a Tramp," and "Johnny One Note."

I'd Rather Be Right (1937) pointed up the foibles and inconsistencies of political life in Washington in a play by George S Kaufman and Moss Hart, one of the characters being President Franklin D. Roosevelt, memorably portrayed by George M Cohan. *I Married an Angel* (1938), a fantasy, returned to the ballet world, in which the episodes starring Vera Zorina revealed an ever increasing spaciousness in Rodgers' musical writing, and *The Boys from Syracuse* (1938) was the first effort to adapt Shakespeare to the modern popular musical stage. The title song of *I Married an Angel* and "Falling in Love with Love" from *The Boys from Syracuse* were some of the unforgettable Rodgers songs from these productions.

Perhaps Rodgers and Hart's most courageous effort to side-step the traditional and the expected in musical comedy and to place musical comedy on an adult level came with *Pal Joey* (1940), based on stories by John O'Hara. The principal characters were scoundrels whose daily operations included blackmail, illicit love, double-dealing, and various other discreditable exploits. Never before had musical comedy dealt with such disagreeable people and involved them in so many offensive actions. Out of this healthy realism came two gems—"I Could Write a Book" and "Bewitched, Bothered and Bewildered."

The collaboration of Rodgers and Hart, which had lasted almost a quarter of a century, ended with *By Jupiter* and a revival of *A Connecticut Yankee*, the former in 1942, the latter in 1943. That of Rodgers and Hammerstein—Oscar Hammerstein II, already one of the musical theater's most distinguished librettists and lyricists —began in 1943 with the epoch-making production, *Oklahoma!* This was an eloquent folk play with music, adapted from a Theater Guild drama by Lynn Riggs, *Green Grow the Lilacs,* a presentation in which old formulas had to be abandoned and original approaches had to be continually sought out. Music, comedy, and production numbers were made basic to the play. In place of the stereotype boy-meets-girl formula, *Oklahoma!* exploited a vital Western folk drama rich in dramatic conflict. Formal dance routines gave way to extended ballets of American identity with choreography by Agnes de Mille. Traditional chorus-girl scenes were dispensed with. (No chorus girls appeared on the stage until midway in the first act.) The music was spread on an ambitious canvas. Besides thirteen principal numbers and ballet sequences, the score included orchestral fragments serving for background to dialogue or for graceful transitions.

It is now a part of theater lore that almost everyone concerned with *Oklahoma!*—with the exception of Rodgers—thought that the play was too highbrow for the musical-comedy clientele and would be a box-office disaster. These skeptics were confounded by one of the greatest triumphs in the history of the theater. Opening in 1943, it was described by the major critics as a "folk opera," "beautiful . . . delightful . . . fresh . . . imaginative," "different—beautifully different." In New York it enjoyed a run of five years with a box-office gross of seven million dollars, both without precedent. A national company toured for ten years, and the original New York company played seventy cities in fifty-one weeks. It was seen in London (where it had the longest run of any production in the almost three-hundred-year history of the Drury Lane Theater), Berlin, Paris, South Africa, Scandinavia, Australia, and other foreign places. It became the first musical whose entire musical score was recorded, initiating a practice that has since become standard in the recording industry. The original investment in the play yielded a profit of over five million dollars, returning to each investor more than $50,000 for each $1,500 invested.

Rodgers revealed altogether new dimensions in his writing. With his lifelong resiliency he adapted himself to the new demands of a folk drama by creating music with the overtones of a folk art. "Oh, What a Beautiful Mornin'," with which the play opened (sung offstage) had the simplicity, spontaneity, directness, and earthiness of a genuine folk ballad. "The Surrey with the Fringe on Top," "The Farmer and the Cowman," and "Kansas City" were other songs with a distinct Western personality. Only the main love duet, "People Will Say We're in Love," can be described as characteristically musical-comedy. But even here—as in other traditional numbers like "Out of My Dreams" and "Many a New Day,"—Rodgers' lyricism is touched with a new kind of enchantment.

Oklahoma! is one of the few American musical stage productions where the description "masterwork" is not misplaced. The same is true of three subsequent musical plays by Rodgers and Hammerstein—*Carousel* (1945), *South Pacific* (1949), and *The King and I* (1951). Ever richer and deeper grows Rodgers' music to match the glow, warmth, humanity, and simplicity of Hammerstein's dialogue and lyrics. Ever more penetrating grows their insight into character, ever more subtle their delineation of mood and atmosphere.

Carousel was an adaptation of Ferenc Molnar's play *Liliom*, with basic changes of story and a shift of setting from Budapest to the New England of 1873. It opens musically with a waltz prelude of symphonic dimensions, and a vocal highlight of the score is an expansive narrative, "Soliloquy," in which the popular song breaks through all restrictions to assume the ample structure and varying style of the German *Lied*. A spiritual, religious feeling is present in a song like "You'll Never Walk Alone," and a heightened expressiveness can be noted in songs like "If I Loved You," "June Is Bustin' Out All Over," and "What's the Use of Wond'rin'?"

With *South Pacific*, Rodgers and Hammerstein achieved another artistic and box-office triumph of the magnitude of *Oklahoma!* This was an adaptation by Hammerstein and Joshua Logan of James A. Michener's Pulitzer Prize winning stories of World War II. A practice which Rodgers had begun in *Oklahoma!* and continued with *Carousel* became normal procedure. Numerous orchestral passages and interludes helped underscore the dramatic action, provide an emotional base for some of the dialogue, introduce a character, set a mood, or comment upon something that has happened or is about to happen. Rodgers went even further in making music an inextricable part of the dramatic action. His songs penetrated deeply into the inmost personalities and emotions of his characters, more so than heretofore—"A Cockeyed Optimist," "I'm in Love with a Wonderful Guy," and "I'm Gonna Wash That Man Right outa My Hair," for the girlish, exuberant heroine Nellie Forbush, magnificently played by Mary Martin; "Bali Ha'i" and "Happy Talk" for the matronly Tokinese, Bloody Mary; "Younger than Springtime" for the romantic Lieutenant Cable; "Some Enchanted Evening" and "This Nearly Was Mine" for the wise, mature, and debonair hero, De Becque, a role portrayed by Ezio Pinza.

The King and I was based on Margaret Landon's novel, *Anna and the King of Siam*, which had already been made into an impressive motion picture. The exotic setting of Siam and a cast of characters consisting mostly of Orientals seemed hardly the materials for a Broadway musical; nor was the plot, in which there was almost no love interest between the two principals, calculated to win audiences. Yet *The King and I*—with Gertrude Lawrence and Yul Brynner—proved a spellbinding experience, "a flowering of all the arts of the theater," as Danton Walker described it.

Music and dance proved vital in projecting the story. Without directly attempting to imitate Oriental music, Rodgers often flavored his score with delicate Oriental spices, both in the melodic structure and in the harmonic and instrumental coloration. The march of the royal Siamese children, "My Lord and Master," and the king's expansive narrative, "A Puzzlement," are cases in point. So is the music of the ballet, "The Small House of Uncle

Thomas," in which Jerome Robbins' choreography retells the story of *Uncle Tom's Cabin* in terms of a Siamese dance, in which Rodgers utilized only percussive effects by ancient cymbals and wood block as the background to a spoken chorus. The exquisitely sensitive mood and atmosphere maintained in this ballet are found throughout the play, continually caught and held in compelling songs, of which the most significant are "Hello, Young Lovers," "Getting to Know You," "I Have Dreamed," and "Shall We Dance?"

There are numerous rewarding musical episodes even in the Rodger and Hammerstein plays of lesser consequence than those already discussed. Out of *Allegro* (1947)—an absorbing though not always successful experiment in telling the biography of a doctor through lights, colors, and dance, as well as through dialogue, lyrics, and music—came "A Fellow Needs a Girl" and "The Gentleman Is a Dope." *Me and Juliet* (1953) produced an excellent musical narrative in "The Big, Black Giant" and a hit song in "No Other Love," the latter a tango melody that Rodgers had previously used for the music to a documentary film, *Victory at Sea*. *Pipe Dream* (1955) was the source of one of Rodgers' best inspirational numbers, "Everybody's Got a Home but Me" and a fine love song, "All at Once You Love Her." *The Flower Drum Song* (1958) boasted a sure-fire winner in "I Enjoy Being a Girl" and two lesser delights in "Love, Look Away" and "You Are Beautiful." *The Sound of Music* (1959)—whose setting was Austria and whose main characters were the Trapp Family Singers—brought a new exalted inspirational number in "Climb Every Mountain" and such joyous musical experiences as "Do Re Mi," "My Favorite Things," and the title song. As it turned out, *The Sound of Music* was destined to be the last of the Rodgers and Hammerstein musicals, for Hammerstein died in August, 1960.

Rodgers and Hammerstein wrote only one original score for motion pictures, *State Fair* (1945), including "It Might as Well Be Spring," which won the Academy Award. The score included a second remarkable song in "It's a Grand Night for Singing." (A screen remake of *State Fair,* in 1960, called for a few new musical numbers, and, since Hammerstein was no longer alive, Rodgers decided to be his own lyricist for the first time.) For television, Rodgers and Hammerstein wrote *Cinderella* (1957), starring Julie Andrews, who charmingly delivered "In My Own

Little Corner" and collaborated in the rendition of "Do I Love You?" Also for television—but this time without the assistance of Hammerstein—Rodgers wrote the music for a series of documentary films about naval operations in World War II entitled *Victory at Sea*. For this series he produced thirteen hours of accompanying music, the best sections of which were gathered by Robert Russell Bennett into a nine-movement suite for symphony orchestra. In 1960 Rodgers completed another ambitious musical-background score for a television series, this time one based on the war memoirs of Winston Churchill—*Winston Churchill: The Valiant Years*, spanning the years from the close of World War I to the aftermath of World War II and consisting of twenty-six chapters.

Cole Porter (1893—   ) did not come out of Tin Pan Alley. Like that of Richard Rodgers, his song writing career was born, nurtured, and carried to maturity in the Broadway theater. He was born to wealth in Peru, Indiana, and music played a significant role in his boyhood. He started studying the violin when he was six and the piano two years later. At ten he wrote an operetta, and at eleven he had one of his piano pieces published. His academic education, however, was not neglected. After being graduated from the Worcester Academy in Massachusetts, he entered Yale, where he continued his musical activity by writing football songs (two became famous, "Yale Bull-Dog Song" and "Bingo Eli Yale"), directing the glee club, and helping write and produce college shows. Upon receiving his degree from Yale he went on to Harvard to attend Law School, but after a year he changed his mind and decided to concentrate on music and transferred to the Harvard School of Music.

His first Broadway musical comedy, *See America First* (1916), was a fiasco. Porter temporarily abandoned music to join the French desert troops in North Africa. When the United States entered World War I, Porter was transferred to the French Officers School in Fontainebleau, after which he was assigned to teach American soldiers French gunnery. While fulfilling his military duties, he occupied a luxurious apartment in Paris, the scene of lavish parties continually enlivened by his performances of his own sophisticated songs.

Immediately after the war, while on a visit to the United States, he was commissioned by Raymond Hitchcock to write several numbers for the revue *Hitchy-Koo,* which Hitchcock was then producing annually on Broadway. Porter contributed twelve songs to the *Hitchy-Koo of 1919,* one, "An Old Fashioned Garden," of more than passing interest.

Still maintaining his elaborate establishment in Paris and occasionally renting a palace in Venice, Porter continued his musical diversions while leading the gay life of a wealthy dilettante. He managed to study composition for a time at the Schola Cantorum with Vincent d'Indy, and he kept on writing both the lyrics and the music for popular songs.

He again had a try at Broadway in 1924 with five songs for the *Greenwich Village Follies,* and once again he failed completely to attract attention. His friends insisted that both as lyricist and composer he was much too smart, unconventional, and debonair to enjoy a widespread reputation. "But one day," Elsa Maxwell told him prophetically, "you will haul the public up to your own level, and then the world will be yours."

The first time he made any kind of an impression on theater audiences was in *Paris* (1928), starring Irene Bordoni. Two of his songs for this musical had the smart pose and impudent manner that would henceforth identify so much of his writing—"Let's Do It," and "Two Little Babes in the Wood." In 1929, he wrote the music for *Fifty Million Frenchmen,* his breezy songs including "You've Got That Thing," "You Do Something to Me," and "Find Me a Primitive Man." In 1930, "What Is This Thing Called Love?" was introduced in *Wake Up and Dream.*

He had by now established his identity both as a composer and as a lyricist. As composer he was best in sweeping, sensual, often Slavic-style melodies in a minor key, carried to exciting climaxes and set against a throbbing rhythm. As a lyricist he distinguished himself for his provocative and suggestive verses filled with all kinds of sophisticated allusions and molded with the greatest technical skill.

From 1930 on, Cole Porter was one of Broadway's ace composer-lyricists. His greatest successes came with *The Gay Divorce* (1932), starring Fred Astaire, in which Porter's classic, "Night and Day," was introduced; *Anything Goes* (1934), with Ethel Merman, William Gaxton, and Victor Moore, its brilliant score including "Blow Gabriel, Blow," "You're the Top," and "I Get a Kick

Out of You"; *Leave It to Me* (1938), a satire on the Soviet Union and a hapless American ambassador portrayed by Victor Moore, in which Mary Martin made her unforgettable stage debut singing "My Heart Belongs to Daddy"; *Du Barry Was a Lady* (1939), *Panama Hattie* (1940), and *Something for the Boys* (1943), all three starring Ethel Merman; *Let's Face It* (1941), with Danny Kaye; *Mexican Hayride* (1944) for which Porter wrote "I Love You"; *Kiss Me Kate* (1948), which will be discussed in a separate paragraph; *Can-Can* (1953), memorable for "I Love Paris," "It's All Right With Me," and "C'est magnifique"; and *Silk Stockings* (1955), the musical-comedy adaptation of Greta Garbo's motion picture, *Ninotchka.*

One of Porter's greatest songs, "Begin the Beguine" came from a Broadway failure, *Jubilee* (1935), and even the song failed to excite interest and passed unnoticed. A decade or so later "Begin the Beguine" was revived on records and over the radio with startling results, and its popularity has not yet died down.

Kiss Me Kate was the greatest box-office triumph of Porter's career, with a Broadway run of over one thousand performances and successes in many European capitals (the first American musical to reach Poland). The book by Sam and Bella Spewack was based in part on Shakespeare's *The Taming of the Shrew*—but only partly. Actually *Kiss Me Kate* is a play within a play, in which a modern troupe is performing the Shakespeare comedy. The amatory complications of the troupe's two stars spill over into the Shakespeare presentation, and a final reconciliation between these two players takes place during an actual performance of *The Taming of the Shrew.* For this amusing text, Porter wrote the best score of his career—romantic, sensual, nostalgic, satirical, malicious, and provocative. "So in Love," and "Were Thine That Special Face" were the leading ballads; the humorous or satirical numbers included "I Hate Men," "Always True to You," "Brush Up Your Shakespeare," and "Wunderbar"; the sophisticated songs, rich with sex innuendos, included "Too Darn Hot" and "Where Is the Life That Late I Led?"

We have thus far commented only on Porter's stage music. He was also a bountiful provider of hit songs for the motion-picture screen, the best of these being "Don't Fence Me In," "I've Got You Under My Skin," "Easy to Love," "In the Still of the Night," "You'd Be So Nice to Come Home To," and "True Love." Porter was also the subject of an impressive screen biography, *Night and Day*, released in 1946.

While Porter was writing much of his magnificent music, he was the victim of considerable physical pain. Riding horseback in 1937 he suffered a serious accident in which both legs were crushed and his nerve tissues severely damaged. He spent two years in a hospital and several more in a wheel chair and underwent over thirty operations until the amputation of one leg was found necessary in 1958. The fact that through all these difficult years he was able to continue working and reaching an ever higher level of achievement evidences his courage and spirit as well as his creative power.

13—Other Voices in the Theater

Others besides the "mighty five" contributed significant music to the Broadway stage in the 1920's and early 1930's. The most important were Vincent Youmans, Ray Henderson, Harry Tierney, and J. Fred Coots.

Vincent Youmans (1898-1946), who was born in New York, was directed by his parents to engineering. When that field failed to interest him he left the Sheffield Scientific School without a degree in 1916 and found a job in a Wall Street brokerage house. All the while he had been playing the piano, having received his first lessons when he was only four. During World War I while in the Navy he helped produce musicals for the servicemen. For some of these he wrote songs, and one became especially popular with the Navy after John Philip Sousa had played it with his various bands. A decade later, Youmans used the same melody for one of his greatest song hits, "Hallelujah."

After the war, Youmans went to work in Tin Pan Alley as staff pianist for Harms and helped Victor Herbert rehearse singers for some of Herbert's operettas and musicals. In 1918, Youmans contributed his first song to the Broadway stage, "Who's Who with You?" in *From Piccadilly to Broadway*. Four years later Youmans enjoyed a major success with *Two Little Girls in Blue*, a musical comedy for which he collaborated with Paul Lannin writing the music and for which young Ira Gershwin (then hiding under the pseudonym of Arthur Francis) wrote the lyrics. The two leading songs in this score were the title number and "Oh Me! Oh My!"

Wildflower (1923), book and lyrics by Harbach and Hammerstein, was an even greater success and remained on Broadway for well over a year. This time collaborating with Herbert Stothart, Youmans was responsible for two solid hits in the title song and "Bambalina."

Two later Youmans musicals, in which the scores were entirely his own, rank among the most successful seen on Broadway in the 1920's. *No, No, Nanette* (1925), book by Harbach and Frank Mandel and lyrics by Irving Caesar, introduced two all-time Youmans favorites in "Tea for Two" and "I Want to Be Happy." *Hit the Deck* (1927), adapted by Herbert Fields from the Broadway play *Shore Leave*, also had two outstanding musical numbers—"Hallelujah" and "Sometimes I'm Happy." The latter was a melody Youmans had written two years earlier for a different lyric, "Come On and Pet Me."

After 1927, one after another of Youman's musicals collapsed at the box office. But one of these failures deserved a better fate. *Rainbow* (1928), book by Laurence Stallings and Hammerstein and lyrics by Hammerstein, was an ambitious attempt at a musical folk play, in which the background, atmosphere, characterization, dialogue, lyrics, and music were all sensitively adjusted to one another. The music was particularly noteworthy. Some of the choral numbers and dances had a genuine folk flavor, but, coming as it did so long before *Oklahoma!* had won audiences over to this kind of adult entertainment, *Rainbow* was too far ahead of its time to be appreciated.

There was hardly a Youmans musical, however badly it might fare at the box office, that did not yield an outstanding song. Out of *Great Day* (1929) came "Without a Song" and "More Than You Know." *Through the Years* (1932) brought the poignant title number and "Drums In My Heart." *Take a Chance* (1932), the last of Youmans' Broadway musicals, introduced "Rise 'n Shine." "Time on My Hands," one of Youmans' best songs, was written for *Smiles* (1930), but Marilyn Miller, the star, refused to sing it, and it was deleted from the production and issued as an independent number.

In 1933, Youmans went to Hollywood where his first assignment was a Fred Astaire-Ginger Rogers musical, *Flying Down to Rio*. This was the score that included "Carioca" and "Orchids in the Moonlight." After 1933, Youmans wrote little. A victim of tuberculosis, he spent most of his time in sanitariums. He planned a return to Broadway in 1943 with a somewhat pretentious production called *The Vincent Youmans Ballet Revue*, which passed out of existence during tryout performances in Baltimore. Youmans' health broke down again after that, and he spent the last year of his life in a Colorado sanitarium.

Ray Henderson (1896-   ) was a member of the productive song writing team of De Sylva, Brown, and Henderson. Though Henderson was its composer and Buddy De Sylva and Lew Brown provided the lyrics (with De Sylva often collaborating in the writing of musical-comedy texts), the three men worked together so closely that their greatest songs are usually referred to not as those of Henderson but as those of all three.

Henderson, born in Buffalo, New York, received his musical training from his mother and at the Chicago Musical College. While studying music he earned his living playing the piano in jazz bands, performing at parties, and appearing as accompanist for vaudeville artists. After he had completed his musical education, he found employment in Tin Pan Alley as staff pianist for the firm of Shapiro-Bernstein. To lyrics by Lew Brown he wrote two songs published by Shapiro-Bernstein in 1922, "Humming" and "Georgette," the latter introduced in the *Greenwich Village Follies.* In 1925, Henderson scored major successes with "Alabamy Bound" and "Five Feet Two, Eyes of Blue."

The team of De Sylva, Brown, and Henderson came into existence in 1925 when the three were put under contract by George White to provide songs for his *Scandals* as successors to George Gershwin, who had just withdrawn from this assignment. For the editions between 1925 and 1928 De Sylva, Brown, and Henderson created such outstanding numbers as "The Birth of the Blues" and "Black Bottom." But the trio did not confine itself to the *Scandals.* In 1927, joined by Laurence Schwab, it invaded the field of musical comedy with *Good News,* a formidable success. Three songs from this production were in the brash, youthful, rowdy spirit of the college-town texts of De Sylva and Schwab: "Varsity Drag," "The Girls of Pi Beta Phi," and the title song. One was in a more romantic style, "The Best Things in Life Are Free," a title later used by Hollywood for the screen biography of this trio of song writers. For *Hold Everything* (1928)—in which Bert Lahr became a Broadway musical-comedy star—De Sylva, Brown, and Henderson wrote "You're the Cream in My Coffee" and "Don't Hold Everything"; for *Follow Through* (1929) they wrote "Button Up Your Overcoat" and "I Could Give Up Anything but You"; and for *Flying High* (1930), "Thank Your Father," "Happy Landing," and "Wasn't It Beautiful While It Lasted?".

For a while the three were also successful song writers for the screen. For Al Jolson's triumph, *The Singing Fool*, they produced one of the most successful theme songs ever written for the screen, "Sonny Boy." Two other De Sylva, Brown, and Henderson favorites were heard in this picture—"It All Depends On You" and "I'm Sitting on Top of the World." They also wrote the score for *Sunny Side Up*, one of the most delightful musicals in the early era of talking pictures. The best songs here were "Keep Your Sunny Side Up," "I'm a Dreamer," and "If I Had a Talking Picture of You."

Then the partnership broke up. De Sylva became a powerful Hollywood and Broadway producer. For a while, Henderson continued writing songs for various Broadway musicals—at times with Lew Brown, at times with other lyricists—but without ever regaining the magic touch with which he had previously fashioned his greatest melodies. Henderson's achievements as a composer belong exclusively to the time when he worked so fruitfully with De Sylva and Brown, a fact of which we were once again reminded in 1956 with the release of their motion picture biography, *The Best Things in Life Are Free*.

Harry Tierney (1895-   ) was the composer of two resounding musical-comedy successes of the 1920's—*Kid Boots* and *Rio Rita*. Born in Perth Amboy, New Jersey, Tierney received his musical education at the Virgil Music School in New York. In 1915 he went to London, where he worked as staff composer for an English music publisher, wrote and had published several songs, and composed some music for the stage. He returned to the United States a year later and went to work in Tin Pan Alley. Several of his songs were immediately interpolated in Broadway musicals. Frances White introduced "M-I-S-S-I-S-S-I-P-P-I" in Ziegfeld's *Midnight Frolics* in 1916, and Anna Held scored with "It's a Cute Little Way of My Own" in *Follow Me* in 1917. In 1919, Tierney wrote his first complete Broadway stage score, *Irene*, which made stage history by enjoying the longest run of any Broadway musi--

cal up to its time (670 performances). Much of the charm of this Cinderella-story musical lay in Tierney's music, particularly in "Alice Blue Gown" (lyrics by Joseph McCarthy), one of the most famous of all popular American waltzes. In 1922, Tierney reappeared on Broadway with *Up She Goes*, whose best number was "Lady Luck, Smile on Me." *Kid Boots*, in 1923, was a starring vehicle for Eddie Cantor, cast in the role of a caddie master at a swank Palm Beach golf club. Tierney's best songs were "Someone Loves You, After All" and "If Your Heart's in the Game." But neither of these proved the hit song of the production; that role was filled by the interpolated song, "Dinah," by Harry Akst. *Rio Rita*, in 1927, was a lavish musical set in Mexico with which the master showman, Florenz Ziegfeld, opened a new theater bearing his name on Sixth Avenue. The title song became one of the hits of the year.

J. Fred Coots (1897-   ) was a comparative novice in Tin Pan Alley when he solidly established his success on Broadway with *Sally, Irene and Mary* in 1922. Though up to 1922 he had written and published only a handful of songs, none of them of particular importance, he managed to persuade the Shuberts to gamble on him when they planned the musical starring Eddie Dowling. *Sally, Irene and Mary* proved a striking box-office attraction, running for about a year, and one of the reasons for its success was Coots' tuneful score, including such ingratiating numbers as "I Wonder Why," "Something in Here," and "Time Will Tell."

During the next decade, Coots wrote songs for many Broadway productions put on by the Shuberts—revues like *Artists and Models* (1924 and 1925) and *A Night in Paris* (1926) and musical comedies like *June Days* (1925), *Gay Paree* (1925), and *Sons o' Guns* (1929), for the last of which he wrote "Why?" and "Cross Your Fingers." After 1930 Coots also wrote songs for motion pictures. Some of his finest songs, however, were meant for neither the stage nor the screen but appeared independently—"I Still Get a Thrill Thinking of You," "Santa Claus Is Coming to Town," "You Go to My Head," and "Love Letters in the Sand," the last published in 1931 and successfully revived a quarter of a century later by Pat Boone.

In the early 1920's a revolution took place in the presentation of Broadway revues. As they became increasingly elaborate and sumptuous under the management of showmen like Ziegfeld, Earl Carroll, and George White, a wave of reaction set in and carried the intimate and sophisticated revue on its crest. Young and enterprising producers and writers started placing less stress on lavish sets and costumes, big numbers, and glamorous stars, and more stress upon wit, satire, charm, and adult entertainment. Undoubtedly economy was the underlying cause of this revolution, since the younger men could hardly compete with their more affluent rivals on their own ground. But if lack of funds led these newcomers to make a virtue out of necessity by replacing huge productions with clever material, it is also true that these young men had the courage to try the unorthodox and both the talent and the imagination to create something new in the musical theater.

The intimate revue was born not on Broadway but further downtown on Grand Street with a series of productions called *The Grand Street Follies*. Described in its initial program in 1922 as "a low-brow show for high-grade morons," *The Grand Street Follies*, nevertheless, was entertainment for the intelligent and the mature. Its strong suit was satire—devastating take-offs on famous shows of the past and present and on the stars of stage, screen, ballet, and opera.

The Grand Street Follies, which continued to operate until 1929 (the last few years on Broadway), inaugurated a vogue for smart, bright, economical revues, and the vogue lasted for many years. The first of the *Garrick Gaieties*, with which Rodgers and Hart achieved their first success, appeared in 1925. After that came the first edition of *Americana* (1926), the three *Little Shows* beginning in 1929, *Three's a Crowd* (1930), *Shoot the Works* (1931), *Walk a Little Faster* (1932), and the first edition of Leonard Sillman's *New Faces* (1934). *Pins and Needles*, which opened in 1937, accomplished a feat never before equalled by a revue by accumulating a run of over a thousand performances. This revue, a production by the International Ladies Garment Workers Union, introduced to our theater a trenchant social consciousness and a keen awareness of the political problems and conflicts of the times. The intimate revue continued to flourish in the 1940's with *Meet the People* (1940), *Lend an Ear* (1941, revived in 1959), *Straw Hat Revue* (1941), and *Call Me Mister* (1946).

Since the emphasis of these productions was on fresh new talent, the intimate revues provided a means by which young writers could find an outlet for their songs. Some of these composers joined the leaders of Broadway after having profited from this valuable apprenticeship. Besides Rodgers, three talented men received their first recognition in the sophisticated revue—Arthur Schwartz, Harold Rome, and Vernon Duke.

Arthur Schwartz (1900-   ) became famous in the first *Little Show*, in 1929. Born in Brooklyn, he received his academic schooling at New York University and Columbia University and was admitted to the bar in 1924. All the while he found diversion in music, mainly in writing songs. At college he wrote marching tunes for football games, and later, in 1923, one of his numbers was interpolated into a Broadway musical, *Poppy*, starring W. C. Fields. In the next few years other songs by Schwartz found a place in *Dear Sir* (a lesser Jerome Kern musical), the *Grand Street Follies, Merry-Go-Round*, and *Good Boy*.

In 1928, the lyricist Howard Dietz convinced Schwartz to give up law for good and work in earnest on his music, and the two began to collaborate on a permanent basis. Their first major effort together was a winner, the first *Little Show* (1929), for a long time the model for the intimate revue. They wrote for this production "I've Made a Habit of You" and "I Guess I'll Have to Change My Plan" among other tunes. But the two most remarkable songs from that first edition came from other composers— "Moanin' Low" by Ralph Rainger and "Can't We Be Friends?" by Kay Swift.

The *Second Little Show* (1930), once again with songs mainly by Schwartz and Dietz, did not have the vitality and imaginativeness of its predecessor. *Three's a Crowd* (1930), however, with almost the same cast of principals as the first *Little Show*, was a triumph. Here the best song by Schwartz and Dietz was "Something to Remember You By," and Johnny Green added a remarkable song of his own in "Body and Soul."

Among later revues by Schwartz and Dietz the best was *The Band Wagon* (1931), book by George S. Kaufman, which con-

tained one of Schwartz's greatest ballads, "Dancing in the Dark,"
as well as "New Sun in the Sky" and "I Love Louisa."

Two other song classics by Schwartz and Dietz belong to one
of their musical-comedy failures, *Revenge with Music* (1934), a
modern adaptation of Alarcón's story, *The Three-Cornered Hat*,
which had been the source of Manuel de Falla's celebrated ballet
—"You and the Night and the Music" and "If There Is Someone
Lovelier Than You," whose immense permanent appeal, no doubt,
led television to revive this otherwise uneventful musical production.

Two of Schwartz's Broadway musical comedies have been
moderate successes, and both of them profited greatly from
the performance of the same star, Shirley Booth. The first, *A Tree
Grows in Brooklyn* (1951), was a musical-comedy version of Betty
Smith's best-selling novel, and three years later came *By the
Beautiful Sea*. In both these musical comedies Schwartz parted
company with Dietz and used the lyrics of Dorothy Fields.

Harold Rome (1908-   ) emerged on Broadway with the
sensational revue, *Pins and Needles* (1937), with which he instantly established his fame as an ace lyricist and composer. Rome
came from Hartford, Connecticut, graduated from Yale, and received a degree from the School of Architecture in 1934. From
boyhood he had been interested in music, and at college he supported himself by playing the piano in jazz groups. After coming
to New York in 1934 to work as an apprentice architect, he supplemented his meager salary by writing and marketing songs. One
of his lyrics was published, and one of his songs was used by the
Ritz Brothers in a movie. In summers, between 1935 and 1938, he
worked at Green Mansions, an adult camp in New York's Adiron-
dack Mountains, helped to produce the weekly show, and wrote
much of the material and music.

When the International Ladies Garment Workers Union of
New York planned an amateur revue, with union members for
the cast, it asked Rome to write the songs. Several of these numbers were in the socially conscious attitude of the revue as a
whole—"Sing Me a Song of Social Significance" and "Doing the
Reactionary." Others had a sentimental approach, and one of
these, "Sunday in the Park," received an award from ASCAP.

Having now become identified with a successful revue of political and social interest, Rome was called upon by other producers to write songs for similar productions. He wrote one of his best political numbers, "Franklin D. Roosevelt Jones" for *Sing Out the News* (1938), and in 1942 he wrote the score for a leftist revue entitled *Let Freedom Ring*.

After more than two years in the army during World War II—when he wrote songs and special material for shows presented for army personnel in the United States and the Pacific combat area—Rome created the songs for one of the most successful revues of the post-war era, *Call Me Mister* (1946). One of these was the greatest hit Rome had yet produced, "South America, Take It Away," introduced in the revue by Betty Garrett; another was an eloquent tribute to President Roosevelt, "The Face on the Dime."

Since 1952, Rome has written music for several successful musical comedies. *Wish You Were Here* (1952) had a hit song in the title number. *Fanny* (1954)—S. N. Behrman's adaptation of Marcel Pagnol's trilogy of plays, *Marius, Fanny,* and *César*—was Rome's most ambitious score up to then, particularly in its ballet music and in its dramatized numbers providing a penetrating insight into the emotions and inner conflicts of the principal characters. *Destry Rides Again* (1959) was a rousing, rip-roaring Western set to music, a musical version of Max Brand's story.

Vernon Duke (1903-   ) was another composer to find the intimate revue of the early 1930's a convenient showcase to exhibit his tunes. Born Vladimir Dukelsky in Pskov, Russia, he was trained at the Kiev Conservatory. Immediately after the Russian Revolution the Dukelsky family fled to Constantinople. At a YMCA there Duke came upon Gershwin's "Swanee," his first contact with American popular music. This proved an unforgettable experience, for it converted him into a dedicated enthusiast of both Gershwin and the rest of our popular music. After coming to the United States in 1921, Duke met Gershwin, who encouraged him to pursue popular composition and who coined for him the name of Vernon Duke. While producing ambitious works for the Ballet Russe de Monte Carlo and the Boston Symphony, which were performed under the name of Vladimir Dukelsky, Duke devoted himself to more popular media. In 1930 he placed two songs in the third edition of the *Garrick Gaieties* and one in *Three's a Crowd*. "Let Me Match My Private Life with Yours" was heard in the 1932 edition of *Americana*.

This year also marked the production of his first full score, the revue, *Walk a Little Faster*, one of whose numbers was "April in Paris," Duke's greatest hit to date. The song was not in the original score but was interpolated during the Boston tryout. When it was heard on Broadway, "April in Paris" was completely ignored by critics and audiences. Some years later it began to catch on, first in night clubs, then in an excellent recording by Marian Chase.

A second Vernon Duke standard, "Autumn in New York," was featured in the revue *Thumbs Up* (1932). For the *Ziegfeld Follies* of 1934 and 1936, Duke contributed several fine numbers, including "I Can't Get Started with You," lyrics by Ira Gershwin, and "What Is There to Say?"

Besides participating in these and other revues, Duke also wrote the music for some distinctive musical comedies. *Cabin in the Sky* (1940), his first, was a musical fantasy with book by Lynn Root and lyrics by John La Touche. It was a beautiful folk play with music, sensitive in characterization, subtle in dramatic pulse, powerful and imaginative in the choreography by Kathrine Dunham, and restrained and dignified in its portrayal of Negro life and backgrounds. "Takin' a Chance on Love," another of Duke's distinguished songs, came from this play, as did the title song and "Honey in the Honeycomb."

In 1941, Duke wrote the music for *Banjo Eyes*, adapted from the Broadway horse-racing comedy, *Three Men on a Horse*, and starring Eddie Cantor. Though Duke wrote the music for half a dozen other productions after that, none of these was successful.

Since 1943, the year of *Oklahoma!*, the American musical theater has simultaneously pursued two directions. One was a well-trodden route, the other broke new ground. The first was musical comedy along well established patterns—however slicker the methods or more mature and sophisticated the approaches. The other was the musical play, which continually sought to achieve artistic unity of drama, music, and choreography. Some important composers since 1943 have preferred to work exclusively within the framework of musical comedy. Others have graduated with honors from musical comedy to the musical play.

Harold Arlen (1905-   ) is one of the former, and, up to present writing, has been content with the more traditional and formal musical theater. A native of Buffalo, Arlen spent much of his boyhood playing the piano in night clubs and on steamers; he also founded and played in a jazz ensemble and wrote arrangements for it. In 1925, Arlen brought his jazz group into a New York night club and, while in New York, found employment as pianist in the orchestra of George White's *Scandals* and as rehearsal pianist for the Vincent Youmans musical *Great Day*. In 1930, his first song, "Get Happy," was interpolated into the *9:15 Revue*, which closed seven performances after its Broadway opening. But the song was a hit, drew high praise from Gershwin, and helped land Arlen a post with Remick's and an assignment to provide music for the Harlem night spot, The Cotton Club. For The Cotton Club Arlen wrote the first songs in which the unmistakable stamp of his personality can be detected—"Between the Devil and the Deep Blue Sea," "Minnie Moocher's Wedding Day," "I Love a Parade," "I've Got the World on a String," and a song now recognized as a classic, "Stormy Weather," first made popular in a recording by Leo Reisman and then identified with Ethel Waters. These are probably the first significant songs written directly for a night club production.

In 1931, Arlen wrote his first complete musical comedy score, *You Said It*. In 1934, working mainly with the lyricist E. Y. Harburg, Arlen produced ten numbers for the revue, *Life Begins at 8:40*, and in 1937, once again with Harburg, he wrote songs for the Ed Wynn extravaganza, *Hooray for What?* Though some of these productions boasted pleasant songs—such as "Sweet and Hot" and "I've Gone Romantic on You"—it was not on Broadway but in Hollywood that Arlen came to full maturity as a composer.

Hardly had Arlen arrived there than he revealed his rich creative powers by writing "It's Only a Paper Moon" for *Take a Chance* (1933). During the next decade the following Arlen standards appeared on the screen: "Blues in the Night," "That Old Black Magic," "Accentuate the Positive" (all three to lyrics by Johnny Mercer), "Let's Fall in Love," "Happiness Is a Thing

Called Joe," "One for My Baby," "My Shining Hours," and the song with which he won the Academy Award in 1939 and that since then has become the signature of Judy Garland, who introduced it, "Over the Rainbow," from *The Wizard of Oz*, lyrics by E. Y. Harburg.

Arlen returned to Broadway in 1944 with a box-office bonanza, *Bloomer Girl*, lyrics by Harburg and book by Sig Herzig and Fred Saidy. This was a period piece set during the Civil War in New York, where Dolly Bloomer (a historical figure whose real name was Amelia) was a passionate feminist, an advocate of temperance, and a propagandist for bloomers in place of hoop skirts as women's apparel. An excellent score and some remarkable choreography by Agnes de Mille were the strong points of the production, Arlen's best numbers being "I Got a Song," "Evelina," and "T'morra, T'morra."

St. Louis Woman (1946) was an all-Negro production—book by Arna Bontemps and Countee Cullen and lyrics by Johnny Mercer—in which Pearl Bailey delivered two fine numbers in "A Woman's Prerogative" and "Legalize My Name." An outstanding song in a more sentimental vein was "Come Rain or Come Shine." *St. Louis Woman* was radically revised about a decade later and, renamed *Free and Easy*, began a brief and unsuccessful European tour late in 1959.

For his next two musicals Arlen went to the Caribbean for exotic settings and colorful characters. *House of Flowers* (1954) had a book and lyrics by Truman Capote. In *Jamaica* (1957) Lena Horne made her musical-comedy debut as star. In tune with their settings, Arlen wrote music for both plays that was heavily spiced with the melodic and harmonic condiments of calypso and other West Indian folk songs and dances, of which "Incompatibility" and "Take It Slow, Joe" from *Jamaica* are memorable examples.

The composer of *Bloomer Girl* returned to a rich American background of a bygone era in *Saratoga* (1959), adapted from Edna Ferber's novel, a dismal failure from every point of view. Since 1944 Arlen has also worked for Hollywood. For *A Star Is Born*, starring Judy Garland, he wrote one of his most poignant torch songs, "The Man That Got Away," lyrics by Ira Gershwin. With Gershwin, Arlen also contributed the songs for *The Country Girl*, with Bing Crosby.

Like Arlen, Burton Lane (1912-   ) achieved recognition in Hollywood before moving on to a triumphant career on Broadway. Lane was born in New York and attended local public schools and the Dwight Academy, for which he wrote two marches that were published. He then went to work in Tin Pan Alley, where he met the lyricist Howard Dietz, through whose influence (and with whose lyrics) he made his Broadway bow with two songs for *Three's a Crowd* in 1930. One year later Lane's songs were heard in the *Third Little Show* and in Earl Carroll's *Vanities,* this time with lyrics by Harold Adamson.

Lane began working for Hollywood in 1933 with three songs for *Dancing Lady* starring Clark Gable and Joan Crawford. In the next decades, Lane's songs appeared in over thirty-five motion pictures, the most important songs being "Says My Heart" (lyrics by Frank Loesser) and "How About You?"

Lane came back to Broadway to write the music for Al Jolson's last Broadway play, *Hold On to Your Hats* (1940). Four years after that Lane wrote the music for the Olsen and Johnson extravaganza, *Laffing Room Only,* which included one of Lane's biggest hits, "Feudin' and Fightin'," lyrics by Al Dubin.

Then came the greatest artistic and commercial triumph of Lane's career, the remarkable musical comedy, *Finian's Rainbow* (1947), book by Fred Saidy and E. Y. Harburg, and lyrics by Harburg. This outstanding production, surely one of the shining adornments of our theater, was a curious but always effective blend of sentiment and sophisticated wit, of romance and trenchant satire, of Irish fantasy and bitter commentary on the American social and political scene. Harburg's lyrics were consistently brilliant both in the suppleness and dexterity of their versification and in the sharp thrust of their satire, and never before or since has Lane created a musical score of such dimension and variety. "How Are Things in Glocca Morra?" and "Look to the Rainbow" were ballads with an Irish character which stepped out of the play to join the year's song hits. In "The Begat," "Something Sort of Grandish," and "When the Idle Poor" the grace and flash of Harburg's lines found a match in Lane's scintillating melodies.

Jule Styne (1905-   ) is another composer for whom musical comedy, rather than the musical play, proved fertile soil. Styne was born in London, England, but settled in Chicago when he was only eight. In music he was a child prodigy and appeared as piano soloist with the Chicago Symphony and won a scholarship for the Chicago Musical College. After his studies ended in 1931, Styne abandoned serious music in favor of jazz by forming a jazz group which performed in hotels and clubs and for which he wrote all the arrangements. He was soon called out to Hollywood to write background music, make arrangements, and work as a vocal coach for Shirley Temple, Alice Faye, and others. In Hollywood he teamed up with the lyricist Sammy Cahn, with whom he wrote many song hits, all for motion pictures—"I'll Walk Alone" (an outstanding ballad of World War II), "There Goes That Song Again," "Love Me," "Give Me Five Minutes More," and "It's Magic." They received the Academy Award in 1954 for "Three Coins in a Fountain."

Jule Styne and Sammy Cahn came to the Broadway stage for the first time with a resounding box-office success, *High Button Shoes* (1947). Its best songs were "Papa, Won't You Dance with Me?" and "I Still Get Jealous." Three later musicals by Styne were also great successes. In *Gentlemen Prefer Blondes* (1949) Carol Channing became a star with "Diamonds Are a Girl's Best Friend" and "A Little Girl from Little Rock," lyrics by Leo Robin. With *Bells Are Ringing* (1956), Judy Holliday made a sensational debut in musical comedy. Three of its songs are of particular interest, "Just in Time," "The Party's Over," and "Long Before I Knew You," lyrics by Betty Comden and Adolph Green. *Gypsy* (1959) was the musical-comedy adaptation of Gypsy Rose Lee's autobiography, starring Ethel Merman in one of her greatest roles. "Together, Wherever We Go" and "Everything's Coming Up Roses," lyrics by Stephen Sondheim, were two of the principal songs. *Do Re Mi* (1960)—book by Garson Kanin, based on his own novel—starred Phil Silvers in a briskly moving musical about the jukebox business. One of its hit songs was "Make Someone Happy."

Several other composers of musical comedies deserve attention. Robert Wright (1914-   ) and George "Chet" Forrest (1915-   ) have functioned as a team in writing both words and music. They have been particularly successful in re-fashioning the music of classical composers for the commercial theater—that of Edvard Grieg in *The Song of Norway* (1944), whose hit song was "Strange Music," and that of Borodin in *Kismet* (1953), where we find "Stranger in Paradise" and "And This Is My Beloved."

Richard Adler (1923-   ) and Jerry Ross (1926-1955) have also worked harmoniously together writing lyrics and melodies. Two of the greatest box-office successes of the 1950's are theirs. *The Pajama Game* (1954) received one third of the seventeen Antoinette Perry Awards, a record previously held only by *South Pacific*. *Damn Yankees* (1955) was hardly less successful. Before undertaking their first stage assignment, Adler and Ross had to their credit several song hits including "Rags to Riches," which sold over a million copies of sheet music and over a million records. Their list of song successes was extended by those in their two musical comedies with "Hey There" and "Hernando's Hideaway" from *The Pajama Game* and "Whatever Lola Wants" and "Heart" from *Damn Yankees*. Jerry Ross' premature death at the age of twenty-nine disrupted this fruitful partnership.

Since 1950 several other significant newcomers have made profitable contributions to musical comedy. Bob Merrill (1921-   ) wrote lyrics and music for several highly commercial songs, including "Sparrow in the Tree Top," "Doggie in the Window," and "Honeycomb" before he was discovered by George Abbott and brought to Broadway. Merrill's first stage score was a winner, *New Girl in Town* (1957), a musical version of Eugene O'Neill's drama, *Anna Christie*. Its leading songs were "Look at 'Er" and "Sunshine Girl." Merrill's second Broadway venture was another adaptation of a Eugene O'Neill play, the heartwarming comedy, *Ah, Wilderness!*, and proved an even greater success. It was called *Take Me Along* (1959), starred Jackie Gleason, and provided several musical pleasures, among them the title song, "That's How It Starts," and "I Would Die." Merrill's third Broadway musical, *Carnival* (1961), was a stage adaptation of the motion picture *Lili*.

Albert Hague (1920-   ) wrote two outstanding songs for his musical-comedy success about the Amish sect in Pennsylvania, *Plain and Fancy* (1955)—"Young and Foolish" and "Plain We Live." This impressive effort was followed by another in *Redhead* (1958), starring Gwen Verdon, for which he wrote "Just for Once" and "Look Who's in Love."

Before he turned his impressive talents to the stage, Meredith

Willson (1902-   ) had long been a successful writer of popular songs, among them "You and I," "Two in Love," and "Whose Dream Are You?" His debut on Broadway proved a sensation, for it was made with *The Music Man* (1957), a nostalgic, sentimental comedy of small-town life in America in 1912, for which he wrote the book and the lyrics as well as the music. A tuneful score embraced a resounding hit in "Seventy Six Trombones." In Meredith Willson's second musical, *The Unsinkable Molly Brown* (1960), a character out of America's past is vividly brought back to life. She is Molly Brown, an ignorant Missouri backwoods girl who makes a fortune in the mines of Colorado, conquers the social world of Europe, and then, on her way home, becomes one of the few survivors of the "Titanic," which collided with an iceberg in 1912. One of its most attractive and musical numbers was "I Ain't Down Yet."

A rich vein of Americana was also tapped by two musical comedies by Jerry Bock (1928-   ), a young composer working with Sheldon Harnick, lyricist, and Jerome Weidman, librettist. *Fiorello!* (1959) was a colorful picture of political life in New York at the turn of the century, profiting greatly from its brilliant characterization of its hero, Fiorello H. La Guardia, New York's bouncing, rambunctious mayor. The musical traces his career from his law practice in Greenwich Village in 1914 to his election as mayor on a Fusion ticket. Satire, as well as realism and nostalgia, helped make *Fiorello* an unforgettable stage experience—the satire being at its best in the songs, "Politics and Poker" and "Little Tin Box." A resounding box-office triumph, *Fiorello* won the Pulitzer Prize and the Drama Critics Award as the best play of the season. In *Tenderloin* (1960)—by the same authors who created *Fiorello*—Maurice Evans made his musical-comedy debut as a Presbyterian minister out to clean up a disreputable neighborhood in New York in the 1890's.

Several composers achieved fame in musical comedy and then went on to greater achievements with musical plays. The most important of these, of course, was Richard Rodgers, whose two careers—the first with Lorenz Hart and the second with Oscar Hammerstein II—have already been discussed.

Kurt Weill (1900-1950) was already one of Broadway's top composers of musical comedy with *Knickerbocker Holiday, Lady in the Dark,* and *One Touch of Venus* when he wrote music for two of the most poignant musical plays of our time, *Street Scene* and *Lost in the Stars.* Weill had been trained as a serious composer in his native Germany, and success first came to him there with operas in which a popular musical style—sometimes jazz and sometimes even pop tunes of the Tin Pan Alley variety—was skillfully used. The most famous of these operas is *The Three-Penny Opera* (*Die Dreigroschenoper*), a modern adaptation of John Gay's *The Beggar's Opera* with a satirical new text by Bertholt Brecht and breezy melodies by Weill. *The Three-Penny Opera* enjoyed over four thousand performances in about 120 different theaters in the first year of its eventful history. Since then it has become a monument in the theater, performed in all parts of the civilized world and on several occasions made into motion pictures. In 1954, with a text modernized and revised by Marc Blitzstein but with Weill's music unchanged, it began an off-Broadway run that has lasted for several years and over two thousand performances. One of its leading melodies, "Mack the Knife," became an American hit song, selling over two million records in Bobby Darin's recording in 1959.

The rise of the Nazi regime in Germany drove Weill from his native land to the United States, of which he subsequently became a citizen. His first Broadway assignments were the writing of a score for a sardonic anti-war play by Paul Green, *Johnny Johnson* (1936), and for a pageant of Jewish history by Franz Werfel produced by Max Reinhardt in 1937. The American identity of the first score (with its ballads, cowboy songs, and Tin Pan Alley ditties) and the religious exaltation of the music of the second play gave evidence of Weill's great range. Success on Broadway came to Weill with *Knickerbocker Holiday* (1938), a musical comedy with book and lyrics by Maxwell Anderson, with Walter Huston providing an unforgettable portrayal of Peter Stuyvesant in the New Amsterdam of 1647. "September Song" from this play is still Weill's most famous song. *Lady in the Dark* (1941) was Moss Hart's trenchant play about the psychoanalytic treatment undergone by its heroine, brilliantly enacted by Gertrude Lawrence. Weill here produced various sequences serving as transitions from one scene to the next, lending an emotional thrust to some of the dream sequences, or evoking an appropriate mood. There were also a few excellent songs, with lyrics by Ira Gershwin—"The Saga of Jenny," "My Ship," and "Tchaikovsky," in the last of which Danny Kaye won an accolade for his rifle-precision delivery of the names of Russian composers.

One Touch of Venus (1943), in which Mary Martin appeared as a statue come to life, and *Love Life* (1948), with book and lyrics by Alan Jay Lerner, were also in the more or less recognizable format of musical comedy. From the latter play emerged another celebrated Weill song, "Green-Up Time."

In 1947 appeared the exciting musical version of Elmer Rice's realistic, Pulitzer-Prize-winning play, *Street Scene*. The musical play became even more compelling than the stage drama in its portrayal of elemental passions, frustrations, and aborted dreams. Much of the credit for this achievement belongs to Weill, who here created one of the best integrated scores of his career on Broadway. *Lost in the Stars* (1949)—Maxwell Anderson's adaptation for the musical theater of Alan Paton's novel, *Cry the Beloved Country*—also touched depths of passion and reached for heights of humanity in telling a story of racial conflicts. Eloquent pages of choral music, stirring musical narratives, and powerful songs penetrating in their psychological understanding of character and deeply moving in their emotional content gave Weill's music the dimensions of opera. Indeed, the operatic character of both *Street Scene* and *Lost in the Stars* has been recognized by the New York City Opera Company when it included these productions in its regular operatic repertory.

Frank Loesser (1910-   ) wrote lyrics and music for two remarkable musical comedies, *Where's Charley?* and *Guys and Dolls,* before extending his horizon as Weill did. Loesser was born in New York City, the brother of Arthur Loesser, famous as a concert pianist and teacher. Frank's musical education ended abruptly after one year at the College of the City of New York. His contact with music was not through any formal instruction but from experiments on a harmonica and at a piano keyboard. He floundered about in several poorly paid jobs before he came to the conclusion that he wanted to become a song lyricist. For a while he was employed by the firm of Leo Feist, who published his lyric "I'm in Love with the Memory of You" to music by William Schuman, who subsequently became one of America's most significant serious composers as well as the president of the

Juilliard School of Music. Recognition came to Loesser in time, and he was called to Hollywood to write lyrics for several of movieland's most successful composers including Hoagy Carmichael, Arthur Schwartz, Burton Lane, Jule Styne, and Jimmy McHugh.

The first songs for which Loesser wrote both the music and the lyrics were inspired by World War II. The first was "Praise the Lord and Pass the Ammunition," written immediately after Pearl Harbor. It sold over two million records and a million copies of sheet music—a sale that probably would have been even greater if powerful members of the clergy had not condemned it for coupling the name of the Lord with ammunition. "The Ballad of Roger Young," Loesser's second song with his own music and lyrics, was requested by the Infantry and is one of the most eloquent ballads to come out of World War II. For the rest of the war, as a Private First Class in Special Services, Loesser wrote other songs for various branches of the armed forces. One is permanently identified with the foot soldier, "What Do You Do in the Infantry?"

After the war Loesser continued writing music to his own words. After becoming one of Hollywood's major composer-lyricists, he came to Broadway for the first time with *Where's Charley?* (1948). This was George Abbott's adaptation of *Charley's Aunt,* long a popular farce by Brandon Thomas. With Ray Bolger as a most engaging Charley—and sparked with hit tunes like "Once in Love with Amy" and "My Darling"—*Where's Charley?* accumulated a Broadway run of almost eight hundred performances.

The triumph of *Guys and Dolls* (1950) was even greater. Its run on Broadway exceeded 1200 performances, and the box office grossed twelve million dollars. Some critics described it as the ideal of what musical comedy should be. Damon Runyon's stories about and characters from Broadway provided a wealth of mirth-provoking situations and complications, a reservoir of racy dialogue, and a cross-section of gamblers, chiselers, and crackpots from the Main Stem. Jo Swerling and Abe Burrows, as the adaptors, took full advantage of this spicy material, as did Loesser in his music and lyrics. Rarely if ever before had he shown such a diversified style in melodies and such brilliance, wit, and dexterity in the writing of lyrics. His best romantic numbers were "I'll

Know," "I've Never Been in Love Before," and "If I Were a Bell." Broad humor, burlesque, and satire overflowed in "Adelaide's Lament," the opening "Fugue for Tinhorns," "Take Back Your Mink," and "A Bushel and a Peck."

Loesser's musical gifts now demanded a larger, more ambitious canvas than musical comedy. *The Most Happy Fella* (1956) was that canvas—a musical production which he himself adapted from Sidney Howard's Pulitzer Prize play, *They Knew What They Wanted.* A prodigious score included about thirty numbers— arias, duets, choruses, instrumental passages, folk songs, parodies, canons, and dance music. The music made such a potent contribution to the changing passions and humors of Howard's play that Brooks Atkinson was led to say in his review that Loesser "has told everything of vital importance in terms of dramatic music." There were also several commercial items in this soundly conceived score—"Standing on the Corner," "Big D," and "Happy to Make Your Acquaintance."

Meanwhile, Loesser combined his rich activity on Broadway with significant work in Hollywood. In 1949 he received the Academy Award for "Baby, It's Cold Outside" from *Neptune's Daughter,* and in 1952 he created a charming score for the Danny Kaye motion picture, *Hans Christian Andersen,* among whose best numbers were "Anywhere I Wander" and "Thumbelina."

The songwriting duo, Lerner and Loewe, has brought the American theater two of its most magnificent musical creations— *Brigadoon* and *My Fair Lady.* Frederick Loewe (1904-   ) was born in Vienna, the son of a famous operetta tenor. Frederick was a prodigy pianist and at thirteen was the youngest soloist ever to appear with the Berlin Symphony Orchestra. His piano training took place with two masters—Ferruccio Busoni and Eugène D'Albert—and in 1923 he was honored with the Hollaender Medal for piano playing.

Loewe came to the United States in 1924 and, unable to make any headway as a virtuoso, deserted music completely. For many years he wandered about the country, taking on any job that came along, including gold-mining, teaching horseback riding, boxing, and punching cattle. His return to music took place in the 1930's when he found jobs as pianist in various night spots in Yorkville and Greenwich Village. At this time he began writing popular songs. One was sung by Dennis King in the non-musical play, *Petticoat Fever;* four found their way into an unsuccessful Broadway musical, *Great Lady.*

Meeting Alan Jay Lerner proved a decisive turning point in his life. Lerner, a graduate from Harvard, was a radio script writer whose ambitions lay in the direction of the theater. He joined forces with Loewe in writing a musical comedy commissioned by a Detroit stock company, and immediately thereafter they went to work on their first Broadway musical, *What's Up?* (1943), which lasted only eight weeks. Their second Broadway effort, *The Day Before Spring* (1945), was also a failure.

Both Lerner and Loewe achieved maturity and met success with *Brigadoon* (1947), with book as well as lyrics by Lerner. The first musical to win the Drama Critics Award as the best play of the season, *Brigadoon* was an enchanting fantasy set in a Scottish magic village which appears once each century, and on which two present-day American tourists stumble during its single day of existence. Lerner's deft touch in creating a sensitive balance between contemporary realism and the timeless world of dreams endowed the play with much of its charm. Loewe's contribution was equally significant, for it was here that he first achieved eminence as a composer, frequently with numbers delightful for their Scottish personality—"The Heather on the Hill," for example, or "Come to Me, Bend to Me," and a song that was among the hits of 1947, "Almost like Being in Love."

Paint Your Wagon (1951), though one of the less successful of the Broadway efforts of Lerner and Loewe, had much to recommend it—its authentic American folk character, the impressive choreography of Agnes de Mille, and the effective way it traced the disintegration of a mining camp from a boom town to a ghost town.

With their next musical, *My Fair Lady* (1956)—a musical version of Bernard Shaw's comedy, *Pygmalion,* starring Rex Harrison and Julie Andrews—Lerner and Loewe realized not only the triumph of their careers but one of the greatest triumphs in the history of the American theater. Brooks Atkinson went all out in proclaiming it one of the best musical plays of the twentieth century. The musical retained much of Bernard Shaw's bite and sting, irony and malice; but to these it contributed some things of its own, sentiment and a heartwarming romantic glow, compassion and humanity. Moss Hart's direction, Hanya Holm's choreography, Oliver Smith's sets, Cecil Beaton's costuming were all on a par with Lerner's dazzling dialogue and lyrics and Loewe's ingratiating music. The last was often touched with a winning Viennese *Gemütlichkeit* that suited the London setting of 1912 most admirably, as in the "Ascot Gavotte" and the "Embassy Waltz." At other moments the music had a most ingratiating lightness of mood and humor, for example in the two cockney songs, "With a Little Bit of Luck," and "Get Me to the Church on Time." It also had its quota of solid hits in "I Could Have Danced All Night" and "On the Street Where You Live."

Later Lerner and Loewe contributed a chapter to motion-picture history with *Gigi*, their debut as writers for the screen. In 1959, *Gigi* broke all precedents for a musical motion picture by winning more Academy Awards than any other motion picture, nine in all, one of which was for the title number. The return of Lerner and Loewe to Broadway after *My Fair Lady* took place late in 1960 with *Camelot*, a musical-play setting of the legend of King Arthur and the knights of the Round Table. Arriving on Broadway with the largest advance sale in theater history—over three million dollars—*Camelot* inspired high expectations which were not completely fulfilled. This was not another *My Fair Lady*. Though many of the same people who had helped *My Fair Lady* become the miracle it was were gathered together again for *Camelot* (not merely Lerner and Loewe but also Moss Hart, Hanya Holm, Oliver Smith, Julie Andrews, Robert Coote, Franz Allers, and Robert Russell Bennett), the old recipe did not add up to a consistently succulent dish. Perhaps what was lacking was the most significant ingredient of all: a brilliant play by Bernard Shaw as the point of departure. Nevertheless, *Camelot* was a spectacle to dazzle the eye, filled with components that were highly attractive in themselves. In the musical department there were songs like the title number, "How to Handle a Woman" and "What Do Simple Folk Do?"

Leonard Bernstein (1918-   ), whose phenomenal achievements in the theater represent only one facet of a varied musical career, wrote the music for two outstandingly successful musical comedies and one triumphant musical play. Bernstein, of course, is one of the world's foremost symphony conductors, the musical director of the New York Philharmonic Orchestra. He has also been acclaimed as pianist, composer of concert music and ballets, lecturer, teacher, and author. In the Broadway theater, as elsewhere, he was destined to win instantaneous acclaim. His first musical comedy was *On the Town* (1944), book and lyrics by Betty Comden and Adolph Green, in which Jerome Robbins undertook his first assignment as choreographer. One of the freshest musicals to come to Broadway in several years, *On the Town* played for over a year, was made into a movie, and was revived by two different companies in New York in 1959. Though Bernstein carried to his popular writing his extraordinary technique in orchestration, harmony, and rhythm—particularly in the ballet episodes—he did not lack the common touch so necessary to musical comedy, as is proven by "New York, New York," the ballads "Lonely Town" and "Lucky to Be Me," and the comic song, "I Get Carried Away."

Wonderful Town (1953), Bernstein's second Broadway show, was the musical-comedy treatment of Ruth McKenney's *My Sister Eileen,* originally a series of short stories and afterwards a Broadway stage comedy. Rosalind Russell, playing Ruth, an innocent come from Ohio to Greenwich Village with her sister Eileen to seek a career, was the dynamo who charged the stage with a perpetual flow of electric energy. She was, however, just a single element in a powerful production which, abetted by George Abbott's sure-fire direction, maintained a breathless pace from the opening to the final curtain. The vitality, exuberance, and excitement that were generated by the performers flowed out of Bernstein's score, which opened with a racy, headstrong overture, continued immediately with an abandoned ragtag dance, and progressed through a succession of breezy numbers, ballads, and volcanic rag music. "Ohio," a take-off on sentimental songs about home, was the number which found greatest favor outside the theater, but within the theater the ballads "A Quiet Girl" and "Never Felt That Way Before," the volcanic "Wrong Note Rag," and the comic "Story Vignettes" were equally appealing.

A transition from musical comedy to musical play took place with *Candide* (1956), for which Bernstein produced an iridescent score to Lillian Hellman's book based on Voltaire's famous satire. Here Bernstein uncovered new creative resources as a popular composer, and he now stood ready to undertake his most ambitious stage assignment. *West Side Story* (1957), book by Arthur Laurents and lyrics by Stephen Sondheim, was a grim, turbulent, hypertense story of life in New York's West Side among teen-age gangs and specifically among Puerto Ricans. Its tragic love story was a translation of Shakespeare's *Romeo and Juliet* into modern jargon and modern symbols. Rarely before had our commercial musical theater turned to so realistic and tragic a story, so concerned with social problems and so timely in its discussion of juvenile delinquency. The story was projected not only through the long-accepted techniques of the stage but also through several imaginative dances conceived by Jerome Robbins, and much of the savagery and neuroticism of the play were echoed in Bernstein's music for these dances. The play's bitter satire was also found in songs like "America" and "Gee, Officer Krupke," and the play's inherent tenderness, pity, and hope found eloquent expression in songs like "Tonight," "Maria," "Somewhere," and "I Feel Pretty."

14—Other Voices in Tin Pan Alley

As has been shown above, Richard Rodgers, Cole Porter, Ray Henderson, and Vincent Youmans are some of the composers who received their first significant musical experiences within the theater, and it is there that they achieved their first major successes. Many other popular composers since 1910, however, have been children of Tin Pan Alley. There they not only served their apprenticeship but also did much of their most significant work. In the true tradition of Tin Pan Alley, these composers ground out their songs with mechanical precision and with the principal goal of achieving a huge sheet-music and record sale. Any work they did for the theater or for motion pictures was supplementary, often incidental.

Because the number of such Tin Pan Alley composers is legion, we can do no more here than single out the activity and accomplishments of a representative handful and to discuss these in alphabetical order.

Milton Ager (1893-   ) received valuable training in Tin Pan Alley. After working as a song plugger for the Chicago branch of Waterson, Berlin and Snyder, he came to New York to work as an arranger at its main office and later for the firm of William Jerome. His career as composer began with a few piano pieces written in collaboration with Pete Wendling, several of which were published by Waterson, Berlin and Snyder and recorded on small ten-cent discs. With Grant Clarke as his lyricist and in collaboration with George W. Meyer, Ager produced a hit in 1918 in "Everything Is Peaches Down in Georgia," which Al Jolson made popular at the Winter Garden. In 1919 and 1920 he wrote two more hits, this time in collaboration with Cliff Hess, "Freckles" and "I'm in Heaven When I'm in My Mother's Arms." In 1920, Ager began working with Jack Yellen, lyricist,

and it was with him that Ager produced his greatest successes—
"A Young Man's Fancy," which sold over a million records,
"Who Cares?", sung by Al Jolson in *Bombo*, "I Wonder What's
Become of Sally?", "Crazy Words, Crazy Tune," and, most
popular of all, "Ain't She Sweet?"

Ager's contribution to the Broadway stage consisted of several
scores for musical comedies and revues, most significantly *Rain
or Shine* (1928), starring Joe Cook. In 1929 he began working
in Hollywood. His most famous songs for motion pictures have
been "I'm the Last of the Red Hot Mamas," written for and sung
by Sophie Tucker in *Honky Tonk*, "Happy Days Are Here Again"
(since 1932 a favorite theme song for the presidential campaigns
of the Democratic Party), "A Bench in the Park," and "Happy
Feet." "Forgive Me," an independent number written in 1927,
was successfully revived in 1952.

Fred Ahlert (1892-   ) was also an employee of Waterson,
Berlin and Snyder. His most important experience in music, however, came from making arrangements and providing special
material for various musical groups and vaudeville performers
and from preparing the scores for Fred Waring's Glee Club.
His first published song was "Beets and Turnips," in 1914, written
in collaboration with Cliff Hess. His first hit came six years later
with "I'd Love to Fall Asleep and Wake Up in My Mammy's
Arms," and his first million-copy sheet-music sale came with "I'll
Get By," lyrics by Roy Turk, in 1928. Later successes included
"Walkin' My Baby Back Home," made famous by Harry Richman,
"Where the Blue of the Night Meets the Gold of the Day," Bing
Crosby's theme song, "I Don't Know Why," and "I'm Gonna Sit
Right Down and Write Myself a Letter," written in 1935 and
revived two decades later by Pat Boone. Ahlert also wrote for
several motion pictures beginning with *Marianne* in 1929 and for
Sonja Henie's first New York ice show, *It Happened on Ice*, in
1940.

Joseph Burke (1884-1950) was an arranger for a Philadelphia
publisher when, in 1916, he had his first song published, "Down
Honolulu Way." With Benny Davis as his lyricist he produced
several hits including "Oh, How I Miss You Tonight" in 1925 and,
soon thereafter, "Yearning Just for You" and "Carolina Moon,"

the last of which became Morton Downey's radio theme music. His most important songs after that included "For You" and "A Little Bit Independent." Burke also wrote songs for motion pictures, beginning with the *Gold Diggers of Broadway* in 1929, in which, to Al Dubin's lyrics, he introduced "Tip Toe through the Tulips."

Hoagy Carmichael (1899-   ), whose "Star Dust" is an American classic, supported himself while studying law by playing the piano at resort hotels and booking dance orchestras for university affairs. His first opus was "Riverboat Shuffle," published in 1925 as an instrumental composition. It was successfully recorded by the Wolverines and in 1939 acquired a set of lyrics. After he abandoned law, Carmichael worked as demonstrator of Tin Pan Alley songs and as pianist with various groups in Bloomington, Indiana, the city of his birth. It was during this period, in 1929, that he wrote "Star Dust," its original version being a piano rag. An instrumental arrangement in slower tempo was then prepared by Victor Young, introduced by Isham Jones, and later recorded by the Emile Seidel Orchestra with a piano obbligato by Carmichael himself. Not until Mitchell Parish fashioned for this melody a set of sentimental love lyrics did "Star Dust" begin its phenomenal ascent to national popularity. Artie Shaw's recording sold over two million records within five years and several million records were sold with performances by the Mills Brothers, Eddie Duchin, and André Kostelanetz, among others. To date "Star Dust" has received about five hundred different recordings. It is probably the only song ever presented on both sides of a single disc in two different performances, one by Tommy Dorsey and the other by Benny Goodman. It has appeared in almost fifty different arrangements, and its lyrics have been translated into more than forty languages.

In 1930, Carmichael came to New York, where he wrote "Rockin' Chair" to his own lyrics, and in 1933, "Lazy Bones," to lyrics by Johnny Mercer. After 1936, Carmichael worked for motion pictures, his leading screen songs being "Small Fry" and "Two Sleepy People," lyrics by Frank Loesser, and "In the Cool, Cool, Cool of the Evening" from *Here Comes the Groom*, lyrics by Johnny Mercer. The latter song won the Academy Award in 1951.

Con Conrad (1891-1938) had been a vaudeville entertainer from his seventeenth year, before he started working for Waterson, Berlin and Snyder in 1920. In the same year he had published his first big song success, "Margie," written in collaboration with J. Russel Robinson to lyrics by Benny Davis. After that came "Ma, He's Making Eyes at Me," and, to Billy Rose's lyrics, "Barney Google." With his success now firmly established in Tin Pan Alley, Conrad wrote songs for several Broadway musical comedies and revues. From 1929 his main activity was in Hollywood, where in 1934 he became the first composer to receive an Academy Award, for the song "The Continental," lyrics by Herb Magidson, introduced by Fred Astaire and Ginger Rogers in *The Gay Divorcée*.

Walter Donaldson (1893-   ) was a staff pianist and song plugger in Tin Pan Alley when in 1915 he wrote and had published "Back Home in Tennessee," lyrics by William Jerome, still one of the favorite songs about that state. When Irving Berlin formed his own publishing house, Irving Berlin, Inc., immediately after World War I, Donaldson joined its staff and at once made a name for himself with "How Ya Gonna Keep 'Em Down on the Farm?" and "You're a Million Miles from Nowhere," both to lyrics by Sam Lewis and Joe Young. In 1920, again with Lewis and Young, he wrote "My Mammy," inevitably associated with Al Jolson, who made it famous at the Winter Garden. Between 1922 and 1925 Donaldson wrote, to lyrics by Gus Kahn, "My Buddy," "Carolina in the Morning," "Beside a Babbling Brook," "Yes Sir, That's My Baby," "That Certain Party," "My Sweetie Turned Me Down," and "Isn't She the Sweetest Thing?" One of Donaldson's all-time favorites, "My Blue Heaven," lyrics by George Whiting, appeared in 1927. Afterwards Donaldson frequently wrote his own lyrics, as for "You're Driving Me Crazy," "Little White Lies," and "You Don't Have to Tell Me."

Donaldson was also active on Broadway and in Hollywood. In 1928, with Gus Kahn, he wrote the songs for *Whoopee!*, the successful Broadway musical produced by Ziegfeld and starring Eddie Cantor. Donaldson's best numbers here were "Makin' Whoopee!" "My Baby Just Cares for Me," and "Love Me or Leave Me," the last used many years later as the title for the screen biography of Ruth Etting. After 1929, Donaldson produced songs for a succession of outstanding screen musicals, including

Kid Millions with Eddie Cantor, *The Great Ziegfeld, Panama Hattie,* and *Follow the Boys.* Songs worth remembering from these productions include "It's Been So Long" and "Did I Remember?" both to lyrics by Harold Adamson.

Sammy Fain (1902-   ) was a staff pianist and song plugger in Tin Pan Alley and after that a performer over radio and on the vaudeville circuit, before "Nobody Knows What a Red-Head Mama Can Do" was published in 1925. His first hits began appearing in 1927, when he started writing music to Irving Kahal's lyrics, a collaboration that lasted seventeen years. Their first success was "Let a Smile Be Your Umbrella," which was soon followed by "There's Something About a Rose," "Wedding Bells Are Breaking Up That Old Gang of Mine," and "When I Take My Sugar to Tea."

Before going to Hollywood, where he became one of the leading composers of the motion-picture industry, Fain wrote the music for the two fabulous Olsen and Johnson Broadway extravaganzas, *Hellzapoppin'* (1938) and *Sons o' Fun* (1941). Among his best Hollywood songs were "You Brought a New Kind of Love to Me" (introduced by Maurice Chevalier in *The Big Pond*), "By a Waterfall," and "I Can Dream, Can't I?" all to lyrics by Kahal. For still another Fain movie song success, "That Old Feeling," Lew Brown provided the lyrics. One song written in Hollywood, but not directly for the screen, also became highly popular—the ballad "I'll Be Seeing You," which, written in 1938, was revived in 1943 to become one of the favorite sentimental songs of World War II.

After Kahal's death in 1942, Fain worked with other lyricists, most notably Paul Francis Webster, with whom he won the Academy Award twice—for "Secret Love" from *Calamity Jane* in 1953, and for "Love Is a Many Splendored Thing" from the picture of the same name in 1955. Still another distinguished screen song to Webster's lyrics was the title song from *April Love.* To Joe Young's lyrics Fain wrote "Was That the Human Thing to Do?" and, to lyrics by Bob Hilliard, "Dear Hearts and Gentle People."

George W. Meyer (1884-1959) was an oculist before he decided upon music as a permanent profession. He reached this decision in 1909 after his song, "Lonesome," which he wrote with

Kerry Mills to Edgar Leslie's lyrics, sold over a million copies. "When You're a Long, Long Way from Home" was Meyer's second big hit, published in 1914, and soon thereafter popularized by many blues singers, including Sophie Tucker and Grace La Rue. "For Me and My Gal," lyrics by Edgar Leslie and E. Ray Goetz, published in 1917, is probably the most successful song he ever wrote and the one by which he will always be remembered. A quarter of a century after it was written, it was used as a title for, and revived in, a motion picture starring Judy Garland. After 1917, Meyer's leading songs included "Everything Is Peaches Down in Georgia" in collaboration with Milton Ager, "Now I Lay Me Down to Sleep," which Bert and Betty Wheeler used in their vaudeville act for many years, "Tuck Me to Sleep in My Old 'Tucky Home," "Brown Eyes, Why Are You Blue?", "Happy Go Lucky Lane," and "My Song of the Nile."

Harry Ruby (1895-   ), like so many other song writers of his day, was a Tin Pan Alley staff pianist and song plugger for many years. He then toured the vaudeville circuit as a pianist and met Bert Kalmar, a young lyricist who was also part owner of a publishing house. When Kalmar retired from vaudeville to concentrate on writing lyrics and publishing songs, Ruby became his composer. Their first song was "He Sits Around," which Belle Baker sang in vaudeville. Then came "When Those Sweet Hawaiian Babies Roll Their Eyes," "So Long, Oo-Long," and "The Vamp from East Broadway," the last featured by Fanny Brice in the *Ziegfeld Follies of 1920*. Their greatest hit appeared in 1923, "Who's Sorry Now?", for which they wrote the lyrics to Ted Snyder's music, a number effectively revived on records and in night clubs thirty-five years later by Roberta Sherwood.

Between 1923 and 1941, Ruby and Kalmar wrote songs for several important Broadway musicals, including *The Ramblers* (1926), *Five O'clock Girl* (1927), *Good Boy* (1928), and the Marx Brothers farce, *Animal Crackers* (1928). Among their best numbers from these plays were "All Alone Monday" in *The Ramblers*, "Thinking of You" in *Five O'clock Girl*, "I Wanna Be Loved By You," made famous by Helen Kane in *Good Boy*, and "Watching the Clouds Roll By" in *Animal Crackers*.

Ruby and Kalmar went to Hollywood in 1930, where their first assignment was *Check and Double Check*, for which they created one of their greatest hits, "Three Little Words." Out of later screen musicals came "I Love You So Much," "Keep On Doin' What You're Doin'," and "Do You Love Me?", the last with Ruby's own lyrics. A screen biography of Ruby and Kalmar, entitled *Three Little Words*, was produced in 1950.

Richard A. Whiting (1891-1938) was made office manager of Remick's branch in Detroit just before World War I. As its employee he wrote "It's Tulip Time in Holland" in 1915, which sold a million and a half copies of sheet music. A year later Whiting had two more hits, "Mammy's Little Coal Black Rose" and "Dixieland." These, however, were just the preliminaries to one of Tin Pan Alley's song triumphs and one of the most memorable ballads of World War I, "Till We Meet Again," lyrics by Raymond Egan. Over five million copies were sold. Among Whiting's best songs after World War I were "Japanese Sandman," "Ain't We Got Fun?" "Ukulele Lady," and "Horses."

Beginning in 1929 Whiting sank his roots deep into Hollywood soil. His first song there was a winner, "Louise," lyrics by Leo Robin, introduced by Maurice Chevalier in his first American movie, *Innocents of Paris*, and since become one of his stand-bys. Later years brought to the screen such outstanding Whiting songs as "Beyond the Blue Horizon," melody written in collaboration with W. Franke Harling, "My Future Just Passed," "My Ideal" and "One Hour With You," two more Chevalier favorites, the former written in collaboration with Newell Chase, and "When Did You Leave Heaven?" and "Too Marvelous for Words," lyrics by Johnny Mercer.

For the Broadway stage Whiting wrote the music for the first edition of the George White *Scandals* and for several musical comedies including *Free for All* (1931) and *Take a Chance* (1932). Out of the last of these came "You're an Old Smoothie" and "Eadie Was a Lady," both of them in collaboration with Nacio Herb Brown to De Sylva's lyrics.

There was, then, in Tin Pan Alley, no dearth of composers able to create fresh, salable melodies. But through the years, Tin Pan Alley has tapped another source in the production of hit songs— the classics. It has never hesitated to raid the storehouse of great music for melodies that might serve the commercial needs of popular music. In 1888, for example, Joseph J. Sullivan snatched a motive from Wagner's *Lohengrin* for "Where Did You Get That Hat?", and four years later Percy Gaunt used a theme from the Neapolitan folk song, "Spagnola," for "The Bowery." Ben Harney presented rag treatments of Mendelssohn's "Spring Song," Rubinstein's "Melody in F," and the "Intermezzo" from Mascagni's *Cavalleria Rusticana*. Irving Berlin ragged Mendelssohn's "Spring Song" in "That Mesmerizing Mendelssohn Tune."

A highly profitable use of a classical melody was made in 1918 by Harry Carroll (1892-   ) in "I'm Always Chasing Rainbows," lyrics by Joseph McCarthy. The melody came from Chopin's "Fantaisie Impromptu in C-sharp minor." Before 1918 Carroll had written several Tin Pan Alley hits with his own tunes, notably "The Trail of the Lonesome Pine" and "By the Beautiful Sea." But the greatest hit of his career came with "I'm Always Chasing Rainbows," introduced on the Broadway stage in *Oh Look!* in 1918 and attractively recalled in 1945 for the motion picture, *The Dolly Sisters*.

In 1920, Al Jolson helped to popularize "Avalon," which he had written with Vincent Rose. The resemblance of this melody to the aria, "E lucevan le stelle," from Puccini's opera *Tosca* was by no means coincidental, despite a change of key. Puccini's publisher, Ricordi, brought suit against "Avalon" for infringement of copyright and was awarded damages of $25,000 together with payment of all subsequent "Avalon" royalties.

Although in 1920 Puccini was still protected by international copyright, the music of other masters was free for the taking. In the 1920's a wholesale raid on the classics took place among Tin Pan Alley tunesmiths. Works like *Scheherazade,* "Song of India," and "Hymn to the Sun" by Rimsky-Korsakov, Liszt's "Liebestraum," the "Dance of the Hours" from Ponchielli's *La Gioconda,* Cui's "Orientale," and MacDowell's "To a Wild Rose" were vulgarized either through jazzed-up versions or through use in popular songs. Sigmund Romberg earned a fortune from his popular adaptation of Schubert's melodies for the operetta *Blossom Time*. The income from one song alone, "Song of Love," exceeded $100,000.

So widespread had this practice of lifting tunes from the classics become that from across the ocean, England's leading music critic shouted: "Paws off!" In America, another outstanding music critic, Richard Aldrich of the *New York Times,* excoriated the trend in a stinging Sunday article.

But since this type of crime paid large dividends, the invasion of the property of the masters has continued even to the present day. The following are some of the most successful popular songs derived from the classics:

"Anniversary Song" (Ivanovici's "Waves of the Danube"), "As Years Go By" by Charles Tobias (Brahms' "Hungarian Dance No. 4"), "Concerto for Two" (Tchaikovsky's *First Piano Concerto*), "Don't You Know?" (Puccini's *La Bohème*), "Full Moon and Empty Arms" (Rachmaninoff's *Second Piano Concerto*), "I'd Climb the Highest Mountain" (Dvořák's "Humoresque"), "If I Should Love You" (Tchaikovsky's *Fifth Symphony*), "I Love You" by Robert Wright and Chet Forrest (Grieg's "Ich liebe dich"), "In an Eighteenth Century Drawing Room" by Raymond Scott (Mozart's *Piano Sonata in C*), "In the Valley of the Moon" by Charles Tobias (Mendelssohn's *Violin Concerto*), "I Think of You" (Rachmaninoff's *Second Piano Concerto*), "Kiss of Fire" (Volloldo's "El Choclo"), "The Lamp Is Low" (Ravel's *Pavane pour une Infante défunte*), "Lover Come Back to Me" by Sigmund Romberg ("June" from Tchaikovsky's *The Months*), "Moon Love" by André Kostelanetz with Mack Davis (Tchaikovsky's *Fifth Symphony*), "My Moonlight Madonna" (Fibich's "Poem"), "My Reverie" (Debussy's "Reverie"), "On the Isle of May" by André Kostelanetz with Mack Davis (Tchaikovsky's "Andante Cantabile"), "One Summer Night" (Dvořák's *Songs My Mother Taught Me*), "Our Love" (Tchaikovsky's *Romeo and Juliet*), "Strange Music" by Robert Wright and Chet Forrest (Grieg's "Wedding Day in Troldhaugen"), "The Things I Love" (Tchaikovsky's "Melodie"), "And This Is My Beloved" by Robert Wright and Chet Forrest (Borodin's "Nocturne"), "Till the End of Time" (Chopin's "Polonaise in A-flat"), "Tonight We Love" (Tchaikovsky's *First Piano Concerto*), "When the Lights Go On Again" (Beethoven's "Minuet in G"), and "Wild Horseman" (Schumann's "Wild Horseman").

15—Hollywood

On October 6, 1927, with *The Jazz Singer,* the long silent motion-picture screen suddenly burst into song and speech. In this movie Al Jolson starred as a jazz singer who must forego his big chance on Broadway to substitute for his dying father, a cantor, at the Day of Atonement services in the synagogue. Most of the film was silent, but in several sequences sound was injected to permit a few moments of dialogue and to allow Jolson to sing "Dirty Hands, Dirty Face," "Toot, Toot, Tootsie," "My Mammy," and "Blue Skies." Thus a new age was ushered in—not only for motion pictures but also for show business and for popular music.

The popular song had already been an ally of motion pictures for some time. Just before the era of talking pictures, the writing of theme songs for important screen productions had become a lucrative activity. One of the most successful composers in this field was Erno Rapee (1891-1945), later the musical director of Radio City Music Hall in New York. To Lew Pollack's lyrics, Rapee wrote "Charmaine" for *What Price Glory?* in 1926, "Diane" for *Seventh Heaven* in 1927, and "Angela Mia" for *Street Angel* in 1928. Mabel Wayne created an immensely popular theme song in 1927—"Ramona," for the film of the same name, lyrics by L. Wolfe Gilbert.

It was, however, after talking pictures came into existence that music became a dominant element in Hollywood. In 1929, the first screen revue was produced, *The Broadway Melody.* Its songs —by Nacio Herb Brown with lyrics by Arthur Freed—included the title number and "The Wedding of the Painted Doll." A smash box-office success and the first musical to win the Academy Award as the best picture of the year, *The Broadway Melody* inevitably invited imitation. In the next two years, revues flourished on the screen. Out of these productions came Hollywood's first contributions to the song hit parade. Besides the two numbers already

166

mentioned from *The Broadway Melody*, these new screen songs included Harry Akst's "Am I Blue?" from *On with the Show*, Joe Burke's "Painting the Clouds with Sunshine" and "Tip Toe through the Tulips" from *Gold Diggers of Broadway*, Nacio Herb Brown's "Singin' in the Rain" from *Hollywood Revue of 1929*, and Milton Ager's "Happy Feet" and "A Bench in the Park" and Mabel Wayne's "It Happened in Monterey" from *The King of Jazz*.

Original screen musicals also became popular. After his initial triumph in *The Jazz Singer*, Al Jolson appeared in *The Singing Fool* in 1929, for which De Sylva, Brown, and Henderson wrote "Sonny Boy." In the same year the same song writing team produced the score for *Sunny Side Up*, with Janet Gaynor and Charles Farrell. Maurice Chevalier made his American bow on the screen in 1929 with *Innocents of Paris* singing Richard Whiting's "Louise." Chevalier's Hollywood success was soon thereafter firmly solidified with *The Love Parade* in 1929, score by Victor Schertzinger, and, in 1930 with *The Big Pond*, in which he introduced Sammy Fain's "You Brought a New Kind of Love to Me." In 1929 Fanny Brice was starred in an original screen musical, *My Man*, in which she sang some of her favorites from the *Ziegfeld Follies*, including the title song. Rudy Vallee had a screen musical written for him, appropriately named after a song he helped make famous, *The Vagabond Lover*. Amos and Andy of radio fame, appeared in another tailor-made musical, *Check and Double Check*, in which Harry Ruby made his Hollywood bow as composer with a big song hit, "Three Little Words." Jeanette MacDonald was starred in *Monte Carlo*, in 1930, presenting several excellent songs by Richard Whiting including "Beyond the Blue Horizon."

In its avid hunt for musical-comedy material, Hollywood inevitably raided the Broadway stage and adapted many of its productions for the screen. Among the earliest of these (in 1929) were Sigmund Romberg's *The Desert Song*, Harry Tierney's *Rio Rita*, and Jerome Kern's *Sally* and *Show Boat*.

The net of Hollywood caught not merely famous musical comedies and operettas, but also the leading composers and lyricists of Broadway and Tin Pan Alley. A great invasion of the West by Eastern songwriters began in 1929 and continued for the next few years. Among the earliest arrivals were De Sylva, Brown, and

Henderson, Irving Berlin, Con Conrad, Richard Whiting, Milton Ager, and Walter Donaldson. Sigmund Romberg and Jimmy McHugh wrote their first Hollywood scores in 1930. George and Ira Gershwin, Rodgers and Hart, and Jerome Kern made their first appearances in Hollywood in 1931. In time, most of the other famous writers of songs diverted at least a part of their activity to the needs of motion pictures.

While it is true that most of the music being written for motion pictures came from composers imported from the East, Hollywood was by no means negligent in creating musical careers of its own. Let us therefore consider some of the most significant composers to be raised from obscurity by the talking picture.

Nacio Herb Brown (1896-   ) was a successful real estate broker in California before beginning to write songs for the movies. He was born in Deming, New Mexico, and arrived in Los Angeles in 1904, where he completed his education. He toured the vaudeville circuit for a year as piano accompanist to Alice Doll and then opened a tailoring establishment in Hollywood, which drew its clientele from motion-picture stars. In 1920 he began investing in Beverly Hills real estate—an activity that made him wealthy. In the same year he also had his first song published, "Coral Sea," a hit after being introduced by the Paul Whiteman Orchestra. In 1926 another of his numbers, "Doll Dance," attracted interest in a revue produced in Hollywood. In 1928, Irving Thalberg persuaded him to take a vacation from real estate to write music for *The Broadway Melody*, then being planned for MGM. *The Broadway Melody*, as has already been said, made screen history, and Brown's songs—with lyrics by Arthur Freed—became hits. Thalberg now found it easy to convince Brown to combine real estate with music. In 1929, still with Freed, Brown wrote "Singin' in the Rain" and "You Were Meant for Me," for the *Hollywood Revue of 1929*, and "Chant of the Jungle" and "Pagan Love Song." After that came "Paradise" and "Temptation" among many other numbers.

By this time, Brown had given up all his activity in real estate to concentrate on music. Between 1934 and 1943 he was one of Hollywood's busiest composers, producing songs for more than twenty motion pictures. To Arthur Freed's lyrics he wrote "All I Do Is Dream of You," "You Are My Lucky Star," "Broadway

Rhythm," and "Would You?" To lyrics by Gus Kahn he wrote "You Stepped out of a Dream," and to lyrics by Heyman and Brent, "If I Steal a Kiss" and "Love Is Where You Find It."

Jay Livingston (1915-   ) met his collaborator, the lyricist Ray Evans, while attending the University of Pennsylvania. After college, they played in jazz bands and on cruise ships, wrote special material for radio, and contributed some songs to the Olsen and Johnson Broadway extravaganza, *Sons o' Fun*, in 1941. Livingston and Evans came to Hollywood in 1945 to write songs for *Why Girls Leave Home*. In the next eleven years they won the Academy Award three times—for "Buttons and Bows" from the Bob Hope comedy, *The Paleface*, in 1948; "Mona Lisa" from *Capt. Carey of the U.S.A.*, in 1950; and "Whatever Will Be, Will Be" from *The Man Who Knew Too Much*, in 1956. Other significant screen songs included "Golden Earrings," "Copper Canyon," "*Bonne Nuit*, Good Night," and "Tammy" from *Tammy and the Bachelor*, introduced by its star, Debbie Reynolds. Livingston and Evans wrote their first Broadway musical-comedy score in 1958 for *Oh, Captain!*

Jimmy McHugh (1894-   ) came to Hollywood with a few song hits and an outstanding Broadway revue to his credit, but his career belongs essentially to Hollywood, where for over a quarter of a century he has been one of its ace composers. After publishing his first song, "Emaline," in 1921, McHugh wrote songs for seven years for the Harlem night spot, The Cotton Club. The most famous of these was "When My Sugar Walks Down the Street" and "I Can't Believe You're in Love with Me." In 1928, with Dorothy Fields as his lyricist, he wrote the score for the sensational all-Negro Broadway revue, *Blackbirds of 1928*, among whose principal songs were "I Can't Give You Anything but Love" and "Diga, Diga, Doo." After writing songs for two more Broadway productions, McHugh came to Hollywood in 1930 and almost immediately assumed a place of first importance among its composers. With Dorothy Fields he wrote "Cuban Love Song," "Thank You for a Lovely Evening," the title song of *Hooray for Love*, "I'm in the Mood for Love," and "I Feel a Song Coming On." He also wrote music with other lyricists, principally with Harold Adamson. This collaboration was responsible for "A

Lovely Way to Spend an Evening," "Life Can Be Beautiful," "Say a Prayer for the Boys Over There," "Comin' In on a Wing and a Prayer," and "It's a Most Unusual Day." In 1948 McHugh and Adamson wrote the songs for the successful Broadway musical comedy, *As the Girls Go*.

Harry Revel (1905-1958) was the musical half of one of Hollywood's foremost songwriting teams, Gordon and Revel. He was born in London, and as a young man played in Parisian jazz bands and Hawaiian orchestras. A dedicated admirer of American popular music, before he even set foot on American soil he wrote "I'm Going Back to Old Nebraska," which sold over a million copies in London. He came to the United States in 1929 and soon afterwards met Mack Gordon, a vaudevillian and lyricist, with whom he toured the vaudeville circuit. They started writing songs in 1931 and placed several in two Broadway revues, one of them the *Ziegfeld Follies*, and two musical comedies. They made their first appearance in Hollywood in 1933, putting their best foot forward at once with "Did You Ever See a Dream Walking?" for *Sitting Pretty*. In the next two years they wrote "You're My Past, Present and Future," "Stay as Sweet as You Are," "Love Thy Neighbor," "Goodnight, My Love," "With My Eyes Wide Open I'm Dreaming," and "Don't Let It Bother You." In 1935 they received from ASCAP special awards for no less than nine songs, including "The Loveliness of You" and "From the Top of Your Heart." Between 1935 and 1937 their most significant songs included "A Star Fell out of Heaven," "May I Have the Next Romance with You?", "There's a Lull in My Life," and the title song from *Wake Up and Live*. This fruitful partnership was dissolved in 1942 when Revel engaged extensively in war work.

Dimitri Tiomkin (1899-   ) received a thorough musical training at the St. Petersburg Conservatory and then with Egon Petri and Ferruccio Busoni. He then embarked on a successful career as concert pianist and also achieved recognition in Paris and New York as a composer with avant-garde tendencies. He first came to Hollywood in 1930 to do the scoring for *The Rogue Song*, starring Lawrence Tibbett. He returned to Hollywood three years later to provide the background music for *Alice in Wonderland* and has since then become one of the most productive, highest paid, and most widely sought after composers of background music. He has written the scores for more than one hundred pictures and on fourteen occasions was nominated for Academy Awards. He received the Academy Award for his scoring of *High Noon* in 1952, *The High and the Mighty* in 1954, and *The Old Man and the Sea* in 1958. In addition he received the award for the theme song of *High Noon,* "Do Not Forsake Me," lyrics by Ned Washington. Other highly successful songs for the screen included the title numbers of *The High and the Mighty,* lyrics by Ned Washington, and *Friendly Persuasion,* lyrics by Paul Francis Webster; "The Battle of the Alamo" and "Green Leaves of Summer" from *The Alamo*; "They Call It Love" and "Legend of Navarone" from *Guns of Navarone*; and the score for *The Sundowners.*

Jimmy Van Heusen (1913-   ) attended Syracuse University, where he wrote college shows with Harold Arlen's brother. It was Harold Arlen who first recognized Van Heusen's musical talent and who urged him to come to New York. In 1938, Van Heusen finally had a hit song in "It's the Dreamer in Me," written in collaboration with Jimmy Dorsey. Several other outstanding songs were responsible for bringing him out to Hollywood in 1940, the best being "Heaven Can Wait," "Oh You Crazy Moon," and "Imagination."

One year after his arrival in Hollywood, Van Heusen started a fruitful association with Bing Crosby by writing songs for *The Road to Zanzibar.* For almost a decade thereafter he wrote the music for some of Crosby's most important motion pictures, his lyricist usually being Johnny Burke. For *The Road to Morocco* he wrote "Moonlight Becomes You," for *Dixie,* "Sunday, Monday, or Always," for *Road to Utopia,* "Put It There Pal" and "Personality," for *The Bells of St. Mary's,* "Aren't You Glad You're You?", for *The Road to Rio,* "Smile Right Back at the Sun," and, for *Going My Way,* a song for which he received the Academy Award in 1944, "Swinging on a Star."

But Van Heusen did not confine himself exclusively to Bing Crosby's pictures. Still with Johnny Burke as his lyricist he wrote important songs for numerous other motion pictures—"Suddenly It's Spring," "It Could Happen to You," and the title song for *My Heart Goes Crazy,* among others. He also worked with the lyricist, Sammy Cahn, with whom he wrote the title song of *The Tender Trap*, and songs for the motion-picture biography of Joe E. Lewis, *The Joker Is Wild*, starring Frank Sinatra, and for another Sinatra picture, *Hole in the Head*. "All the Way" from *The Joker Is Wild* received the Academy Award in 1957, and "High Hopes" from *Hole in the Head* in 1959. In 1960, "Second Time Around" from *High Time* was nominated for the Academy Award.

Harry Warren (1893-   ), like Jimmy McHugh, wrote some song hits before coming to Hollywood, but, also like McHugh, he did his finest work for the screen. After finding a job in Tin Pan Alley as song plugger, Warren produced several moderate successes between 1922 and 1925, notably "Rose of the Rio Grande" (with Ross Gorman) and "I Love My Baby (My Baby Loves Me)." Several more modest Tin Pan Alley hits followed in the ensuing years, as well as a few significant numbers for Broadway revues, including "You're My Everything," "I Found a Million Dollar Baby," "Cheerful Little Earful," and "Would You Like to Take a Walk?"

Warren's first contribution to the screen came in 1930 with two songs for *Spring Is Here*. His music, thereafter, appeared in over sixty motion pictures. On three occasions he won the Academy Award—in 1935 for "Lullaby of Broadway," lyrics by Al Dubin, from *The Gold Diggers of 1935;* in 1943 for "You'll Never Know," lyrics by Mack Gordon, from *Hello, Frisco, Hello;* and in 1946 for "On the Atchison, Topeka and the Santa Fe," lyrics by Johnny Mercer, from *The Harvey Girls*.

Most of Warren's other screen successes were to Al Dubin's lyrics. They included "We're in the Money," "Shuffle Off to Buffalo," the title song of *Forty-Second Street*, "The Boulevard of Broken Dreams," "I'll String Along with You," "I Only Have Eyes for You," and "She's a Latin from Manhattan." "You Must Have Been a Beautiful Baby" and "Jeepers Creepers" were to lyrics by Johnny Mercer; "You Wonderful You" to lyrics by Brooks and Chapin; and "That's *Amore*" to lyrics by Jack Brooks.

No higher accolade can be bestowed on a motion picture than the annual award of the Academy of Motion Picture Arts and

Sciences, the so-called "Oscar." Since this prize was instituted in 1928, the Academy Award for the best picture of the year has three times gone to a musical comedy or revue—*The Broadway Melody* in 1929; *An American in Paris,* in which George Gershwin's music was used, in 1951; and the Lerner and Lowe musical, *Gigi,* in 1959. Two other motion pictures that have won the "Oscar" cannot properly be described as musical comedies but did make prominent use of songs within the story texture. In *The Great Ziegfeld* (1936) were heard three songs by Walter Donaldson with Harold Adamson's lyrics and an old Irving Berlin favorite, "A Pretty Girl Is Like a Melody," was revived. Three songs by Jimmy Van Heusen and Johnny Burke were used in *Going My Way* (1944), starring Bing Crosby, one of which, as we have already mentioned, "Swinging on a Star," itself won an Academy Award.

In 1934 the Academy instituted a category for screen songs among its annual awards. The first recipient of this "Oscar" was Con Conrad's "The Continental" from *The Gay Divorcée.* Besides those already mentioned, the following songs have received the "Oscar": 1937, "Sweet Leilani," words and music by Harry Owens, from *Waikiki Wedding;* 1938, "Thanks for the Memory," music by Ralph Rainger and lyrics by Leo Robin, from *The Big Broadcast of 1938;* 1940, "When You Wish upon a Star," music by Leigh Harline and lyrics by Ned Washington, from *Pinocchio;* and 1947, "Zip-a-Dee-Doo-Dah," music by Allie Wrubel and lyrics by Ray Gilbert, from *Song of the South.*

Another yardstick of success for Hollywood, besides the Academy Award, is provided by the box office. Measured by such means, the most significant screen musicals are those which have grossed over five million dollars. They are, in alphabetical order: *The Bells of St. Mary's, Blue Skies, Can-Can, Cinderella, The Country Girl, The Eddie Duchin Story, Gigi, The Glenn Miller Story, Going My Way, Guys and Dolls, Hans Christian Andersen, High Society, Jolson Sings Again, The Jolson Story, The King and I, Meet Me in St. Louis, No Business Like Show Business, Oceans 11, Oklahoma!, Pillow Talk, Porgy and Bess, Pal Joey, Seven Brides for Seven Brothers, Show Boat* (1951), *Snow White, South Pacific, A Star Is Born, This Is the Army, Welcome Stranger, White Christmas,* and *Yankee Doodle Dandy.*

Some of the most ambitious, and at times most gratifying, screen musicals have been based on the lives of famous popular composers. The plot might often be more fiction than fact and might run a gamut of emotions from "A" to "B," but such shortcomings were often compensated for by the fact that these motion pictures provided wonderful entertainment through the presentation of the outstanding musical achievement of our significant popular composers. The following are among the most important of such screen biographies:

George M. Cohan (*Yankee Doodle Dandy*), De Sylva, Brown, and Henderson (*The Best Things in Life Are Free*), Paul Dresser (*My Gal Sal*), Stephen Foster (*Swanee River* and *I Dream of Jeanie*), Fred Fisher (*Oh, You Beautiful Doll*), George Gershwin (*Rhapsody in Blue*), W. C. Handy (*St. Louis Blues*), Victor Herbert (*The Great Victor Herbert*), Joe Howard (*I Wonder Who's Kissing Her Now*), Jerome Kern (*Till the Clouds Roll By*), Cole Porter (*Night and Day*), Rodgers and Hart (*Words and Music*), Sigmund Romberg (*Deep In My Heart*), Harry Ruby and Bert Kalmar (*Three Little Words*), and John Philip Sousa (*Stars and Stripes Forever*).

Biographies of famous stars of the stage or of band leaders and other performers of popular music have also provided rich opportunities for cavalcades of the songs with which these people are most often identified. Here are some of the most interesting of these screen musicals:

Nora Bayes (*Shine On Harvest Moon*), Eddie Cantor (*The Eddie Cantor Story*), Vernon and Irene Castle (*The Story of the Castles*), The Dolly Sisters (*The Dolly Sisters*), The Dorsey Brothers (*The Fabulous Dorseys*), Eddie Duchin (*The Eddie Duchin Story*), Ruth Etting (*Love Me or Leave Me*), Benny Fields (*Minstrel Man*), Eddie Foy (*The Seven Little Foys*), Jane Froman (*With a Song in My Heart*), Benny Goodman (*The Benny Goodman Story*), Al Jolson (*The Jolson Story* and *Jolson Sings Again*), Gene Krupa (*The Gene Krupa Story*), Joe E. Lewis (*The Joker Is Wild*), Ted Lewis (*Is Everybody Happy?*), Glenn Miller (*The Glenn Miller Story*), Marilyn Miller (*Look for the Silver Lining*), Helen Morgan (*The Helen Morgan Story*), Red Nichols (*The Five Pennies*), Lillian Roth (*I'll Cry Tomorrow*), Lillian Russell (*Lillian Russell*), Eva Tanguay (*The I Don't Care Girl*).

16–Popular Music Becomes Big Business

Through the years, technological advances have helped bring popular music to an ever expanding audience. In the 1910's, the player piano was supplanted by the phonograph. It is doubtful whether any piano roll ever helped to make a song a hit, but in 1919 the phonograph record could claim credit for such an achievement when George Stoddard's "Mary," recorded by Victor before the song was either published or publicly performed, sold about three hundred thousand discs in three months.

The record business now became a force not only in swelling the tide of popularity of an already familiar song but, in many cases, in converting an unfamiliar number into a hit. With the sales of records mounting steadily, recorded music has become a medium of the first importance in the distribution of popular songs. The annual sale of popular records reached forty-five million in 1939. The figure reached a hundred million in 1949 and a hundred and fifty million in 1959. There are twenty-five million phonographs in the United States. "More than ever," wrote Abel Green in *Variety*, "an inanimate object—a vinylite platter running three minutes regardless of the 33, 45, or 78 speed—is king of Tin Pan Alley. The popular music business seems to revolve almost entirely around the revolving biscuit."

Each decade has had its recording stars to popularize and sell its songs of the day—Al Jolson, Eddie Cantor, Gene Austin, Kate Smith, Bing Crosby, Rudy Vallee, Eddie Fisher, Frank Sinatra, Perry Como, the Andrews Sisters, Patti Page, Rosemary Clooney, Vaughn Monroe, Frankie Laine, Nat "King" Cole, Pat Boone, Tony Bennett, Elvis Presley, Jimmie Rodgers, Paul Anka, Fabian, Frankie Avalon, Connie Francis, and Bobby Darin. Each decade has had its favored band, from Paul Whiteman to Artie Shaw, from Benny Goodman to Glenn Miller. The impact of a singing star or a band upon a song often has been phenomenal.

The following is only a sampling of songs that have had a sale of a million or more records, the name of the recording artist appearing in parentheses: "Rags to Riches" (Tony Bennett), "April Love" (Pat Boone), "Come on-a My House" (Rosemary Clooney), "Nature Boy" and "Mona Lisa" (Nat "King" Cole), "Temptation" and "Hot Diggety" (Perry Como), "Sweet Leilani," "Dear Hearts and Gentle People," and "Too-ra-loo-ra-loo-ral" (Bing Crosby), "Pistol Packin' Mama" (Andrews Sisters), "Oh, My Papa" (Eddie Fisher), "Young Love" (Tab Hunter), "Mule Train" and "Moonlight Gambler" (Frankie Laine), "Green Door" (Jim Lowe), "Riders in the Sky" (Vaughn Monroe), "Doggie in the Window" and "Tennessee Waltz" (Patti Page), "The Great Pretender" (The Platters), "All Shook Up," "Love Me Tender," and "Don't Be Cruel" (Elvis Presley), "Cry" (Johnnie Ray), "Tammy" (Debbie Reynolds), "Honeycomb" (Jimmie Rodgers), "Young at Heart" (Frank Sinatra), "Diana" (Paul Anka).

Records have frequently drawn renewed attention to and re-vived enthusiasm for songs that first became popular many years earlier. In 1957, for example, Pat Boone revived interest in "Love Letters in the Sand," and in 1958 recordings of "Smoke Gets in Your Eyes" by The Platters and "Who's Sorry Now?" by Connie Francis again made hits of these old favorites. Million-copy rec-ord sales also first carried to recognition many songs now regarded as standards but that were permitted to languish for many years in neglect and obscurity. Cole Porter's "Begin the Beguine" was almost completely unknown for almost a decade before its revival on records by Artie Shaw in a striking new orchestration, and a two-million copy record sale by the same performer was the major influence in bringing deserved fame to Hoagy Carmichael's "Star Dust." Vernon Duke's "April in Paris" was a dud in the revue in which it was first introduced. Many years later, however, it be-came a major success primarily because of Marian Chase's re-cording.

The juke box is an important offshoot of the record business, bringing popular tunes into taverns, cafés, ice-cream parlors, bars, and restaurants throughout the country. In 1959, a half million juke boxes were in operation.

In the 1950's, the record business began tapping a new fertile market, the teen-age trade, and the youngsters' musical tastes were decisive in shaping a major trend of the times, Rock 'n' Roll, a kind of blues song with a steady but simplified beat and a repetitious melodic phrase. Because of the influence of teen-agers, Rock 'n' Roll became the dominant new song style of the 1950's. Invariably the work of newcomers to the song writing business, these primitive and unsophisticated songs—often to completely unintelligible lyrics—spread like contagion: "Rock Around the Clock," "Don't Be Cruel," "Hot Diggety," "Hound Dog," "Why Do Fools Fall in Love?", "All Shook Up," "Blue Suede Shoes," "Jailhouse Rock," and "Bird Dog," to mention only a few.

The radio invaded the American home in the 1920's. With the opening of the first radio network by the National Broadcasting Company in 1926, a single radio program was able to reach an audience of several millions, and a single broadcast could create a hit song. Singing stars became household names—the Happiness Boys, Arthur Tracy (the Street Singer), and Whispering Jack Smith in the early years, and later Kate Smith, Morton Downey, Rudy Vallee, and Bing Crosby. They had the personal appeal and following to create new song hits, some of which became their identifying theme music—"I'm Just a Vagabond Lover" (Rudy Vallee), "Where the Blue of the Night Meets the Gold of the Day" (Bing Crosby), "When the Moon Comes over the Mountain" (Kate Smith), and "Carolina Moon" (Morton Downey).

A historic decision by the United States Circuit Court of Appeals in the 1940's sanctified the marriage of records and radio. One of the major recording companies had filed a suit against several radio stations to prevent the broadcasting of recordings, maintaining that this was an infringement of copyright. In his decision, Judge Hand stated that the broadcaster, in playing records, did not in any way violate the basic rights of the copyright owner. Broadcasting records now became an extensive practice. The disc jockey—a term coined by *Variety* in 1937 to describe radio announcers who devoted programs to recordings and comments—ruled the air waves. After World War II, the disc jockey became a major power in the music business, and about two thousand of them functioned throughout the country. Since he could stimulate and hold a public's interest in a certain record or song through repeated performances and through expressions of his personal enthusiasm, he could actually form the nation's musical tastes. The far-reaching influence of disc jockeys in publicizing records and promoting songs received rather unfavorable publicity in 1959 through the disclosure of the "payola" practices prevailing throughout the industry—bribes to get disc jockeys to plug specific records.

Radio entered more actively into the publication and promotion of hit songs in 1935 with the inauguration of the program *Hit Parade,* which flourished over radio for almost a quarter of a century and for several years until 1959 over television. This was a program devoted to the ten leading tunes of the week based on sales of sheet music and records and on the number of performances given a song on juke boxes. The first *Hit Parade* program placed Jerome Kern's "Lovely to Look At" in the top slot. The program soon became a valuable barometer of the nation's tastes in popular music. Irving Berlin's "White Christmas" was performed on these broadcasts thirty-two times, more often than any other single song. "People Will Say We're in Love" by Rodgers and Hammerstein was heard thirty times; "Harbor Lights," music by Hugh Williams (Will Grosz) and lyrics by Jimmy Kennedy, twenty-nine; and Sammy Fain's "I'll Be Seeing You" and Harry Warren's "You'll Never Know," twenty-four each. "Too Young," music by Sid Lippman and lyrics by Sylvia Dee, was featured most often in first place, twelve times.

Another significant development in radio broadcasting took place the year the *Hit Parade* was born. This was the use of wired radio—baptized "Muzak"—offered to restaurants, night spots, bars, hotels, and later to banks, business establishments, and railroad and bus terminals among other locales. A continual flow of music was provided, uninterrupted by advertisements and often even by announcements. Popular music now penetrated more deeply than ever before into the daily lives and activities of the American people.

Television has also had its influence on popular music. Several songs written expressly for specific television programs have become immediate favorites. "Let Me Go, Lover," music by Jenny Lou Carson with lyrics by Al Hill, became an overnight hit after serving as an integral part of a dramatic television production on *Studio One.* "Love and Marriage" by Jimmy Van Heusen, lyrics by Sammy Cahn, was introduced in a musical adaptation for television of Thornton Wilder's *Our Town* in 1955. (In 1959 the same song returned as the theme music and title of a weekly program.) "The Ballad of Davy Crockett," music by George Burns and lyrics by Tom Blackburn, a hit in 1955, was first popularized in conjunction with a Walt Disney motion picture presented in several installments over television before coming into motion-picture theaters. An established television star like Perry Como could introduce and instantly popularize on his weekly program songs like "Round and Round," "Don't Let the Stars Get in Your Eyes," and "Catch a Falling Star," and a comparative newcomer like Johnny Mathis was able to do a similar service for a song like "Come to Me" on a program of the same name. Theme music for weekly programs sometimes graduated into the hit class either as songs or as instrumental numbers, as happened to Walter Schumann's "Dragnet" and Henri Mancini's "Peter Gunn."

The phonograph, juke box, radio, and television—as well as the stage and the screen—provided new sources of revenue for music. The sale of sheet music, once the backbone of the song industry, was now incidental. Now that the popular music business had become a giant trust, agencies had to be formed to protect the interests of composers, lyricists, and publishers by granting licenses for the use of the work of its members to any organization using it for profit, either in live or canned performances. The first such agency was the American Society of Composers, Authors and Publishers (ASCAP). It came into being as a result of a lawsuit by Victor Herbert against Shanley's Restaurant in New York. While dining there one day in 1913, Herbert heard the restaurant orchestra play some of his compositions. It occurred to him then how unfair it was for a successful restaurant to use the music of composers as a part of its operation without paying the composer. He discussed the matter with his attorney who decided to institute a test action in court. After four years of litigation, the United States Supreme Court ruled in favor of Herbert. Justice Oliver Wendell Holmes maintained that "if music did not pay, it would be given up. If it pays, it pays out of the public's pocket. Whether it pays or not, the purpose of employing it is for profit, and that is enough."

The Shanley case and the litigation it set in motion convinced Herbert of the need for an organization to protect the interests of American composers and lyricists. Together with Sousa, George

M. Cohan, George W. Meyer, about a hundred and fifty other composers and lyricists, and about twenty publishers, he helped organize ASCAP on February 13, 1914, in a New York hotel. Officers were elected, and the preliminary machine was set up to issue, for a fee, licenses for the performance of the music of its members.

It took several years and a considerable amount of court action before business groups were made to pay a fee for the use of music they had so long been using free, but by 1921 ASCAP had signed up about six thousand restaurants, hotels, cabarets, and motion picture theaters. In 1921 the 250 members of ASCAP divided an annual income totaling about $80,000. In 1922 the gross income was doubled, and in 1923 it reached almost $200,000.

With dogged perseverance ASCAP continued and renewed its efforts to make every organization using music of ASCAP members its client for licensing. Now not only restaurants, hotels, and cabarets come under its jurisdiction, but also wire services, night clubs, cocktail bars, radio and television stations, record companies, and theater producers. By the middle 1950's ASCAP had expanded its membership to more than four thousand, and its annual income exceeded twenty million dollars. It had branch offices in about thirty American cities and was affiliated with related groups in over twenty European countries. Since 1950, the share earned by a composer from ASCAP has depended on the number of performances that his works have received through every possible medium. A composer in the first or leading category in number of performances derives about $50,000 a year ($100,000 if, like Irving Berlin or Cole Porter, he is his own lyricist). A composer or lyricist does not have to be alive or productive to be the beneficiary of this system, as long as his work is still heard frequently.

A second important organization of composers, lyricists, and publishers is BMI (Broadcast Music Incorporated), which came into existence in 1940. One year before, ASCAP had demanded from radio an annual fee of nine million dollars, twice what it had received the previous year. When radio refused to meet this demand, ASCAP removed the music of its members from the air waves for more than a year. Since almost all contemporary popular music was the work of ASCAP members, the air was flooded with songs by Stephen Foster and other old stand-bys until a satisfactory compromise was reached. Meanwhile, radio executives created an organization of their own to rival ASCAP, by building up a catalogue of music for use on broadcasts. In short order, BMI was able to create an impressive library of popular songs by new and unknown composers and lyricists and to receive a yearly income of about six million dollars. Within the first three years, several major song hits were in the BMI domain—"The Breeze and I," "I Hear a Rhapsody," "I Don't Want to Set the World on Fire," "Deep in the Heart of Texas," and "Pistol Packin' Mama," among others. The Rock 'n' Roll boom in the 1950's proved particularly beneficial to BMI, since many composers of this kind of music were unknown and owed their development to that organization. Thus such Rock 'n' Roll favorites as the following were BMI numbers: "Bird Dog," "All Shook Up," "Jailhouse Rock," "Be-Bop Baby," "Teen-Age Crush," "Great Balls of Fire," "Teen Beat," and "Red River Rock."

17—New Vistas for Jazz

Composers of popular songs like Jerome Kern and George Gershwin made a conscious effort to bring to their writing some of the rich resources of serious music. Already in 1914 in "They Didn't Believe Me" Kern digressed from seemingly unalterable Tin Pan Alley practices. In the chorus he allowed the melody to expand for eight bars in quarter notes after the simple opening four-bar statement, instead of proceeding at once to his second four-bar theme; he also carried the melody to a compelling climax through a change of key; and finally in the recapitulation of the main melodic thought he suddenly permitted a new idea to intrude before he returned to his original material. Such a maltreatment of the traditional thirty-two-bar chorus was revolutionary. No less iconoclastic was a song like Gershwin's "I'll Build a Stairway to Paradise" in 1922, with its unexpected flatted thirds and sevenths in the melody, its enharmonic changes, and its daring accentuations. After Kern and Gershwin, several other composers extended the structure and heightened the articulation of the popular song. The confining shackles of the thirty-two-bar chorus were once and for all shattered by composers like Harold Arlen and Richard Rodgers. Arlen's "Black Magic" has a chorus that sweeps across seventy-two measures. The "Soliloquy" from Rodgers' *Carousel* is a seven-minute narrative made up of eight different melodic fragments. Added to such new procedures are a harmonic language so varied as to endow the song with a new dimension and a variety of rhythm and meter to contribute a new dynamism.

Borrowing some of the techniques of serious music for the popular song was not exclusively the work of composers. In the early 1920's, several noted arrangers and bandleaders experimented with the presentation of popular music in symphonic transcriptions. The undisputed leaders in such a movement were the bandleader, Paul Whiteman, and his arranger, Ferde Grofé. Whiteman was trained as a serious musician and for several years played the violin in the Denver and San Francisco Symphony Orchestras. While in the latter city he became interested in jazz and formed an ensemble of his own in 1917. After World War I, he reorganized and expanded his jazz ensemble and began filling engagements in California. One of these, at the Alexandria Hotel in Los Angeles, proved so successful that it lasted a year.

In 1919, Whiteman engaged Ferde Grofé as pianist and arranger. Grofé (1892-   ) also had considerable experience in classical music, having played the viola in the Los Angeles Symphony. Then, like Whiteman, he moved from symphony to jazz. He organized a jazz band which he directed, in which he played the piano, and for which he made all the arrangements. Whiteman heard this band in a Los Angeles dance hall and at once hired its director-arranger for his own orchestra. For the next half dozen years and more, Grofé prepared all the arrangements for the Paul Whiteman Orchestra. Grofé was so skillful in his understanding of instrumentation and orchestral color and so resourceful in his handling of sonority that, in Whiteman's carefully prepared performances, his works brought in a new era for popular music. It was the era of symphonic jazz.

At different periods the Paul Whiteman Orchestra included some of the most eminent performers of jazz, among them Bix Beiderbecke, Jimmy and Tommy Dorsey, Red Nichols, and Joe Venuti, and such eminent vocalists as Mildred Bailey and Bing Crosby. In the early 1920's Whiteman's orchestra achieved renown on records, in night clubs and vaudeville, in Broadway musical comedies and revues, and in motion pictures. As a pioneer in the task of providing popular music with a symphonic setting, this orchestra on February 12, 1924, performed in New York's Aeolian Hall, an auditorium for serious concert music. "The experiment," explained Hugh C. Ernst to the audience, "is . . . to point out . . . the tremendous strides which have been made in popular music from the day of discordant jazz . . . to the really melodious music of today." Popular songs were given in symphonic transcriptions. Semi-classical favorites appeared in jazz versions. The climax came with the world première of a symphonic work with jazz idioms and techniques, written expressly for that concert—George Gershwin's *Rhapsody in Blue,* orchestrated by Grofé, with the composer playing the piano obbligato. It was this rhapsody that gave Whiteman's experimental concert its significance. In this remarkably gifted and at times inspired music, proof was provided that jazz could make an original and powerful contribution to the writing of serious music.

The *Rhapsody in Blue* was by no means the first serious work to utilize jazz idioms. European masters like Debussy, Erik Satie, Stravinsky, and Milhaud had already experimented with the techniques and style of jazz in concert music and ballets. Gershwin himself had written a one-act jazz opera in 1922, *Blue Monday (135th Street)*, libretto by Buddy de Sylva, which received a single performance in the *George White Scandals*. *Blue Monday* had been an ambitious attempt to combine spirituals, blues, and pop tunes into an integrated musical organism. Though it boasted some effective lyrical episodes, the opera as a whole lacked conviction because of its diffuse and rambling structure.

Compositions like *Blue Monday*, Satie's *Parade*, Stravinsky's *Ragtime*, and Milhaud's *La Création du monde*, had little influence on the music of their day. These works were regarded as provocative novelties but not as music capable of pointing in a new direction. The *Rhapsody in Blue*, however, was something else again. Its immediate acclaim throughout the music world provided conviction that the procedures, devices, and material of American popular music deserved the most serious consideration by composers everywhere. The writing of operas, concertos, and symphonic and chamber music in a jazz style became a widespread practice in Europe as well as America, largely because of the example and stimulation provided by the *Rhapsody in Blue*. The *Rhapsody in Blue* was fresh, new, vigorous, brash, and exciting music—American to its very core. The frenetic, iconoclastic era of the 1920's was here set to music. The seventeen-note ascent of the clarinet, with which the rhapsody opens, culminating in a saucy jazz tune, set the mood of abandon for the entire work. Sprightly jazz ideas followed in rapid succession until the heart of the work was reached—the broad, majestic song for strings that has since become one of the most celebrated themes in American music.

The *Rhapsody in Blue* has become one of the most frequently heard American compositions in the symphonic repertory. It has been transcribed for every possible combination of instruments and has been the inspiration for several ballets. For all its technical shortcomings—the at times naive harmonic language and its occasional lack of skill in developing germinal ideas—its melodic invention is so fresh and spontaneous that the composition has never lost its audience appeal anywhere in the world.

After the *Rhapsody in Blue*, Gershwin remained a dominant figure in the writing of symphonic and operatic music embodying jazz and popular elements. The *Concerto in F* for piano and orchestra followed the *Rhapsody* by a year and a half—commissioned and introduced by the New York Symphony under Walter Damrosch, with the composer at the piano. Here, as in all subsequent serious works for orchestra, Gershwin did his own orchestration. Then came three *Preludes* for piano (1926), the second of which (in C-sharp minor) is a plangent blues melody that has become famous both in its original version and in orchestral transcriptions; the tone poem, *An American in Paris* (1928); *Second Rhapsody*, for orchestra (1931); *Cuban Overture* (1932); *Variations on I Got Rhythm*, for piano and orchestra (1934); and the folk opera, *Porgy and Bess* (1935). All overflow with lyrical invention, and all use jazz melodies, colorations, and harmonies with extraordinary artistic effect. Each successive composition demonstrates an ever increasing technical sophistication and creative invention. *Porgy and Bess*, which has conquered the world in a way no other American opera and few contemporary European operas have done, represents Gershwin at the apex of his creative powers. Here the marriage of popular and serious music becomes complete and indissoluble.

Gershwin's influence was far-reaching. The French master, Maurice Ravel, readily conceded that it was Gershwin's music that encouraged him to write a "blues" sonata for violin and piano (*Sonata for Violin and Piano*) and to inject jazz writing into his last two piano concertos. American composers have, to be sure, been particularly affected by Gershwin's success. Since 1924, the repertory of American music has been enriched with compositions small and large giving serious consideration to popular ideas and materials. The following are some of the most important contributors to this symphonic-jazz repertory.

Leroy Anderson (1908-   ) has written many instrumental numbers in jazz style beginning with "Jazz Pizzicato" and "Jazz

Legato." His most popular pieces in a symphonic-jazz style include "Blue Tango," "Fiddle Faddle," "The Syncopated Clock," "Sleigh Ride," and "The Typewriter."

Robert Russell Bennett (1894-   ) has for many years been a leading orchestrator for the Broadway stage. In his own compositions he has successfully produced works of ambitious design with both jazz and non-popular elements. Among Bennett's compositions featuring jazz belong *Charleston Rhapsody* for orchestra, *Concerto Grosso* for jazz band and orchestra, *Variations on a Theme by Jerome Kern* for orchestra, and "March" for two pianos and orchestra.

Leonard Bernstein, who has already been discussed as a composer for the Broadway theater, has written the music for two exciting ballets, each score being in a recognizable jazz style— *Fancy Free* and *Facsimile*. It should also be pointed out that jazz passages appear in his symphony, *The Age of Anxiety*.

John Alden Carpenter (1876-1951) was essentially a composer of serious concert music, but he too occasionally used jazz to good effect. His best known work in a jazz style is the ballet *Skyscrapers*, from which an orchestral suite is often performed by major orchestras. Jazz is also prominently used in an earlier Carpenter slapstick ballet, *Krazy Kat*, based on George Herriman's cartoons.

Aaron Copland (1900-   ) is often described as the dean of American serious composers. In his early symphonic works Copland was strongly attracted to the rhythms, tonalities, and melodies of jazz. The most significant of these works were his *Music for Orchestra* and his *Concerto for Piano and Orchestra*.

Duke Ellington, the famous jazz band leader and composer of popular songs discussed in an earlier chapter, has written some fine compositions in forms more spacious and flexible than the song. He prefers describing such orchestral works as "Negro music," but they are all sound jazz: *Black, Brown and Beige*, which Ellington introduced in Carnegie Hall in 1943; *Harlem*, an orchestral suite, first performed by Ellington in the Metropolitan Opera House in 1951; and *Night Creature*, whose première took place in Carnegie Hall in 1955, once again in an Ellington performance.

Morton Gould (1913-   ), like Gershwin, followed two directions, that of serious and that of popular music. In a popular vein he has written the scores for several Broadway musical comedies, most notably *Billion Dollar Baby* (1945) and *Arms and the Girl* (1950). His serious works include symphonies, concertos, suites, and tone poems. As with Gershwin, so with Gould the two paths of serious and popular music have sometimes met on common ground. Gould's principal symphonic-jazz compositions are the *Chorale and Fugue in Jazz* for symphony orchestra, *Swing Sinfonietta* for orchestra, and *Interplay*, for piano and orchestra. Effective use of the blues is made in his *Symphony No. 3* and his *Concerto for Orchestra*.

Jerome Kern, about whom much has already been said, produced two concert works belonging in the symphonic-jazz repertory. The first is *Scenario*, his own symphonic adaptation of melodies from *Show Boat*. The other, with entirely original material, is *Mark Twain: A Portrait for Orchestra*.

Robert McBride (1911-   ) is a serious American composer not averse, on frequent occasions, to exploiting American folk and popular material in his works. In an essentially jazz idiom belong *Swing Stuff*, for clarinet and piano, *Jam Session*, for woodwind quintet, and *Strawberry Jam*, for orchestra.

Igor Stravinsky (1882-   ), a titan in twentieth-century music, is included among Americans despite his Russian birth because he has become an American citizen. In the early 1920's Stravinsky was strongly attracted to ragtime, an idiom in which he produced *Ragtime*, for eleven instruments, and *Piano Rag*, for solo piano. Many years later, in 1946, he wrote a major jazz work, *Ebony Concerto*, for clarinet and swing band, for Woody Herman's orchestra.

The following are some of the most significant European composers to use jazz successfully in serious compositions:

Georges Auric ("Adieu, New York!" a piano fox trot); Paul Hindemith (*Kammermusik No. 1*, and the opera *Neues vom Tage*); Arthur Honegger (*Concertino* for piano and orchestra); Ernst Krenek (the opera *Jonny spielt auf!*); Constant Lambert (*Rio Grande*, for chorus and orchesra); Rolf Liebermann (*Concerto for Jazz Band and Symphony Orchestra*); Frank Martin (*Foxtrot*, for two pianos); Darius Milhaud (*La Création du monde* and *Le Boeuf sur le toit*, ballets; *Rag Caprice* for piano and orchestra; and *Caramel Mou*, a "shimmy" for jazz band); Marcel Poot (*Jazz Music*); Maurice Ravel (*Concerto in D for*

Left Hand Piano and Orchestra, Concerto in G major, for piano
and orchestra, and *Sonata for Violin and Piano*); Erik Satie
(Parade); Kurt Weill (the operas, *The Rise and Fall of Mahag-
onny* and *The Three-Penny Opera*).

The fullest resources of serious music were also applied to real
jazz, the jazz that was born in New Orleans and developed in
Chicago and New York.

In the 1940's, many jazz musicians (some comprehensively
trained in serious music) began to experiment with advanced
harmonic and rhythmic devices. Thus Be-bop as it was first
called, but later renamed Re-bop and then simply Bop, came
into being. (The name is said to have come from a characteristic
sound produced by this new music.) The Bop musician might
affect an eccentric dress—beret, heavy spectacles, and a beard—
and he might often quixotically parade under a Mohammedan
name, but, for all such affectations, he was a serious artist who
helped bring to jazz a new sound through unconventional progressions and intervals and through the avoidance of the usual four-
to-the-beat rhythm for a more subtle pulse, suggested rather
than expressed.

The acknowledged high priest of Bop was Dizzy Gillespie,
trumpeter, who has led his own ensembles—large and small—in
tours of the United States and Europe. One of the most eloquent
spokesmen for Bop was the remarkable alto sax performer,
Charlie "Bird" Parker after whom Birdland, a haven of Bop in
New York, was named. Parker (who died in 1955 at the age of
thirty-five, a victim of dissipation) opened new horizons for
improvisation through advanced harmonic thinking and extremely
subtle and complex rhythmic structures. Another extraordinary
Bop performer is Earl "Bud" Powell (1924-   ), pianist, who
brought to the keyboard an immense technical discipline and a
penchant for exploring new tonal regions and giving expression
to a cyclonic dynamism.

Probably as a reaction to Bop, but no less endowed with
advanced harmonic and rhythmic writing, a more relaxed and
almost dreamy kind of jazz music came into existence. This was
baptized "cool jazz" and first achieved popularity in or about
1949 with Miles Davis, a trumpeter. One of its most significant
practitioners was the pianist, Leonard Joseph Tristano. In the

performance of "cool jazz" Tristano found many willing disciples, the most important being Lee Konitz, alto sax, and guitarist William Henry "Bill" Bauer.

An even more complex form of jazz was expounded by pianists Stanley Newcomb "Stan" Kenton and Dave Brubeck and saxophonist Boyd Albert, among others. Named "progressive jazz," this music absorbed some of the ultramodern idioms of serious contemporary music, notably that of Bartók and Stravinsky—dissonance, polytonality, and polyrhythm.

Bibliography

Armstrong, Louis. *Satchmo: My Life in New Orleans.* New York: Prentice-Hall, 1954.

Arnold, Elliott. *Deep in My Heart (Sigmund Romberg).* New York: Duell, Sloan and Pearce, 1949.

Balliett, Whitney. *Sound of Surprises, 46 Pieces on Jazz.* New York: E. P. Dutton, 1959.

Blesh, Rudi. *Shining Trumpets (A History of Jazz).* New York: Alfred A. Knopf, 1946.

Carmichael, Hoagy. *The Stardust Road.* New York: Rinehart, 1946.

Chase, Gilbert. *America's Music.* New York: McGraw-Hill, 1955.

Duke, Vernon. *Passport to Paris.* Boston: Little, Brown & Co., 1955.

Ewen, David. *Complete Book of the American Musical Theater.* New York: Henry Holt, 1958.

Ewen, David. *Journey to Greatness: The Life and Music of George Gershwin.* New York: Henry Holt, 1956.

Ewen, David. *Leonard Bernstein.* Philadelphia: Chilton, 1960.

Ewen, David. *Panorama of American Popular Music.* New York: Prentice-Hall, 1957.

Ewen, David. *Richard Rodgers.* New York: Henry Holt, 1957.

Ewen, David. *The World of Jerome Kern.* New York: Henry Holt, 1960.

Feather, Leonard. *The Encyclopedia of Jazz.* New York: Horizon Press, 1955.

Fuld, James J. *American Popular Music: 1875-1950.* Philadelphia. Musical Americana, 1955.

Gilbert, Douglas. *American Vaudeville: Its Life and Times.* New York: Whittlesey House, 1940.

Gilbert, Douglas. *Lost Chords: The Diverting Story of American Popular Songs.* New York: Doubleday and Co., 1942.

Goldberg, Isaac. *Tin Pan Alley.* New York: John Day, 1930.

Goodman, Benny, and Irving Kolodin. *The Kingdom of Swing.* Harrisburg, Pa.: Stackpole, 1939.

Green, Abel, and Joe Laurie, Jr. *Show Biz: From Vaude to Video.* New York: Henry Holt, 1951.

Green, Stanley. *The World of Musical Comedy.* New York: Ziff-Davis, 1960.

Handy, William C. *Father of the Blues: An Autobiography.* New York: Macmillan, 1941.

Howard, John Tasker. *Stephen Foster, America's Troubadour.* New York: Thos. Y. Crowell, 1934.

Jablonski, Edward. *Harold Arlen: Happy With the Blues.* New York: Doubleday, 1961.

Jablonski, Edward and Lawrence D. Stewart. *The Gershwin Years.* New York: Doubleday & Co., 1958.

Jordan, Philip D., and Lillian Kessler. *Songs of Yesterday.* New York: Doubleday & Co., 1941.

Kahn, E. J., Jr. *The Merry Partners: The Age and Stage of Harrigan and Hart.* New York: Random House, 1955.

Kaufmann, Helen L. *From Jehovah to Jazz.* New York: Dodd, Mead & Co., 1937.

Marks, Edward B. *They All Had Glamour.* New York: Messner 1944.

Meyer, Hazel. *Gold in Tin Pan Alley.* Philadelphia: J. B. Lippincott, 1958.

Morehouse, Ward. *George M. Cohan, Prince of the American Theater.* Lippincott, 1943.

Paul, Elliott. *That Crazy American Music.* Indianapolis: Bobbs-Merrill, 1957.

Shapiro, Nat and Nat Hentoff, editors. *The Jazz Makers.* New York: Rinehart, 1957.

Smith, Cecil. *Musical Comedy in America.* New York: Theatre Arts Books, 1950.

Spaeth, Sigmund. *History of Popular Music in America.* New York: Random House, 1948.

Spaeth, Sigmund. *Read 'Em and Weep: The Songs You Forgot to Remember.* New York: Arco, 1945.

Stearns, Marshall. *The Story of Jazz.* New York: Oxford University Press, 1956.

Ulanov, Barry. *Duke Ellington.* New York: Creative Age, 1946.

Ulanov, Barry. *A History of Jazz in America.* New York: Viking Press, 1952.

Waters, Edward N. *Victor Herbert.* New York: Macmillan, 1955.

Whiteman, Paul and Mary Margaret McBride. *Jazz.* New York: J. H. Sears, 1926.

Williams, Martin T., editor. *The Art of Jazz.* New York: Oxford University Press, 1959.

Witmark, Isidore and Isaac Goldberg. *From Ragtime to Swingtime.* New York: Lee Furman, 1939.

Wittke, Carl. *Tambo and Bones (A History of the American Minstrel Stage).* Durham: Duke University Press, 1930.

Index

This Index includes all song titles, titles of musical productions, and names of composers and lyricists mentioned in the book. Other subjects, such as performers, places, publishers, and nonmusical productions, are listed only if they have had a direct influence on the development of popular music.